SRI KARUNAMAYI

A Biography

By

MURUGAN

Published by

SRI MATHRUDEVI VISWASHANTI ASHRAM TRUST
(SMVA TRUST)

India - USA – UK

Published by:

SRI MATHRUDEVI VISWASHANTHI ASHRAM TRUST ®
Penusila Kshetram, Nellore Dt., Andhra Pradesh 524342, India

KARUNAMAYI SHANTI DHAMA ®
14/5, 6th Cross, Ashok Nagar, Banashankari 1st Stage,
Bangalore 560050, India

SMVA TRUST, INC. ®
21 Baldwin Hills Road, Millwood, NY 10546, USA

KARUNAMAYI VISWASHANTHI FOUNDATION ®
22 Lingwell Road, London SW17 7NJ, U.K.

1st Edition - 1992	1000 copies
2nd Edition - 1996	2000 copies
3rd Edition - 1997	2000 copies
4th Edition - 1999	2000 copies
5th Edition - 2001	1000 copies
6th Edition - 2003	2000 copies

Copyright 2002

ISBN: 0-9671853-7-8

Printed by: McNaughton & Gunn, Inc.
Saline, Michigan 48176

Cover design: John Rheem
Los Angeles, CA

Website : www.karunamayi.org
Email: smva@karunamayi.org

Dedicated to Ammamma

Smt. Annapurnamma
(Sri Karunamayi's Mother)

DEDICATION

This printing of the biography of Sri Karunamayi marks the fourth anniversary of the passing of Ammamma, Smt. Annapurnamma (1928-1998), the mother of Sri Karunamayi. Ammamma serves as our greatest example of the spiritual tenet: "Service to man is service to God." Indeed, humble sacrifice for all humanity was a part of every breath of Smt. Annapurnamma, and her life will always serve as a model of selfless service.

Those devotees who came to see Sri Karunamayi at the Sri Mathrudevi Viswashanthi Ashram near the Penusila forest had the good fortune to witness Ammamma's kindness, humility and tireless service to everyone. No matter what time of day or night a devotee would arrive, Ammamma would immediately begin preparing food and take care of that person's every need.

It was Ammamma's wish to construct a hospital near the Penusila Ashram for the benefit of all the local villagers, who often had to travel very far to receive basic medical attention. At the time of the publication of this book, this noble cause is well under way. There are so many examples of Ammamma's kindness and sincerity, yet words can never do justice to the fullness of the compassion she showered upon one and all.

This book is dedicated to Smt. Annapurnamma and the example of *nishkama karma*—selfless service—she set for everyone. Whenever any of us help heal a wound or lessen another's suffering, we can experience in our hearts the tender wave of compassion which best describes the abundant love that was her very life.

Jai Karunamayi!
September, 2002

ACKNOWLEDGEMENTS

I gratefully acknowledge the following people for their *seva* contributions in assisting the publication of this sixth edition of Amma's biography: Smriti Dudley, Laurae Durkin, Manorama Agerwala, Geeta Agerwala, Vijay Khanna, Cassia Berman, Lakshmi Prasanna, Geeta Jayaraman, Gayathri Ranganath and Mythily Vaidyanathan.

Jai Karunamayi!

Swami Vijayeswarananda

TABLE OF CONTENTS

Dedication v
Acknowledgements vi
Preface ix
Introduction x

Sri Karunamayi's Biography
    Parentage of Sri Vijayeswari Devi 1
    The Mysore Visit 4
    Birth of Sri Vijayeswari Devi 5
    Childhood and Schooling 7
    Student Life 11
    The Mother about Her Daughter 13
    From the House to the Hermitage 20

From the Diaries of Swami Vijayeshwarananda
    Love of God 23
    Vishwamitra Pond 26
    Sri Guru Purnima: 1983 32
    Bull—the Symbol of Forbearance 36
    Rama Nama and Siva Nama of the Birds 42
    Miraculous Showers of Abundance 45
    Devi Charanam Pranamamyaham 57
    Sarva Sakshini, Mother Karunamayi 65
    The Silent Language of Love 79
    Bhavani Is Won by Devotion 86
    Sri Dakshinamurti Rupini 99
    Amma as Annapurneshwari 124
    Saraswati Answers All Our Doubts 132

Devotees' Experiences
- The Miracle of Transformation 159
- The Embodiment of Love and Affection 170
- Savior of the Distressed 178
- Bestower of Progeny 183
- Mother—The Omnipresent 185
- Wisdom is Essential for Human Evolution 187
- Amma and the Failed Brakes 196
- Jewel of Compassion, Mother of All 199
- Divine Presence 203
- All Paths Lead to the One 206
- Double Darshan 210
- Long Distance Healing 212

Blessed Messages of Sri Karunamayi
- Practice of Meditation in Daily Life 217
- Divine Message 224

Sri Karunamayi's Mission
- Sri Karunamayi's Wish 235
- Amma's Charitable Projects 238
- Sri Karunamayi's Ashrams 244
- Contact Information 246

Appendix
- The Spiritual Tradition of India 249
- Significance of Navaratri 249
- The Greatness of Lalita Devi 250
- Pronunciation Key 252

Stotra, Shloka and Kirtana 254

Glossary 263

PREFACE

This edition of the Biography of Bhagavati Sri Sri Sri Vijayeswari Devi has eight sections. The first of these contains the fascinating and miraculous biographical incidents surrounding Sri Karunamayi, while the second includes stories from my journals, *The Diaries of Swami Vijayeswarananda*. These compelling accounts offer the reader a charming, intimate and moving picture of Amma's early days in the forest. Section three contains the testimony of Eastern and Western devotees. They narrate how Mother transformed their lives and illustrate Her unconditional love and boundless compassion for all. The fourth section is devoted to the blessed messages of Sri Karunamayi to all humanity, while the fifth gives updated information on Amma's mission, Her charitable projects and Her *ashrams*. A short appendix has been added explaining the spiritual tradition of India, the significance of *Navaratri* and the greatness of Divine Mother as *Lalita Devi*. In the final two sections, the reader is provided with a translation of all the *shlokas* Amma has chanted, in addition to a glossary.

Much has changed in the last ten years since the first edition of the Biography was published in English. There has been a great increase in the number of devotees seeking shelter at the lotus feet of Mother. In addition, Amma has made many visits to the western hemisphere, including many cities in the United States, the United Kingdom, Guyana, and also Europe. Her divine qualities and inspiring spiritual discourses have swept the people there with a newfound curiosity to unravel the Truth, rather than confining themselves to mere materialistic living.

We are sure that this sacred gospel will quench the spiritual thirst of all seekers of Truth.

—Murugan
(Swami Vijayeswarananda)

INTRODUCTION

*Sarve bhavantu sukhinaḥ
Lokaḥ samastaḥ sukhino bhavantu*

"May all beings in all the realms of this beautiful cosmos be happy and free from all suffering."

This is the sole and cherished desire of our Blessed Mother Sri Karunamayi, Bhagavati Sri Sri Sri Vijayeswari Devi. There can be no higher aim than this.

In 1958, glowing with divine light, our beloved Amma descended to this Earth in the form of a baby girl born to Smt. Annapurnamma and her husband Sri Subaramanna. The infant was the fulfillment of a prophesy made by the famous sage Bhagavan Ramana Maharshi, and Smt. Annapurnamma's own vision of the Goddess which she had seen at the Chamundeshwari temple at Mysore exactly one year earlier.

Her birth occurred on the auspicious day of *Vijaya Dashami*,[1] which is the culmination of the yearly *Navaratri* celebration. During *Navaratri,* the Goddess is praised for vanquishing the demonic forces of the universe and for restoring light, peace and healing to one and all—hence Her name, Vijayeswari Devi. Every part of creation reverberates with the blessings of that divine creative power, who is in our midst pouring Her invaluable love into Her own creation.

The joy in our hearts is inexpressible. Its very experience is a treasure-trove so bountiful in its truthfulness that it surpasses all boundaries of our mind. We can only thank a million times Bhagavati Devi, our beloved Amma, Sri Karunamayi, for Her divine grace in granting us this enviable opportunity to perceive Her in this world, in our mortal presence, as She casts Her merciful, loving and reassuring glances into every moment of our lives. We leap

---

[1] See appendix

with joy and unbounded happiness, and dance with divine fervor, throwing our minds into the vast emptiness to lose into Her forever the very essence of our selves.

Mother is beyond creation since She Herself is Creation—the sum and substance of it. She is "Enlivened Silence" functioning in Her own completeness. With Her mystical plan She is creating a blissful plane for all mankind—who are Her own form—an abode of joy and happiness for all to grow in Her direction and enter Her divine kingdom. She appeared on the sacred day of *Vijaya Dashami,* heralding the reign of victory for all mankind. Her *lila,* divine sport, this time is to make Her children *amrita putras,* immortals, clad in the shield of purity, *sattva,* armed with inexhaustible energy, *shakti,* guided by supreme Consciousness, *chaitanya,* and wrapped in the cloak of divine awareness, *chidambara.* They are thus empowered to trounce all evil, illusion and imperfection and radiate truth, bliss, peace, and love.

Her every movement and breath is charged with fiery *tapas,* intense spiritual practices, carrying waves of force impregnating every atom with Happiness, Happiness, Happiness! Knowing that the basis for all this *sukham, sukham, sukham* is peace, peace, peace, She has been constructing the empire of joy for all these years, sitting silently in deep meditation in the hidden forests of sacred Penusila Kshetra—the retreat of many sages through the centuries, and the abode of Sri Lakshmi Narasimha Swami. This so that mankind may enter a new kingdom, an abode of positivity on Earth, flourishing in abundance like the celestial Vaikuntha, Kailasa and Manipura and surpassing even Sripura. How can the Mother be engulfed alone in the ocean of joy when Her children are in a sea of misery? This is the secret that has drawn Her into our midst today and She will not spare a moment's effort to guide with Her benign grace, every child into Her fold.

From the moment of creation She has been the awe of the Gods and the wonder of the *rishis,* the great sages. And now a new day has dawned in the universe when the Divine Mother looks upon Her children with pride. Mortals who by Her grace are on the road to immortality are being hailed by the Gods, joyful that Her mystical strength has borne fruit over the passage of time.

To prepare the child to enter Sripura, Her mystical, celestial abode, Divine Mother is now filling all hearts with Her abundant love. Weeding away illusions and misery She is implanting Herself deeply into the fields of the mind as seeds of *Gayatri*—to sprout and strengthen every fiber with divine *tejas,* radiance. With every phase of the moon, Mother is tending the fresh growth, infusing the nectar of *Sri Vidya,* the knowledge of supreme Consciousness, into every nerve of the mind and body.

The spiritual journey is long and the goal distant; so She carries us when we are tired and weary, and shades us when it is hot and sultry. She nudges us along with gentle care and comfort to move forward at every phase of life and, in the reassuring security of Her presence, to reach at last Her eternal abode of peace and everlasting bliss.

Let us cling to our beloved Mother with determination and innocent love, forgetting all fears and confusion. Let us keep pace with Her, knowing that Mother is all we have to escape from the gnawing emptiness of the individual self; for every wrong step draws us into the woods of suffering and the agony of separation. Let us sincerely pray to Her to hold on to us at every moment— to hold us tightly and never let us lose Her on the journey of life.

Mother is *Sat chit ananda*—truth, knowledge and bliss Absolute. The combined divinity of *Lalita Devi, Durga Devi,* and Saraswati Devi has manifested in the adorable form of Sri Vijayeswari Devi. Let us now explore the form Her life has taken.

Jai Karunamayi!

Karunamayi Bhagavati Sri Sri Sri Vijayeswari Devi

Sri Karunamayi's Biography

SRI KARUNAMAYI - A Biography

PARENTAGE OF SRI VIJAYESWARI DEVI

Blessed are the parents of Sri Vijayeswari Devi because they gave birth to the Mother of the Universe! Subbaramanna, Vijayeswari Devi's father, was a trader of mica and an ardent devotee of Sri Ramakrishna Paramahamsa. Sri Subbaramanna was also a Telugu scholar and a proponent of the Sanskrit language. He had studied many books on *Dharma Shastra*, the ancient codes of conduct written by the sage Manu. Obviously an enlightened soul, his desire to serve the Divine was great. Often Sri Subbaramanna would quietly donate great sums to help the needy, thereby deriving much self-satisfaction. His philosophy echoed the biblical maxim, "Inasmuch as you have done it to the least of these, you have done it unto Me."

Greatly devoted to Sri Ramakrishna, Sri Subbaramanna would go to Dakshineshwar near Calcutta as often as he could, offering his prayers in the room where Sri Ramakrishna had lived. Sri Subbaramanna also rendered unique service in the freedom struggle of India. Firm conviction, self-confidence and selfless service were his natural traits.

After the birth of two daughters, Sri Subbaramanna offered special prayers for the birth of a son. One night in a dream, he saw his beloved deity Sri Ramakrishna Paramahamsa utter something. However, since Sri Subbaramanna couldn't determine what his *Gurudeva* had said, as soon as he awoke, he hurriedly left for Dakshineshwar, with the hope that he could unveil the importance of his *Gurudeva's* words.

Smt. Annapurnamma, the devoted wife of Sri Subbaramanna, worshipped Sri Rama and was often a visitor to

Bhadrachalam, the site of the famed Sri Rama temple built by Ramadas on the banks of the Godavari River. There she spent most of her time praying to Sri Rama and writing *Rama nama*, the name of her beloved deity. She would then offer her *Ramakoti*—her written *japa*— at the feet of her *Ishta devata*, her honored God.

Smt. Annapurnamma was also well-known for her compassion, cooperation and service to others. Her other outstanding virtues included simplicity, affection and the ability to convey a feeling of intimacy and warmth towards whomever she encountered.

Often, Smt. Annapurnamma would also visit nearby Tiruvannamalai, the *ashram* of Bhagavan Sri Ramana Maharshi, the incarnation of Shanmukha (also called Subramanya, the brother of Lord Ganesha), who mostly maintained silence, but would occasionally converse with his devotees. One day, in an apparent response to the worship and respect paid by her during her many visits to his residence, Sri Ramana Maharshi called Smt. Annapurnamma close to him. It was early in the morning and, as he stood outdoors next to the cowshed, she affectionately came and prostrated at his feet.

"Would you like to live your life in an *ashram*? Sri Ramana Maharshi asked the shy young woman.

"Whatever your Grace wishes, Bhagavan Ramana," Annapurnamma whispered, marveling that he knew her mind so well.

"Not now," Sri Ramana Maharshi replied. "And not in this *ashram*. You will get *ashram* life, however, as desired by you. You will give birth to the Mother. Everyone will then come to you. You need not live in any other *ashram*." So saying, Sri Ramana Maharshi turned and left the dazed young Annapurnamma alone.

Since she was timid, Smt. Annapurnamma dared not even approach Sri Ramana Maharshi to seek clarification of her doubts. She also felt she was too simple and unworthy to converse with divine souls. For her, Bhagavan Sri Ramana Maharshi was God. As Lord Maha Vishnu was shining as the divine Self in the human body of Sri Rama, so also was Lord Subramanya in the body of Bhagavan Ramana. Belief in him as the highest goal in life was accompanied by her strong conviction that Sri Ramana had descended to Earth as an incarnation to protect his devotees. As such, thinking of Bhagavan Ramana's conversation with her made her tremble with awe and happiness. In the days to come, Smt. Annapurnamma had no courage to divulge this event to anyone.

THE MYSORE VISIT

When her husband requested her to accompany him to Mysore, Smt. Annapurnamma did not ask him the reason for the visit. She never disobeyed her husband's requests, nor did she think it right to question him. She belonged to the category of women who did not consider it right to question their husbands' decisions.

The couple came to Mysore to view the *Dashehra* festivities and on the tenth day, *Vijaya Dashami*, when Smt. Annapurnamma was sitting and praying in the temple of *Devi Chamundeshwari*, she had a divine vision of a great lotus lake. By the edge of this lake was a pearl *mandap*, containing a raised platform supported by pillars. The Divine Mother then descended from Her dais and a divine eternal light in the form of *Sri Chamundeshwari* manifested. Smt. Annapurnamma felt both of these forms of Devi enter her own body. The joy and bliss this experience engendered in the wondrous young woman, was amazing. This, too, she kept to herself and did not confide it even to her husband.

This initial divine experience was subsequently followed by several others.

THE BIRTH OF SRI VIJAYESWARI DEVI

On *Vijaya Dashami* day in the year 1958, on the first floor of Smt. Annapurnamma's house, her husband was going through the office files. Three days earlier Sri Subbaramanna had received the bad news that a steamer holding a mica shipment dispatched by him, had sunk. This report had made him dejected and displeased. Such an accident was a great financial loss, not easily to be recouped. Sri Subbaramanna lived in silence about the matter, however. He did not mention it to anyone.

That evening after taking a bath, Sri Subbaramanna sat down for meditation in front of a photo of Sri Ramakrishna. Diving deep within, he had an experience of absolute serenity and supreme bliss. He also witnessed the emergence of sixteen lights into the *puja* room, one after the other. In the midst of these sixteen lights, he became aware of a beautiful and unusual divine feminine form seated in the center. To Her and to the sixteen effulgences, he offered his adoration. After this vision, every year on *Vijaya Dashami* day, Sri Subbaramannna distributed sweets and clothes to all his family members and workers.

Gudur in the Nellore District of Andhra Pradesh had an extra reason to rejoice on that eventful day of *Vijaya Dashami*, for on that day the Divine Mother took a human form as Sri Vijayeswari Devi. On the very day when Goddess Maha Lakshmi is said to enter every house, Subbaramanna heard the good news that his wife had given birth to a daughter.

The birth of Vijayeswari Devi was immediately followed by another piece of good news. The steamer which had sunk was not the one which had carried the mica consignment and, in fact, the transaction had realized a great profit. Sri Subbaramanna, understanding that his newborn daughter was the boon of the Divine Mother, celebrated the event by distributing *kumkum*, turmeric powder, new *saris*, fruit and other presents to all the blessed women on his street. The entire house was filled with joy. While the nation was celebrating the *Dashehra* Festival, the father adorned the beautiful neck of his little child with pearls and diamonds.

Sri Subbaramanna and Smt. Annapurnamma were truly blessed, for one year after the day when Her mother experienced the miraculous vision of *Chamundeshwari Devi* at Mysore, Sri Vijayeswari Devi's parents were showered with the choicest blessing of the Lord, who indeed gifted to them the most precious jewel, the Mother of the Universe.

SRI KARUNAMAYI - A Biography

CHILDHOOD AND SCHOOLING

From the childhood and schooling of young Vijayeswari, we can easily see that Her omnipresence and omnipotence was visible at an early age. Events occurring during this time clearly signaled to the world that here was an extraordinary being.

One of the most amazing proofs of Vijayeswari's omniscience occurred shortly after Her father showed Her horoscope to a famous astrologer. This well-known figure said that the girl was of a divine nature and that She would settle down for some years in a forest. He also said that She would be the Light of lights to humanity, that She would impart eternal knowledge to the world, and that She would provide shelter to orphans, the poor, sinners and those in distress. He added that She would not get married and that She would be eternal and worshipped by the world.

Upon hearing these predictions by the astrologer, Sri Subbaramanna shuddered. Most of all, he was distressed by the idea that his beloved daughter would have to live in the forest.

One afternoon, disturbed by these same thoughts, Sri Subbaramanna was sitting in his office. In the meanwhile, little Vijayeswari had just returned from school and entered the room. Putting Her books aside, She went and stood next to Her father, addressing him as follows:

"Father, why are you so depressed by such a small issue?"

Surprised, Her father replied: "Why, which issue do you mean?"

"Regarding my life, Father," the girl replied. "I have to live for some time in the forest."

At these words, Sri Subbaramana was speechless. He had never experienced such a thing! What truly amazed him was the all-pervasive knowledge of his daughter, for he had not told anyone, including his wife, about the astrological predictions he had heard. He could not understand how the small girl who had just returned from school could know about them.

While he was engrossed in these thoughts, Sri Subbaramanna suddenly remembered an incident that had happened in Kanchi during a family pilgrimage. The family was just returning from the temple, after having the *darshan* of Mother *Kamakshi* and *Ekambareshwara*, when an enraged elephant was seen running in their direction, chasing a group of people. Without hesitation, little six year-old Vijayeswari had stepped in front of the advancing elephant.

No sooner did the beast see the child, than he sat down on the ground, acting as if he had been tranquilized. Everyone around the scene was spellbound at the girl's amazing powers.

In 1966, another miracle occurred. Sri Subbaramanna had to attend an urgent commercial conference in Chennai in connection with his business. All the files connected with this affair had been kept on top of an iron safe. However, probably due to its weight, the bundle of files had slipped backwards and lodged itself between the wall and the iron safe. There was only an hour before the train's departure, and eight strong men tried to move the heavy safe forward so as to retrieve the files. However, after half an hour's hard effort, the safe could not be moved even half an inch.

At this critical juncture, little Vijayeswari returned from school. Entering the office, She moved the iron safe aside as if She were moving a book. Then She placed the bundle of files before Her astonished father. At the sight of this feat, the eight strong men were also amazed and stood spellbound, wondering whether the little girl was possessed by a devil or had divine power. Addressing them directly, little Vijayeswari told them that She was *Bhima Shankari* of Himachala. So saying, She left the room, wearing a smile.

Soon afterwards, Vijayeswari's father left hurriedly for Chennai on his business affairs. Naturally, his mind kept returning to his daughter's colossal feat. However, since the identity She had claimed, that of *Bhima Shankari*, was unknown to him, he was anxious to discover who She really was.

Therefore, from Chennai he went directly to Kanchi to have the *darshan* of Sri Chandrasekhara Saraswati, the Seer of Kamakoti Pitha. Placing a written note before the Swamiji, Sri Subbaramanna pleaded to know who this *Bhima Shankari* was and where She lived. Swamiji replied in Tamil that *Bhima Shankari* was *Adi Para Shakti*, supreme energy, and that Her abode was in Himachala. Now, after the clarification given by Swamiji and the words uttered by his daughter, Sri Subbaramanna was clearly convinced of Vijayeswari's divine nature.

Returning home, Sri Subbaramanna saw his sweet little girl sleeping innocently under the moonlight. Looking at that beautiful, glowing face, he said to himself that certainly his little darling had the power to rule this world and felt absolutely sure that She had come to Earth to redeem the suffering of humanity. From then on, confident of this, Her father used to frequently consult Vijayeswari on various matters.

Thus Vijayeswari was unusual in both Her early childhood accomplishments and in Her remarkably unique actions. In addition, the child was gifted in other respects, such as an inexpressibly pleasant smile, creativity and an unperturbed stance. She had the ability to win over the minds of others at first sight and to express Herself in a natural and beautifully refined manner. Meditation and discipline were the games of Her childhood.

STUDENT LIFE

For Her primary education, Sri Vijayeswari attended the Pitsley Memorial Girls' School. The child had an immense intellectual capacity along with a photographic memory. Anything She saw or heard once, She could repeat without a flaw. In addition, She used to write beautiful and interesting work in a neat hand, whose finished look resembled knitted pearls. Vijayeswari was fond of education, but She also gave importance to simple daily habits such as cleanliness and maturity of emotional and physical expression.

The young student also showed incredible artistic talent. She loved to draw beautiful pictures depicting landscapes with birds, brooks and the rural life of India. In addition, She would sing melodiously the compositions of Thyagaraja Swami. She had the voice of a nightingale. Along with excelling in intellectual and artistic pursuits, Vijayeswari was always centered on the Divine. She enjoyed preparing flower garlands which would decorate the family *puja* and the image of Sri Rama. She would also assist Her mother in the worship of God with great humility and earnestness.

Even while at college, Vijayeswari's learning went far beyond the prescribed academic syllabus and encompassed spiritual subjects. She assimilated the subtle secrets of *kundalini yoga* and of meditation, teaching the latter, along with the *Bhagavad Gita*, to Her mother. Often She would tell Her mother to take refuge in this unique gospel, saying that it uplifted the oppressed and led people from darkness to light.

When she was in Her first year of college, studying for Her B.A., Vijayeswari gradually felt the urge to discard food and sleep. Most of the time She would sit in the prayer-room of Her home, meditating with closed eyes. She reduced Her sleep at night and, day by day, Her outlook changed. She seemed to have no awareness of Her environment. Most of the time, She appeared to be like an immobile statue. Sometimes for days and even weeks, She was closeted in the room. During such seclusions Vijayeswari Devi neither ate nor conversed with anyone.

During Her meditation, the young Devi would sit in the upstairs wing of the eastern part of Her house. Her beautiful eyes were tranquil. Though She was completely absorbed in Herself, outwardly She looked as if She were pondering the mysteries of another world in order to unravel them for the welfare of humanity.

Members of Vijayeswari's family and others as well felt a wonderful change in Sri Vijayeswari. Certainly Her demeanor was not as intimate as it had been in Her childhood. Noticeable differences were also discerned in Her stature, gesture, and conversation, as She began to emerge from Her cocoon-like state. A generous outlook was apparent in the young woman, and She seemed detached from the distress and dilemmas of the material world. All who knew Her respected the sanctity of Her person, seeing in Her the epitome of broad-mindedness and perfection.

THE MOTHER ABOUT HER DAUGHTER

Thinking back with awe about the miraculous pronouncement by Sri Ramana Maharshi that she would give birth to the Mother of the Universe, Smt. Annapurnamma remarked, "The day and moment in which that merciful Bhagavan Ramana spoke to me will never come again in life. Only out of divine love and everlasting devotion can one get the grace of Bhagavan and not through any other penance."

As Smt. Annapurnamma reminisced about the past, her implicit faith in her *Guru* was apparent. "Soon after the gracious words of Bhagavan Ramana, the sad news of his earthly departure was heard. After that I visited the Ramana *ashram* only twice. Is not Sri Ramana eternal? It is my firm belief that Ramana Maharshi, who cast off his mortal body much as one discards old clothes, remains alive to me forever."

With reference to her third daughter, Smt. Annapurnamma also recalled many loving and miraculous incidents. Her mother fondly remembered how little Vijayeswari loved butter, cheese and milk. Especially, she recalled the pleasure she felt when she fed the baby with rice mixed with cream.

One of the first of a series of miracles occurred during the tonsure ceremony, or shaving of the head, when Vijayeswari was only three years old. On this astrologically auspicious day, the family and some close relatives and friends had gone to the famed temple at Tirupati. After bathing, the group walked around the northern side of the *mandir* where the child had been sleeping. To their great surprise and anxiety, they espied a large cobra shielding the child with its hood. However, after offering prostrations, the king of snakes contracted its hood and slowly moved away from the child. Her mother thankfully took the sleeping girl into her arms, but the priest of the temple, who had witnessed the whole event, informed the gathering that the child was divine.

A second miraculous event occurred in the year 1961, when Vijayeswari was also only three years old. It was the month of *Margashirsha* (November/December). After reading her songs in the *Thiruppavai*, the women worshipped Andal, the 9th century *bhakta*, devotee, who had married and merged into the temple idol of Krishna. During the afternoon of that recitation, Her mother was anointing the head of Vijayeswari and applying black *kajal* to Her eyes. Suddenly, Smt. Annapurnamma was blinded by the dazzling lights of the sun and the moon in the gaze of her daughter. Speaking of that experience, the mother recalls: "I closed my eyes. I felt my body sinking in amazement. After that I was even afraid to touch my own child."

In the year 1962, Vijayeswari's entire family went on a pilgrimage to Kashi. Upon reaching the banks of the river Ganga where they were all bathing, little Vijayeswari showed Her mother a milk white stone, saying that it was a *Narmada Baneshwara lingam*. "This was a miracle," emphasized Smt. Annapurnamma, "because we were all there when Vijayeswari went empty-handed to bathe and, on Her return, She had this divine *lingam*. Indeed, this treasure came to us as a boon from the Lord in the early morning during the month of *Magha* and, from then until now, daily *puja* is conducted to this *lingam*."

Vijayeswari's mother continued in the same vein, "In the year 1966, Vijayeswari's father passed away. After this, Vijayeswari began to sleep every Friday morning in the flower garden."

On one particular day, for the second time, Her mother was awe-struck at the sight of a huge cobra sheltering her daughter with its spread hood. "The tender rays of the early morning sun matched the color of the child's face, and they both looked alike. Seeing this cobra at such close proximity naturally created fear and anxiety in me. However, when I knelt and offered my prayers, the cobra calmly disappeared and could not be traced in any nearby area. Since there was no way out for the cobra, no one could offer any reasonable explanation for its disappearance. In any event, it was very clear that the face of Sri Vijayeswari Devi lying in *yogic* sleep under the shadow of the cobra's head, and the rays of the sun of the *Magha* month, shone together as one color. This sight stays glued to my eyes and can never be erased from my memory."

"On one *Sankranti*," Smt. Annapurnamma continued, "varieties of food had been made to offer to God. Meanwhile, Sri Vijayeswari Devi realized that a few poor *harijans* who had come had eaten no food for the past two days. Therefore, She carried the food which was in a big vessel, ready for worship and distributed it among those people. Then She addressed Her grandmother, my mother, and said: 'Grandma, today you have done a very good thing. This is how the food so nicely prepared by you has been accepted by the Lord.' Since my mother appreciated whatever her granddaughter used to say, she was moved by these words. As a result, she went in and brought out the remaining food, distributing all of it to anyone who wanted it."

This same benevolent outlook permeated all of Sri Vijayeswari's actions. For example, She used to give away all Her dresses to the poor, and Her books to needy students. To the National Defense Fund, Vijayeswari once donated Her gold bangles and ring. "Sacrifice, in fact, was an integral feature of Her personality right from childhood," added Her mother.

"Another wondrous event occurred when Vijayeswari Devi was studying in the seventh standard and cholera struck our maidservant, Chenchita," Her mother recalled. "Even the doctor, who was summoned when she had become very weak, expressed helplessness. Since cholera is an infectious disease, I was afraid to let my child near the sick girl. However, Vijayeswari brushed past us and went right up to Chenchita's bedside. Leaning over, She dropped *vibhuti* and *prasada* into the girl's mouth. I had no idea from where that scented *vibhuti* had come. However, after a few seconds, Chenchita's closed eyelids slowly opened. Within minutes she became markedly better and in a few hours she became absolutely healthy. At this, I felt that my heart had opened up. I just could not believe that this little child could even ward off death!"

"I definitely remember another incredible day—the fourteenth of June 1968," continued Smt. Annapurnamma, "when a close friend of the family came to our house. All of her family, including herself, were devotees of Sri Ramana Bhagavan. Unfortunately, ten years earlier, her son had left home never to return. Incapable of bearing the loss, this friend used to express her sorrow to her friends and well-wishers.

On that particular day, when this lady was crying in our house remembering her son, Vijayeswari, who was sitting at a distance writing, came over and wiped her tears. 'O Mother,' She said, 'Your son will return home on the sixteenth of June, the day after tomorrow and, from then onward, you will not weep, but will be happy.' Hearing this reassurance my friend replied, 'If your words come true, I will regard you as God, and I will seek refuge in you!'

"On the sixteenth of June, at 6 o'clock in the morning when his mother was offering prayers in her *puja* room, the son who had been missing for a decade returned home. With surprise and happiness in her heart, the boy's mother took her son by the hand and rushed to our house. Without any hesitation, she prostrated before the young Vijayeswari.

"At this, I remonstrated with her. 'What is this?' I said. 'How can you, an elderly lady, prostrate before a child, and will it not reduce Her longevity?'

"In reply, my friend shed tears of joy. 'She has brought back my son, whom I thought I would never again see in my life!'

"In contemplating upon the capabilities of my daughter, Sri Vijayeswari Devi, I was wonder struck. The questions that arose in my mind had no convincing answers. It became clear to me that I was incapable of measuring Her greatness. As one cannot see the bright sun with open eyes, I could not guess the strength of my own child. I could not even guess what more I would witness in the future."

"In 1968, on a Friday evening in the month of *Shravana*, I was preparing fresh garlands of *kasturi*, *sevanthi* and other flowers for the evening *puja*. The children, after returning from school, were playing in the garden. As I sat there, I was recollecting my *Shravana* visits to Sri Bhagavan Ramana, which had lessened and then ceased after his departure from this world. I was firmly engrossed in my thoughts about how Bhagavan Ramana was surely eternal and that only merit from thousands of previous births could afford one the privilege of knowing such sacred and holy people.

"Meanwhile, Vijayeswari had come and sat by my side in order to help me arrange the flowers. She casually asked me whether I was remembering Sri Ramana Maharshi. I just quivered at Her words. I could not imagine that She could know what was passing through my mind."

"Vijayeswari had extraordinary powers which none of my other children had. Though my thoughts had been reinforced by hundreds of previous events depicting Her greatness, the satisfaction I derived by thinking of Her as my daughter was something beyond expression."

"One day Vijayeswari said: 'Mother, you are totally without ego. The wall of egoism in the heart of anyone will surely prevent Self-Realization. When one truly knows that the physical form does not belong to him, he gets liberated. Those who have not given up the ego and selfishness cannot step into the spiritual realm.'

"In return, I asked Her: 'I took refuge in Sri Ramana Bhagavan to get Self-Realization. Do I have the eligibility to get his grace?'

"Vijayeswari answered in the affirmative that it is possible to be graced by the Lord. So saying, She placed Her hand on my head.

"At that moment, I felt such heaviness, as if the entire universe were resting there! I heard the sacred Om vibrating through the earth and sky. I felt bodiless and as light as cotton. I heard words like *'vidruma, hema, nila, dhavala,* and *chhayair mukhai.'* Then I had the *darshan* of Sri Gayatri Devi in Her cosmic form, seated on the lotus, bedecked with precious jewels and with five heads. As I was having this vision, light enveloped the entire universe. I felt that everything was Mother Herself. That figure was familiar and a very close one. I experienced in that form all rivers, oceans, mountains, three *crores* of deities, *maha rishis, siddhas, gandharvas, nagas, kinnaras, kimpurushas* and *crores* of *jivas*. The sun and the moon were Her two eyes. Fire was Her third eye. I could hardly look at that vision which was so radiant.

"'O Mother of the Universe, please bless me,' I prayed. Gradually, that cosmic form disappeared. I felt that the all-pervading universal power was my Self.

"I was totally engrossed in that state for two days. As I could not open my eyes, my family members grew anxious, thinking that I was suffering from some disease. This divine experience was the greatest of my life! I had the joy of amassing invaluable diamonds from the diamond mine of Vijayeswari.

"In this manner, my child became my *Guru*, my beacon light, my Goddess, my ideal of life, and my path to salvation."

FROM THE HOUSE TO THE HERMITAGE

The ninth of June 1980 was significant, for it was on this date that Sri Vijayeswari Devi, divine knowledge Absolute, moved from Her home in Gudur to Sri Penusila Kshetram, the abode of Sri Narasimha Swami.

From the Diaries
of
Swami Vijayeswarananda

LOVE OF GOD

January 14, 1986:

As it was winter, the entire *ashram* was covered with mist. The time was 9:00 a.m. Any object which was seven or eight feet away was not at all visible. Amma, in a simple white *sari*, was seated on the circular platform under the banyan tree. She was enjoying the beauty of nature's atmosphere. We could hear some whispers, but we were not able to see the persons coming towards us. The figures prostrated to Amma. They were a group of three who had come from Chennai, and they offered a light pink scented rose garland specially brought all the way from home. One of them was a known devotee by the name of Sri Sivaramakrishna, and the other two, his friends, were new visitors.

Sri Sivaramakrishna was a staunch devotee of Sri Ramakrishna Paramahamsa. Often he said he loved Divine Mother Sri Sharada Devi more than Paramahamsa. I like to read about Sharada Devi," he said. "In fact, I go on reading the same book repeatedly. Many a time I think how lucky I would have been if I was alive during the time of Divine Mother Sharada Devi. But after seeing Karunamayi Amma, I think my desire has been fulfilled.

"During my first visit, on August 3, 1981, when I first had *darshan* of Amma in the forest, I saw very clearly the form of Sri Sharada Devi in Amma. Sri Karunamayi has blessed me with this *darshan*. Amma is the embodiment of love! What tremendous capacity the name 'Karunamayi' has to save and carry forward the multitude of souls, eager to follow Her towards the goal of realization, universality, true love and compassion for every living creature."

Sri Karunamayi, with compassionate looks, received his love and affection. "Are you coming directly from Chennai?" She asked.

"Amma, we started yesterday from Chennai. We reached Rapur (a nearby town, thirty miles away) late at night. As there were no buses, we again started this morning and came on foot from Gonupalli (four miles from the *ashram*)."

"You must be tired. Are your legs paining? Go to Ammamma (Amma's Mother), have breakfast and come back."

After ten or fifteen minutes they returned.

Sri Sivaramakrishna had one question. "Amma, we are not able to love God as we love worldly things. What is the reason, even though we know clearly that we have to love God alone?"

The atmosphere was extremely chilly and it was silent. Amma, in a very soft and sweet voice, started to speak. "Let us search our hearts and examine well the inner recesses of our minds to discover what we love most. Is it God we love or things of the world? Many people think they must concern themselves only with the food they eat, discussions, home life, and the comforts and pleasures of the body. God is the supreme one from whom all things come. We cannot afford to build a wall of false superiority, distinctions and degrees, and then hope to know God. The world's way of pettiness, jealousy, hatred and envy leads one far from the path of God.

"Then you may inquire, Amma continued, 'Cannot a worldly person attain God, as well as one who has renounced the world?' Attainment of God does not necessitate retiring from the world and renunciation in the outer sense. But it certainly does demand complete renunciation of all lower feelings such as jealousy, hatred, envy, pettiness, dishonesty, untruthfulness and selfishness. No one can rob us of our spiritual birthright but ourselves. We are wholly responsible for what we attain, or do not attain. We may be surrounded by great spiritual men and yet pass them by, because our minds are filled with petty thoughts, so we do not have the room to accept holiness.

"The mind must be holy to perceive holiness. It must be pure to know purity. Initially all of us are pure and holy, but thoughts of an impure nature have clouded and spoiled our inner hearts to such an extent that our vision cannot reflect purity. Fortunate is the one who has a pure heart and mind and seeks God as the natural object of love.

"Christ tells us, 'Blessed are the pure in heart, for they shall see God.' When we are quiet, calm, self-controlled and surrendered to God, then holiness and purity are reflected. Thus, wherever these qualities shine, we perceive them."

There was silence for some time. Slowly the mist was fading away. Amma stood up and started walking on the small path in the *ashram* garden. As it was the month of January, it was a delight to see different colored flowers on either side. Suddenly, Amma knelt down and started caressing a tiny blossom. It was not a colorful flower—it was an ordinary grass flower. Looking at Sivaramakrishna, Amma said, "This also is one of the creations of Divine Mother. Its life will be blessed if we offer it to the lotus feet of Devi."

Very gently Amma plucked the flower, came to the *Lalita Devi* Mandir, and offered it at the lotus feet of Divine Mother.

Amma sat once again on the small *pitham* (wooden plank) and told the visitors to meditate for at least an hour. Immediately She was absorbed in meditation.

After taking lunch from Annapurnamma, all took their leave.

VISHVAMITRA POND

Sri Ram Gopal Sharma of Mangalore, accompanied by a few friends, came to Penusila for the *darshan* of Amma. Some fifteen other persons had been there since the previous day, also anticipating Amma's *darshan*. Amma, however, did not return from the forest.

Next morning, more than thirty of us marched towards the region where Sage Vishvamitra had performed penance, carrying with us fruits, snacks, and food for Amma. I separately carried *atta*, beaten and broken rice and dough, mixed with sugar. We were all extremely happy to find Amma beside a pond at the peak of the Garudadri Hills, and we prostrated before Her.

"Amma," said Dr. Sharma, "I have been meditating on *kundalini* for a long time. I am not at all satisfied with my progress. Depression and grief are gripping me. I am not able to sit for long in meditation. What is the reason? Amma, please bless me to sit for longer periods."

"Dear son, if *kundalini shakti* has to be awakened through meditation, it is to be preceded by *yoga siddhi*. The most important practices for yoga siddhi are *pranayama* and *yogic* postures. When practiced regularly, *kundalini shakti* is awakened. Only by practice of *pranayama*, is steadiness of the mind obtained."

Amma, sitting on the bank of the pond, was sliding the balls of *atta* and beaten rice into the water with overwhelming love. From nowhere, thousands of fish jumped up to share the food released by Amma's hand and then went away.

After a few minutes, Dr. Sharma asked, "Will steadiness

of mind definitely occur by the practice of *pranayama*, Amma?"

"Son," Amma replied, "inhalation and exhalation during *pranayama* reaches the *muladhara*, and is held there for a while. This results in destroying the wavering nature of the mind, which then achieves steadiness. But then, this should be practiced under the guidance of a *Guru*.

If one succeeds in the retention of the vital force, *prana* vayu, in the *kumbhaka* state, one will certainly secure steadiness of mind. The most speedy flow of thoughts will be mellowed, and gradually the mind will completely calm down."

"Amma, what state of mind is necessary to become a sage?"

Amma replied, "By giving up worldly attachments mentally, quietude prevails in life. A thought-free state is the mind of a sage. Only by silencing the mind does a seeker acquire the qualities leading to Self-Realization."

Dr. Sharma sighed. "Amma, is the human life span sufficient for this?"

Amma simply smiled. "Dear one, how long can a ball thrown up stay in space? If you have the wisdom to recognize the goal of life, even a moment spent in divine thought is sufficient and valuable."

Dr. Sharma's friend, Mathi Manjari, also asked Amma: "Mother, I have been worshipping Devi for years. I was worrying as to when my *puja* would yield fruit. I have obtained a lot of peace by meeting You. But even after so many years, anger and egoism have not lessened in my heart. At least, after meeting You, please bless me to get rid of these qualities, so that I don't carry them back with me."

Amma graciously replied, "*Nanna*, don't despair! If there is a hole somewhere in a vessel, only after it is closed can anything poured into it stay there. By the very thought of *Amba*, the human mind becomes Manidwipa, the abode of *Sri Lalita Parameshwari*. All qualities and anger in the mind are destroyed and, gradually, the mind is lit up. Prayer is not mere uttering of words knit together, but should be said with utmost sincerity. The mind will then be filled with peace. Impatience and anger will decrease. Their waning is the index of the fruit of worship. May you get all that is blissful!"

Pouring sugar, broken rice and flour into the hole next to Her, Amma said, addressing the ants like human beings, "Children, come and have your food." All of us were stunned at the sight that followed: One by one, and then in hundreds and thousands, the ants patiently moved in, partook of the feed, and began to disperse. Amma was glancing at them with kindness.

Others took the rare opportunity to ask Mother about their doubts. "Mother," said one, "nowadays there are many hypocrites in spirituality. What will be the result?"

Amma responded. "It is not that easy for men to change their natural low qualities. They just go through the cycles of birth and death. Such people are of no use at all to this world! Just think how much we have suffered because of this body. During time spent devotionally, the negative qualities appear to be silent, but they continue to remain inherent within. Just by sitting on a lotus, can a frog attain the glory of Maha Lakshmi Devi? As it descends into the slush, it exhibits its natural traits! The result of one's hypocrisy will cause harm to one's self."

Another devotee had a question. "Amma, what is meant by *atma linga puja*, Self-worship?"

"Crossing the barriers of the mind and intellect and getting liberated. If one revels in the highest divine state, one attains the natural liberated state by worship of the Self."

Amma continued, "If the mind just thinks about philosophy, will that be philosophical thought? Or, if it is not understood, will it be philosophical thought? The Supreme can be attained only when you do not enter the track of thoughts at all."

Another devotee wondered, "Is there any use of the pilgrimages undertaken by many people who neither have devotion nor any spiritual transformation in their lives?"

"Just by a holy dip in the Godavari River, can a cat turn into a lion? When your mind is pure, you can see God within yourself. However holy a pilgrimage, if it does not bring about transformation in you, it turns out to be a waste."

"Who is referred to as the best of all?" asked another. "The one who is silent," Mother replied. She gazed into the water of Vishvamitra Pond for a long time after that.

Finally, one devotee said softly: "We want to hear and know about the philosophy of *Brahman* through great people, Amma."

"Experiencing the knowledge of *Brahman* by hearing is difficult. It is like trying to dig a well with sound, not with a shovel."

"How does a realized person move about in the *samadhi* state?" someone else wanted to know.

After a moment, Amma replied, "Such a realized soul would be firm, ever immersed in a deep ocean of silence. He will not respond even if called. Whatever efforts are made to bring him back to this world, even by patting, are useless. He does not get identified with the body and remains unconcerned. Whatever one may think about him—whether he is flattered or scorned—he will remain quiet and unconcerned, with a smile. He will remain as the highest principle of Self (Siva) being himself this vital force, the all-knowledgeable Self, as well as being everything else. Such is the state of a realized soul in the monistic state."

"Mother," another wished to know, "will I experience *Brahman*?"

"It is improbable for the divine light to glow in a heart full of layers of worldly ignorance. If the *tamasic* and *rajasic* attributes of the mind are reduced, then the knowledge of the Self arises."

The devotee continued: "I am wandering from place to place for the knowledge of the Self. My belief in experiencing the Supreme in this life has waned. I am feeling restless. What is your advice to me, Amma?"

"For the fruit of good deeds, wandering about without controlling the mind will result in minimal benefit. Withdrawing the mind from external things, controlling the mind and meditating on the Supreme, one can realize the *Atman*. Do not allow despair to envelop you."

Amma went on giving satisfactory replies very calmly to all questions.

One of those assembled said, "Amma, we have come here tired after traversing with hearts parched by the dreary paths of the world. Your words have given us a lot of peace. We are desirous of spending one day in Your holy presence in meditation. Please permit us."

Then Mother said with great compassion, "All of you have come so far, climbing up these hills with a lot of spiritual thirst and sincerity. Meditate here with a peaceful mind, forgetting everything for a day."

Amma distributed fruits and sweets to all of us with incomparable love. Eating them and drinking pure sweet water, we spent that day with Mother, in *dhyana*.

That whole night we spent under the cover of huge trees. Some meditated, while others fell asleep.

The next day having dawned, all took their baths in the river flowing not far off, plucked wild fruits and ate them in haste. By then, Sri Ravi had brought two bags full of rice and curry from the *ashram*. Amma's mother had arranged for this, knowing that the visitors, being without food the previous day, could not climb down the hills.

Unfortunately, the person who brought the food also announced that he had to convey some bad news. Some unidentified persons had set fire to the cattle-shed and to Amma's hermitage the previous night. Fortunately, there had been no causalities, but the hermitage had completely burnt down!

I was anxiously looking at Amma, as to what She would say. But Amma was in Her own composed state. On that very sober and calm face, Her smile continued without any abatement. "All of you have your food. It is already afternoon," was all She said.

The food was served to all on the green leaves of the forest. Having been hungry, everyone ate to their heart's content.

Amma kept some food on a huge plate-like stone for a group of monkeys, who came towards Her. Amma invited them, "Come, come, eat!"

Even before Amma's invitation reached them, the huge group of monkeys had formed a circle around the food. They began hastily eating.

Amma was full of love for the peacocks, deer, rabbits and cheetahs of the forest. They enjoyed Amma's love without hankering for it. Not only that, but the cows and calves, and the dogs and the cats have all experienced Amma's incomparable love at the *ashram*.

Taking permission of Amma, we all left for the *ashram* once again.

SRI GURU PURNIMA: 1983

The waterfall was flowing from the peak of the mountain. The beauty of Sri Lakshmi Gayatri Kundam has a special attraction. The main trees to be found there are the *banyan*, *pipal*, gooseberry and incense trees. Near this place we also find *kusha* grass in abundance. Many devotees had assembled at Sri Lakshmi Gayatri Kundam on the auspicious occasion of *Sri Guru Purnima*. It was cloudy and very chilly.

Back in the days when Amma used to return from the Garudadri Hills where She meditated, a small lily plant had attracted Mother's attention. It was as though it were asking Amma to take it with Her. With utmost care, She had brought it to the *ashram* and planted it in a small pot. That particular plant had the marvelous habit of blooming a couple of flowers, but only on the day of *Guru Purnima*. It seemed as if they had bloomed for Amma only, because they would be facing and bending towards Amma's lotus feet. Hence, we used to call them *Guru Purnima* lilies. Filled with fragrance, they used to dance gaily during Amma's *Sri Pada Puja*. Not only the devotees, but also the plants, flowers, birds and animals were interested in this *puja*.

So, taking utmost care on that day, one of the devotees placed the plant on his shoulders and brought it all the way to Gayatri Pond—four miles from the *ashram*. The plant was fluttering gaily in the breeze, thinking that it would also have the opportunity of participating in *Guru Puja*. We were able to see clearly that its two flowers were ready to bloom during the *pada puja*.

Sri Karunamayi also loved the small white calf that lived in the *ashram*. Not only that, but a pair of peacocks which Amma used to feed with grains daily in the forest, had one day followed Amma to the *ashram*, and stayed there.

So, when we all started for Lakshmi Gayatri Pond, Siva, the small calf, and Aruna, the peacock, wanted to accompany us. We tried in vain to control them, but they had escaped and were well ahead of us.

Devotees from different places had brought varieties of flowers for Amma's *pada puja*. These short-lived flowers were in eager anticipation of falling on Amma's lotus feet.

The whole atmosphere was echoing with *mantras* of *vedic pundits*, songs of devotees, and added to this, the sweet singing of hundreds of birds. Everywhere was the fragrance of incense sticks and the smoke of *sambrani*. Everyone had *ghee* lamps in their hands, and one hundred eight ladies with *kalashas* were praising Amma with *Sri Shodashi Stotra*.

Amma's divine feet had been decorated with *surya* and *chandra*, the sun and moon, on either foot. These lotus feet were resting on a small *pitham* decorated with cloth and raised a little so that all could have convenient *darshan* from afar.

As this arrangement was made, Aruna, the peacock, was the first to come close and gaze at Amma's decorated feet. Siva, the small calf, then came forward, crossing all the devotees, and sat near Amma's blessed feet thinking, "I am the best pet for Her." After some time it stood, came very close and kept its head on Amma's lotus feet. The calf was blessed with Amma's caressing touch. First, it placed its head on one foot only, and then it covered both Her feet. This incident was photographed in every movement.

Many devotees who had come from Kashi, Kashmir, Tamil Nadu, Rajamundry—most of them well-versed in *shastras* and *Vedas*—one by one offered flowers to Amma's lotus feet. After the *puja* everyone sat in meditation.

With compassionate looks, Amma was sitting in front of us like the effulgent light of *purna jnana*. Sri Neelakantha Shastri prostrated to Amma's lotus feet and spoke: "Amma, Your *charana sannidhi* itself is Kashi for us! Your *charana dhuli* is *moksha prasada* for us! Being in front of Your lotus feet is like being in front of Sri Sharadamba of *Satya loka*."

Amma blessed us by placing Her hand on our heads.

Amma then began to speak and told us all that had happened that day before we reached Her in the forest—about the peacock and the calf and also about a devotee bringing the lily plant on his shoulders. Though Amma appears to be a normal person externally, there is nothing in the world that is not known to Her. It would have been very foolish on our part if we had mentioned all these things to Amma. But with Her divine insight, Amma knew—as She can know what has taken place in your previous birth—what is taking place at present, and what is going to take place in the future. Almost all devotees have experienced this.

Being insignificant creatures in front of Amma, we cannot measure the depths of Amma's love, compassion and kindness towards us. If we have at least a ray of love in our hearts, then only can we understand Her a little.

Amma was in silence. "Silence is the language of Lord Siva," She often says. We were all immersed completely in that silence. The waves of stillness from Amma were directly touching everyone's heart. There was silence for some time. Amma's silent message was washing away all our doubts. A person becomes without thought when he sits in front of Amma.

The entire *tapovana* of Sri Gayatri Kunda was filled with the fragrance of *shanti*. Everyone's hearts were filled with the desire to experience *Brahma jnana*. We were able to clearly see what the aim of life is—not to waste time in mundane matters and that Self-Realization is the ultimate goal.

Amma inscribed the *Sri Saraswati Bijakshara Mantra* on the tongues of some of the devotees with tulasi and honey. After the *Maha Sri Pada Puja* and special *aratis*, *prasadam* was distributed to all.

On that day Amma inscribed the *Sri Saraswati Bijakshara Mantra* on my tongue. I felt as if some great power were engulfing me. Something was inspiring my mind to write: I never knew from where the inspiration came. Taking a pen in hand, I started to write in my dairy the *shlokas* which flashed into my mind. I offered them at Amma's lotus feet.

Many stayed back on that cool full-moon night and did meditation. That was the first time devotees had spent the night in the forest.

BULL—THE SYMBOL OF FORBEARANCE

Two early devotees of Amma, Kumaraswamy, headmaster of a municipal high school in Sri Kavali, and Balramareddy, a humble villager from Chennur, tireless in his devotion and *seva*, along with myself, were walking from Lakshmi Gayatri Pond. It was on a narrow path that was very hard, rough, stony, and hurt the feet, where the following conversation took place.

Kumaraswamy asked me, "Swamiji, can you tell me if Amma, who is always calm and composed, has been agitated at any time by any incident?"

"Yes, it is rare," I replied. "But there was one time I will never forget. Two years ago, at the time of *Brahmotsavam* in the Narasimha Swami Temple at Penusila Kshetram, many devotees had assembled. One among them lit a large quantity of camphor, on account of which the darbha grass tied to the *dhvaja stambham* caught fire. It happened between 3:30 and 4:00 a.m. The fire then spread to the entire *shamiana*, and hundreds of pilgrims were caught in that fire. From a distance of half a mile people could hear the screams and cries of the devotees trapped in the blaze. The intensity of the heat was so great that the *Garuda vahana* brought from Sri Venugopala Swami Temple melted! You can just imagine the extent of pain and agony of the burn victims! The people were in critical condition with burn injuries, and their suffering was unbearable.

As there was no telephone facility in the vicinity, messages could not even be sent to Nellore for medical help. The little first aid and few medicines available within the *ashram* were also insufficient.

Amma was shaken with their pain and said, "How can these people travel seventy miles in this condition? How I wish we had a small hospital here!" Saying so, She broke down in great anguish as any mother would, sobbing to see her children in critical condition. For many days Amma refused to take food.

"It was a tragic event! Everyone was heartbroken!" Balramareddy broke in.

I continued, "This incident had a severe impact on Amma, and Her aim became to build a private medical center at Penusila Kshetram to render medical aid to the remote villages. However, because the *ashram* land at that time belonged to the temple authority, we could not do so. Meanwhile, after applying to the government for possession of the land, due to Amma's *sankalpa*, it was temporarily allotted to the *ashram* for a school for two hundred children. Thus the school was started to provide free education."

Amma's *sankalpa* to build a hundred-bed hospital for the villagers was not just because of that one fire. Once, a worker died of a heart attack because medical aid was not available. There was no bus to take him to Nellore to give him proper medical help. If timely help had been rendered, if a proper medical center had existed in this remote area for the poor, his life could have been saved. When needy people come for any sort of help, Amma shares their grief and extends whatever help they need.

By this time, we had all reached Chandi Saptashati Tapovana. Because Amma had done *tapas* for a long time there, we offered our *pranamas*. Amma's feet had purified the place. Kumaraswamy, Balramareddy and myself bowed down and smeared the holy dust on our foreheads as *tilakam*. We also carried a little dust with us. From here we could see the Garudadri Hills, which very much resemble the nearby Tiruvannamalai Hills.

Sri Kumaraswamy wanted to know whether Amma had related any incident atop these hills about Her earlier days.

"Yes," I said. "I was there once myself just after a huge Ongole bull had skidded and fallen down the ravine, breaking its leg. The bull is the symbol of forbearance, and the sight of the pain and agony it suffered was unbearable! Fortunately, Sri Karunamayi had come from the other side on hearing the animal's cries. Looking at the tears of the bull, Amma's heart melted.

Seeing Amma, the bull shook more, as if showing the pitiable condition of its broken foot. By the time the devotees and I reached there, Amma had set the broken leg in its proper position and it looked normal.

Amma washed the wound with cold water and wiped the bull's tears with Her *sari pallu* saying, "Is it still paining? I will take your pain, and you will get relief."

When Amma lovingly touched its leg, the bull got up and started walking normally. Tears of joy rolled down from its eyes as it looked at Amma and bowed its head thankfully. Amma comforted it as if She were caressing a small child.

This incident we witnessed clearly illustrates the hidden power of Amma and portrays Her boundless compassion. A wealth of love, compassion, and riches, when not shared with others, is not worth having. With surprise we had watched Amma, filled as She is with motherly love and compassion. Amma has come down from beyond the aura of colors, planets and *Omkara*. She has descended to Earth only for the love of humanity. She has made us feel the presence of the Divine.

Kumaraswamy asked further: "Did you ever see that bull again?"

"Yes!" I replied. "After that, the bull came many times and sat in front of Amma's feet. It expressed its love and gratitude silently."

Amma extends help and compassion to everybody, thinking of them as Her very own. She does not expect anything in return from anyone. This is Her specialty.

"Our Amma is golden-hearted and good," Balramareddy said. "Amma has taken the responsibility of making us aware of *atma jnana* and has changed the course of our lives towards peace and harmony. We must consider this our good fortune earned from previous births. I have become whole and complete after coming to Amma."

Kumaraswamy was interested to know if Amma talked with the tribal people.

"Again, yes," I replied. "Amma talks with a lot of love and compassion to these village folk. On *Dashehra* day She joyously distributes sweets, fruits, and clothes. *Kumkum* and bangles are given to the ladies. She also takes the responsibility of performing marriages and giving mangala sutras and new clothes to the needy.

At the time of *Brahmotsavam*, the *harijans* here offer honey, nuts and root vegetables to the deity Narasimha Swami at Penusila Kshetram. They sing and dance to the accompaniment of music to celebrate the glory of the Lord. During this festival they look upon Amma as Chenchu Lakshmi, a deity of their family. They offer Her cooked vegetables dipped in honey. Amma is a spectator of these festivities."

"Does Amma strictly adhere to orthodoxy?" Kumaraswamy asked me.

"Amma follows certain principles to set an example for us. Her principles regarding religion and speech are so deep that She follows them Herself and is never seen hurting anyone. But whoever the person may be—of any caste or creed—if he offers *prasadam* with affection, She accepts it with boundless compassion and goes beyond orthodox levels to make them happy."

"For more than two years, an old *harijan* lady climbed the hill with difficulty to where Amma stayed and offered

Her *ragi* gruel. Amma used to take it like *amritam*, nectar, and the leftover porridge was taken by the old lady as *prasadam*.

"This same lady worked for three years for Amma in her old age. When she knew her end had come, she called a shepherd boy and asked him to get a small cloth bag, in which she had kept the holy dust of Amma's feet. She asked the boy to put a little on her chest, and then took out one rupee, which she had saved for a long time. She requested the boy to give it to Amma for the construction of Bharata Mata Mandir. She told him this would fulfill her last wish. Then, when the boy put the holy dust in her mouth, she muttered, 'Amma, have you come? Have you come for my sake?' and left her body.

"The boy, as per her wish, gave that *rupee* to the *ashram*. Even now Amma, with a lot of sentiment, has preserved the coin in a frame. Amma's relationship with the village folk is very subtle and intense. She gives a lot of importance to their small but deep feelings with great reverence."

Kumaraswamy asked another question. "Has Amma got any special food habits, likes and dislikes?"

I told him, "Amma has no special liking for any particular food and never says that the food is not tasty. When food is served to Her, She offers prayers and takes very little. I have never heard Her talking of taste. She takes simple food such as *dal* and *roti*."

"As far as Amma's schedule is concerned," I continued, "every day Amma goes through all the letters written by devotees. She goes to bed around 1:00 a.m. She gets up early at 3:00 a.m., before anyone else is up and does *dhyana* in a scheduled place. She is not particular about things or food, but loves nature abundantly. She loves even a little grass flower. Amma cannot bear to see any difficulty come to these forests."

"What does 'difficulty to the forests' mean?" Kumaraswamy looked puzzled.

"I will explain." I told him. "In those days we were new to these forests, which were filled with *bodha* grass. The villagers used to go to the forests to collect firewood. One day, just for fun, somebody threw a lighted matchstick on the grass. Slowly a fire started with a little smoke, but by nightfall it had spread, devastating all the nearby big trees. Seeing this spectacle, the villagers started clapping their hands. They felt that by destroying the cleared brush, the land would become more fertile.

"When Amma felt very sad, the people said that the big trees would not be affected, and that when the rainy season began, the plants would grow again.

"Amma replied, 'Lighting a fire is easy and joyful to you, but the eggs and little birds in the nests, the rabbits, squirrels, peacocks, deer, anthills, snakes, tigers and birds will all be burnt overnight. How many years does it take for the forests and trees to grow? When anyone lights a fire for fun, you should stop them.'

"Later, Amma gave them food and taught them to show concern for living beings and lead responsible lives."

By that time, the three of us had come out of the forest and were nearing the *ashram*.

SRI KARUNAMAYI - A Biography

RAMA NAMA OF THE PARROTS AND SIVA NAMA OF THE BIRDS

In the deep forests of Kanva in Penusila Kshetram, the trees are so tall that it looks as if they are touching the skies. After crossing a place called Bhairavakona, the atmosphere is filled with the buzzing of bees and the sweet fragrance of wild mango flowers in full bloom. Many types of birds chirp on treetops and wild sweet-gourd fruits grow in plenty.

The birds were sitting around Amma, some on Her shoulders, some on Her hands and on Her head. Eating the ripe fruits from Amma's hands, they were sweetly repeating the name "Sri Rama, Sri Rama" as taught to them by Amma. Their rendering of the name was as sweet as honey! Forgetting ourselves entirely, Amma's mother, Sri Kavali Kumaraswamy, Sri Balramareddy and myself were watching this wonderful scene. Amma was wearing a light orange *sari*, but the countless light green colored parrots sitting all over Amma made Her whole body green! If we had only had a camera, we could have taken a photograph of this rare scene. The birds were reciting in chorus:

> *Śrī rāma rāma rāmeti rame rāme manorame
> Sahasranāma tattulyam rāma nāma varānane*

and

> *Śrī rāma nāmalu śata koṭi oka oka peru bahutepi*

Our hearts were touched by their sweet recitation. Amma was in a sweet, calm and composed state which, though seen by us personally, cannot be imagined. Kumaraswamy, his eyes filled with tears of joy, exclaimed, "Just as the parrots are reciting *Rama nama* today, may Amma give *bhakti rasa* and *Sri Rama nama* to all of humanity in the future!"

In the meantime, the forests were also filled with the sounds of *bulbuls*. Amma had taught them *Siva nama*. As a result, the entire forest was filled with *Siva* and *Rama nama* songs, and the rhythmic beat of the tender leaves as they fluttered in the gentle breeze was like a *tala*, a beat, to the songs. This beautiful sight was indescribable and reminded us of Sita in the forests during the *Treta Yuga*. For a long time we were unable to forget this wonderful scene. The singing of the parrots and *bulbuls* mingling with Amma's happy laughter left an indelible impression in our hearts.

Sri Kumaraswamy was a devotee of Siva, and he used to recite *Siva nama* all the time. He was overjoyed at the bulbuls singing *Siva nama*. Sri Kumaraswamy's prediction of the future has come true: Amma, who at that time had never come out of the forests, has now come to visit many places in the country to spread spiritual truths, divine love, and the divinity of God to all mankind.[2]

Amma, who is the embodiment of spirituality and *atma jnana*, like the cool, serene rays of the autumn moon, generously sprinkles the elixir of sweet inspiring nectar-like words of philosophy on mankind.

Amma has come to impart human values, not only to us Indians, but to all humans, so that all of mankind in the world may experience this divine love. Our compassionate, loving Mother has poured love and affection on all our hearts, just as She taught *Siva* and *Rama nama* to the parrots for their spiritual upliftment.

---

[2] At the time of the publication of this volume, Amma has traveled to several countries of the world and spread Her eternal message to countless people.

SRI KARUNAMAYI - A Biography

Mother has initiated us with *Omkara Mantra* by writing *Om* on our tongues with *tulasi* stems dipped in honey, purifying us and making us *jivan muktas*. Being our Mother in all our previous births, due to Her divine love, She has showered us with *atma jnana*. She is the eternal light of our hearts. Though Her human form looks tiny, the light in Her is the light that illumines the entire universe and millions of planets. Wherever Her devotees may be, and whenever they call out "Amma," She runs to their rescue. I humbly offer myself at the lotus feet of holy Mother.

MIRACULOUS SHOWERS OF ABUNDANCE

Amidst the dense Kanva Forests, which shelter many free birds, lies beautiful Penusila, bordered by the Garudadri Mountain peaks touching the blue sky. Sri Karunamayi is beyond this materialistic ether. Sri Vijayeswari, the Supreme Swan who always moves in the *chidakasha*, the inner space of the heart, was the initiator of the following incidents.

Sri B.V. Subba Rao, a close devotee from Giddatharu village, had arranged a week long *Chandi yaga* at his place, for obtaining Amma's grace. Amma had accepted his invitation to bless the villagers with Her maternal love, by gracing the occasion during the last two days. The priests for the *yaga* were Sri Balavishwanatha Sharma and Sri Brindam, both known to Amma.

Amma's car, along with three others filled with many devotees, left Penusila in the morning and reached Giddatharu village by evening. The village chieftains had dressed up traditionally in the Indian style. Amma was received with *purna kumbham, nadaswaram*, a bandset, and by hundreds of devotees holding decorative white umbrellas.

The town was decked up for Amma's reception with colorful welcoming banners, strings of mango leaves and flowers, plantain trees, colorful buntings and the illumination of lights. Amma's divine presence brought peace and added to the beautification.

The street of Subba Rao's residence, where Amma's stay was arranged, was neatly cleaned up and decorated with *pandals* of coconut leaves and fresh lotus flowers. As Amma entered, a garland of newly blossomed manoranjani flowers was offered to Her lotus feet. A mala of *mandara* flowers adorned Amma's neck. Amma is fond of *mandara* flowers! She is *Mandara kusuma priya*, isn't it?

All the ladies offered *arati* with *jyotis* on either side, as Amma moved on. The evil glance was warded off by breaking nine coconuts and five pumpkins. Ladies sang welcome songs. By Amma's much awaited arrival, all hearts were filled with waves of joy. All eyes, too, twinkled with joy, and some others shed tears. Ladies sang aloud, offering the auspicious *arati*, thus:

"Sri Lakshmi Devi, please accept our worship! Sri Vijayeswari Devi, please accept our worship! O Goddess, born in the lotus, please come fast, tinkling Your anklets, to accept our *puja*. You who took eight forms as *Ashta Lakshmi*, please come away from the abode of Vishnu at once! Bless us with the shower of Your compassion. In the milky ocean, on the serpent bed, Sri Lakshmi, You are caressing the lotus feet of Lord Vishnu. Please be kind to us and allow us to see your real form."

Sprinkling lotus petals, they continued singing. The final *arati* of *kumkum* water and camphor was offered, chanting the *shloka*:

> *Aruṇa bīja pūrṇa padmāsana samsthite*
> *Hé svarṇāmbarāvṛte manohara manju gate*
> *Udyana manojna smita pankaja manjulasye*
> *Sampat pradāyinī śrī vijayeśwarī lakshmī*
> *naumi nityam*

The devotees bowed to the *arati*. In spite of the daylong tedious journey, Sri Karunamayi exchanged pleasantries with the ladies. Amma blessed Mrs. Subba Rao with *kumkum*, bangles and a silk *sari*. She also blessed all the assembled. Around 9 p.m., Amma took leave of the people.

The upper floor of Subba Rao's house had been fixed for Amma's stay. The house was crowded with friends, relatives and devotees. Arrangements for food were on a large scale. At three, in the wee hours of the morning, the auspicious clarinet was played. Later that morning, *Rudra abhishekam* and *mantra pushpam*—the final *puja*, offering one's own self as a flower at the feet of Devi—was complete.

The sixth day of the *Chandi yaga* commenced at 7:30 a.m. The place for the *yaga* was the spacious site on the premises of a paper factory on the outskirts of town. Large scale arrangements for poor feeding, distribution of clothes, offering of cows to *pundits*, and gifts of turmeric and *kumkum* powders to ladies, as well as platforms for spiritual discourses had been made.

Amma moved slowly on the red carpet, which led to the *yagashala*, as thousands of people on either side of Her looked on. Amma continued blessing the devotees by placing Her divine palm on their heads. She held the infants in Her arms and returned them to their mothers after blessing them. The old with poor vision were trying to catch a glimpse of Amma and hurriedly bowed to Her with folded palms. Sri Karunamayi did not walk to the dais as arranged. Instead She walked to the devotees who were eagerly waiting. Many of them had come from neighboring villages. She talked to them with utmost affection. Amma instructed the volunteers not to stop those who wanted to come close to Her. The people expressed their problems and troubles to their beloved Mother. Amma wiped the tears of the unfortunate and depressed devotees, and Her *pallu* got drenched with tears in the process. She comforted and blessed them with the touch of motherly love. Their joy was boundless, when Amma spoke to them, even for a second. They felt relieved and all their troubles were washed away. Their hearts were filled with immense peace.

In spite of the pressure of the impatient and eager crowd, Amma's patience and tolerance were matchless.

You can never trace even an iota of anger, impatience, discontent or commotion in Sri Karunamayi. Amma is even beyond peace. Ever contented is Mother Karunamayi! Who can ever offer anything to satisfy or please such a Mother?

The joy experienced by thousands of people at the *darshan* of Amma—Her gentle touch, the consoling words in Her soothing voice, Her glance showering maternal love, cooler than the light of the full moon—is indescribable!

Subba Rao, concerned for Amma's welfare, interfered.

"Amma, it is very sunny here. So, please come and take Your seat. The people will come to You."

Amma replied, "It is very difficult for them to reach me. They have to follow so many restrictions and it is difficult for them to pass through the crowd. They cannot come to me! My reaching them is easier, dear one. I shall stay here for some more time."

The real, invisible, divine seat of Amma, which is in the hearts of Her children, is great! This Empress, Karunamayi, occupies the divine seat in those heart temples of Her children which are pure, clean and full of love, and which can never equal any royal thrones, though made of gold and set with rows of precious gems.

The relationship between Amma and Her children is not the temporary bond of blood. It is the incomprehensible, indivisible, eternal bond of souls. This bond is alike whether the child is a king or a commoner! Whether Her child is a great scholar, like Vasishtha Maharshi, or an illiterate, Amma's love is the same! Karunamayi is the real Mother for all souls, since *crores* of births. They are all really Her own children.

The steady, pure and unshakable throne in the heart of Her child is the highest one for Sri Karunamayi. The richest *pancha brahmasana* throne at Manidwipa—where Divine

SRI KARUNAMAYI - A Biography

Mother resides as *Sri Lalitamba*—also cannot equal the pure love of Her children. The delightful motherly love of Amma affirms this.

Meanwhile, the sorrow that brimmed out of thousands of hearts was relieved by Amma's soothing love.

Amma proceeded to the sacrificial fire and offered the *purnahuti*. The yaga was over. The closing *vedic mantras* were chanted in a high pitch, praying for universal peace to flourish in the world, and for happiness and prosperity to bless all of mankind. More than a *lakh* were fed that day. The poor were given clothes. This was a huge gathering with people everywhere! Every mouth chanted Sri Karunamayi's divine name.

The physical presence of Sri Karunamayi made the day's program gracious and complete. After all this, Sri Subba Rao prostrated to Amma.

"Amma," he said, "many people have been eagerly waiting for Your *darshan* since a long time. Now many are blessed and feel contented. All of them are thanking me for this, but I am only an instrument in Your hands. I am Your servant. I am Your child. You were kind enough to come here, and You have filled thousands of hearts. You gave peace to many of them. Please bless them with Your compassion forever," he requested with tears.

"Dear son, your mother has discharged the duties of a mother and nothing more. I always like to be your mother only," Amma said with a broad smile. Wearing a garland of lotus flowers, Amma was Herself radiating like a divine lotus. Such a form was worthy of prostration even by the Gods!

Amma was leaving for a neighboring village at four in the afternoon. There, for many years, children and calves had been dying soon after their birth. There had been no timely rains. The people were suffering from famine and scarcity. Some who knew about Sri Karunamayi's visit at their village, had decided to consecrate the image of the Goddess Shitala Devi at the outskirts of the small town. They wished the consecration of the *murti* to be done with Sri Karunamayi's blessings and by the auspicious touch of Her divine hand.

Accepting everyone's invitation, to please Her children, Amma went to that village with love and affection.

The village chief said, "Amma, you have had no relaxation. We have troubled you; please excuse us."

Amma immediately set him at ease. "Don't say that, my son! This visit is like a holy pilgrimage to Kailasa. I have come here most willingly."

As Amma stepped into the village, the sounds of a band—drums, clarinet, etc.—echoed through the entire place. The happiness and enthusiasm of the villagers were beyond words. There was a display of fireworks such as crackers, sparklers, flower pots, etc. Accompanied by trumpets, the ladies sang, while offering *arati* and breaking coconuts. Such a celebration had never been witnessed in that small village.

The entire village had gathered near a huge boulder, and the installation of the image of Shitala Devi was completed with Amma's divine blessings. Then it started drizzling! The farmers, who had not seen rains for years, started dancing with joy. Gradually, men, women and children—the old and the young—all joined the dance. The musical instruments were played more vigorously. All were drowned in an ocean of joy. The scene was delightful. It is needless to say that the village has never faced that misfortune again.

An exclusive seat was arranged for Sri Karunamayi, under a *neem* tree. Amma gave Her divine message and later conveyed blessings to everyone. One of the devotees had brought sweets, *mysorepak*, which Amma Herself distributed. Thus, the program was concluded.

SRI KARUNAMAYI - A Biography

It was already dusk. The car started to move and people followed it for quite a distance until it picked up speed. At the outskirts of the village, amidst the fields, there was a small hillock. There we could see a small hut under a big guava tree. Amma asked the driver to stop the car and said, "Dear son, I will just go to that house for a minute and come back." As per Amma's wish, taking a flashlight, I proceeded without question, lighting the way for Amma.

I did not know the reason for visiting the small hut. It was already dark. Amma stopped at the doorstep of that hut, which was lit by a small twinkling lamp. The two eyes of a child, who was lying on the bed under the thatched roof, looked at the beautiful lotus feet, like hibiscus flowers, walking softly in.

"Who is it? Please come in. Please come in," the voice of a small boy invited. Amma had to bend Her head to enter the hut. There, an eight-year-old disabled boy lay in bed, crippled. Upon seeing Sri Karunamayi, for a second, he could not move. He was confused and was in shock as he recognized Her. "Amma... Karunamayi...," he stammered, trying to sit up. As Amma approached the boy and stood before him, tears of joy rolled down his cheeks.

"Amma, Amma, look there!" said the boy, showing Amma's photo, which he had hung on the wall. His tender heart was overflowing with joy. He felt as though all the pain he had endured for so long had been wiped out.

"My friends told me that the villagers have been tying colorful buntings, since a week. Amma, Ranga also told me that Your feet are so beautiful with golden anklets and are red in color. Amma, Ranga is my friend. It seems You gave him a pomegranate. All the villagers had come to see You. Even I very much desired to see You. But how is it possible? I am injured and bed-ridden. If only I could have come to You, I could have seen You. How can You come to everyone? Amma, I too wanted to tie the buntings along with others and see You at least once. My grandma also had Your *darshan*. She spoke very highly of You. I cried in my bed thinking of You.

I was picturing the events of the program—that all would have seen You, except me. I am unfortunate, and that is why I could not come to see You," the boy cried broken-heartedly. The pain hidden inside his heart, and his disability due to his legs combined together, made him cry even louder.

Sri Karunamayi, with utmost love and compassion, stepped forward. Stretching out Her hands, She held him in a close embrace. The boy continued to sob. It is true that this boy was helpless and bedridden. It is very true that Sri Karunamayi was comforting him, wiping away all his sorrow.

I now realized that the sweetness of invisible maternal love is beyond imagination! I felt that I clearly understood something that day, which I had not, all these days. I also felt that I had a rebirth, then and there, at that moment.

Amma accepted the invitation that had come from the inner depths of this small boy's heart—hence this personal visit.

Through the boy's words we gradually learned that his name was Gopal and that he studied in a school nearby. Four months earlier, he had fallen into a well at ground level while playing. He had suffered serious injuries with many broken bones and had become bedridden. He had also lost his parents in a fire accident, a long time back.

Now his grandmother was bringing him up in acute poverty. At an age when a boy should be active, jumping and playing, he was helpless, alone and isolated in one room. Months had passed. Treatment was going on with village medicines, but there were no signs of improvement. He was unable to attend school. His grandma went away during the day, working to earn daily wages. Throughout the day, he felt very lonely, lying in bed in pain. Friends did not visit him every day and when they did, once in a while, they went away soon.

Gopal had been bearing all these sufferings silently. He had gone through such agony all these months that his tears had nearly dried up. With the unbearable physical pain and loneliness, he wished many times that his deceased mother could come to comfort him. How nice that would have been, if it were possible. He sobbed uncontrollably, missing his mother.

"Many people are concerned when wealthy people fall sick," he said. "But for me, who else is there other than grandma?" He suffered so much that he had become very dull. He was still like a frozen river in winter. He was helpless on the bed like a lifeless statue.

Gopal's grandma had heard that a Holy Mother was visiting their village. She had also heard that this Mother was compassionate, that whoever approached Her with their problems, got rid of them by Her grace. She wished to take Gopal to Amma and seek Her blessings so that he could become a normal boy again. But at her ripe old age, she could not walk that distance, crossing the fields, carrying him. Above all, it was so crowded that there was no space to place even the tip of a needle.

The previous day, the old lady had visited Amma and received new clothes from Her. But she had had no opportunity to talk about Gopal. Even in such a crowd, she was lucky enough to have the *darshan* of Amma's feet, to touch them and to prostrate.

At home, she had narrated all this to Gopal, who insisted on hearing it again and again from her. The intense desire of having Mother Karunamayi's *darshan* filled his tender heart. He wished he, too, could touch the Mother's feet, as his grandma had done. Perhaps, she would have given him also a fruit as Ranga had received. "But how could it be possible," he thought? "At the age of eight I am crippled, bedridden and also orphaned."

That evening, as usual, Gopal was in bed and grandma had not yet returned. A portion of the thatched wall of the hut had fallen. If anybody approached the hut, their feet outside were visible. Gopal could see the light of a torch coming towards the hut, and the feet that followed the light. He had never seen them before. He had never imagined they would look so lovely! The lotus feet were decorated beautifully by reddening the instep! They are the feet which go in search of the distressed! They are all-pervading feet!

The boy's joy knew no bounds when Sri Karunamayi in person stood before him, while he was lost in Her thoughts only.

Gopal had never known a mother. His grandma, who was looking after him, was everything to him. Many a time laying in bed, he wished his mother were alive. His tender heart had longed for a mother's love and compassion.

Gopal melted at the love of Sri Karunamayi—showered naturally like the love of a birth mother—who held him close to Her. He got the maternal love for which he had yearned all those years! Gopal relished to his heart's content that universally honored and boundless motherly affection.

Stretching out Her arms and saying, "Get up, my child," Amma helped him. Gradually the boy tried to sit up. His heart filling with abundant energy and immense confidence, the boy started rising. Wonder! Great wonder! Wonder of wonders! He succeeded in his efforts. He sat. He stood up. And he walked a few steps, too!

With uncontrollable joy, he hugged Amma like a child hugs his mother. With unbearable joy, he was sobbing.

The divine energy which offered a helping hand was Sri Karunamayi. Now Gopal was a free bird. Sri Karunamayi had given him freedom! The little boy was blessed with a normal life. He was relieved from the hell of loneliness and the jail of his disabling ailment.

In this dark hour, Sri Karunamayi had visited this hut on the hillock, amidst the fields, to bring an unhappy young boy back to normalcy! Mother Karunamayi's divine hand had wiped away the suffering of the little boy permanently. Gopal had no more agony! No loneliness any more! No ill health, also!

Gradually, I recovered from the blessed shock of this unusual incident. As I understand it today I had witnessed the divine reality of Mother Karunamayi—owning each and every one of Her children in the entire universe! The taste of this feeling cannot be explained or described in words.

By now, the grandmother of the boy arrived. Astonished, she stood like a statue. Her eyes shed tears of joy, expressing her gratitude. Grandma's and Gopal's faces were glowing with the radiance of joy, like *crores* of lights lit in rows. The little hut was illumined by the radiance of their joy.

I had known about great souls blessing the devotees from their own seats, when the people go to them for *darshan*. But without anybody informing or inviting, Herself walking to the boy, lying alone, helplessly, and understanding the agony, consoling and wiping the tears with Her hands, this was seen by me only in Sri Karunamayi.

The boy took Amma's hands into his own—the hands which had embraced him—and took them to his eyes with reverence and gratitude. He felt he was at the shore, rescued from an ocean of grief and pain. When viewed philosophically, everybody is sailing in the same boat in this world! Only a compassionate Karunamayi can save us!

The little boy may not truly understand the divinity of Amma, but Sri Karunamayi is the manifestation of Maha Lakshmi Devi:

The one who took birth in a lotus,
The one beautiful as a lotus,
The one who is fragrant like a lotus,
The one who is seated on a lotus,
The one whose complexion is that of a lotus,
The one whose feet are like lotuses,
The one whose eyes are shaped like the petals of a lotus,
The one who is the consort of *Sri Padmanabha,*
The one who wanders in the garden of fragrant lotuses,
The one who is adorned with a garland of lotus blossoms,
The one who is worshipped with lotuses,
The one who resides in the heart lotus of Lord Vishnu,
The one whose face has blossomed like a lotus,
The one who holds a lotus in either hand,
The one addressed as *Padmavati Devi, Padmini,* who resides in the milky ocean,
The bestower of wealth and prosperity,
Maha Padmeshwari, Sri Vijayeswari Devi.

It is a fact that Gopal was showered by Her heavy downpour of kindness. This shower of affection is not physical.

Sri Karunamayi, Herself, is an ocean of kindness. She is the waves of infinite compassion that rise to the sky! Her maternal love and affection are beyond humanity, and they lead us on the royal path—to the achievement of the boundless, eternal freedom of Self-Realization!

SRI KARUNAMAYI - A Biography

DEVI CHARANAM PRANAMAMYAHAM

By dusk, we were about to reach the Mallanna Forest. For nearly a week, Sri Balramareddy, Ammamma (Annapurnamma) and myself had been searching for Sri Karunamayi in the forests of Penusila. As the tribal people said that they had sighted Raja Rajeswaramma (Sri Karunamayi) in the Mallanna Forest, Ammamma immediately asked them how to get there. We had started in the morning and reached the Mallanna region by evening.

"Dear brother, have you seen Amma anywhere here?" Ammamma asked a person cutting grass, with lots of hope.

Ammamma's anxious voice revealed that she could not bear the disappointment of a negative reply. The ray of hope in her heart—that he had seen Her—shone brighter when she heard the answer:

"Salutations, O Mother!' Viranna replied. "Yes, I saw that Holy Mother in penance in this region itself. Come, Mother, I will show you." Thus saying, he accompanied us, showing the way.

"Dear son, Karunamayi will certainly bless you and your family, and you shall prosper for a hundred years to come with peace and happiness. I shall never forget your favor!" Ammamma blessed him heartily, her eyes filled with tears of joy and relief.

"Dear son, we are desperate to have Amma's *darshan*," she added. "We have been searching for Her, wandering and trekking for one week. We came here with great hope, as somebody had told us that She was somewhere in this area. Amma shall bestow good upon you. She shall!" Ammamma said, wiping her tears.

"What humility, Ammamma." said Viranna. "I shall never forget those days when you fed me a stomachful when I came starving to your doorstep. You are really compassionate! I can never repay those favors. Where is Penusila, and where is Mallanna Forest? What a distance you have come! How did you walk this distance, Mother? And why does this *Raja Rajeshwaramma* trouble you like that?"

As we walked along the narrow path, Ammamma could not bear to hear this remark and innocently patted her own cheeks—a way of seeking forgiveness from God. She replied immediately: "Oh, no, dear Viranna, Amma has not troubled me! How can I live without seeing Amma, who is like the brilliant moon of the full moon day? How can I eat and sleep? I myself have come walking all this way. Amma never troubles me. Not only me—She cannot hurt the feelings of even an ant."

"Whatever you say, Mother, but *Raja Rajeshwaramma* could have sat for penance close to your place so that you could have avoided walking all this distance, isn't it? I feel very sorry for you."

"Viranna, don't talk like that! This Divine Mother Karunamayi has come into this world not only for me, but to grace all the people in this world. She has descended to this Mother Earth after the prayers made by many sages and devotees. She has come down to console the suffering, the downtrodden and the needy, as well all nature—these trees, the water, the birds, all the creatures and everything in this world."

Viranna, who was making way for us to walk by cutting the branches of bushes and trees which were obstructing the path, was surprised to hear this and said, "What is this, Mother? *Raja Rajeshwaramma* is your daughter. Your child is your own. How can She be for the entire world?"

"Sri Ramachandra!" Ammamma exclaimed. "Karunamayi is none other than Mother *Sitamma*. How am I to explain to you? The sun is in the sky, but the rays of the sunlight are not for a single person. It is for the whole world that the sun shines. Similarly Karunamayi is for everyone."

The innocent tribal man could not understand the hidden meaning of her explanation.

"Karunamayi is none other than Divine Mother *Sitamma*. Can't you understand? Okay, let me explain it to you this way. Though Sri Rama was born to King Dasharatha, His arrival was eagerly awaited not only by Hanumana, Shabari, Sugriva, Guha, Vibhishana, and Kabandha, but also by many sages and many devotees, too. Now tell me, was the incarnation of Sri Rama only for his father, Dasharatha, or for the upliftment of all the creatures in this world?"

Viranna looked relieved."Oh! I did not understand very well, dear mother! My son, five others and myself have been cutting grass for ten days in this forest. Whenever we see Karunamayi, She has been sitting still, unshaken, similar to a Goddess in the sanctum of a temple. We can smell the fragrance of sandal, turmeric and *kumkum* coming from Her, though She is far away from us. In this dense forest, the home of wild animals such as bison, tigers, cheetahs and snakes, She has been sitting undisturbed, day and night with closed eyes. We have not seen Her either taking food or drinking water. Neither has She looked at us, opening Her eyes. She reminds me of Lord Siva in the calendar in my house, who is in deep meditation. This Mother is also like Siva! I am not an educated person. I expressed what came to my mind only. Please don't think otherwise."

Saying this, he bowed to Ammamma who was listening to him, her eyes welling with tears. Viranna was afraid that his crude expression must have hurt her feelings, so he became silent.

The green grass had grown to a good height. The plants were full of blossomed flowers. The tall trees were standing still—undisturbed, like the *rishis*. But it was not easy to walk through the tall grass, so we were proceeding with difficulty. Suddenly, we saw a huge cobra sliding away swiftly in front of us. Ammamma was petrified for a while! She stood still. Then she relaxed, and we entered more deeply into Mallanna Forest. We were nearing a place where there were two very tall trees, between which there was a *Sivalinga* upon a hill. There was a small river, too, flowing nearby. Balarama, Ammamma and I continued searching for Amma.

At last we spotted Sri Karunamayi on the other side of the *Sivalinga*, amidst tender leaves. We shed tears of joy! She was sitting on the hillock next to the *Sivalinga*, looking very thin. Her clothes were full of dust. Sri Karunamayi was radiating divine brilliance, and She was in the deep state of *samadhi*. Amma had merged in Her own supreme boundless form. Sri Karunamayi resembled that divine flower of the Himalayan forests which blossoms during midnight. She looked like that Sati Devi, who had done *tapas* for the grace of Lord Siva. The entire atmosphere was filled with an enchanting fragrance emanating from Sri Karunamayi.

We prostrated and sat down at a distance for nearly half an hour. Each of us experienced a great divine energy in the surroundings.

Meanwhile, we suddenly heard cries of distress from a distance. Some people soon brought into view the twelve-year-old son of Viranna, who had been bitten by a poisonous snake.

Viranna was shocked! He became deeply distressed seeing the condition of his son. He collapsed and started crying. All of them took refuge at Amma's feet. "O Mother!" they cried. "Please save this child!" Saying so, they laid the boy, Chinnodu, before Her.

The boy had suffered a wound, which was bleeding, and white foam was flowing from his mouth as a result of the serpent's bite. The boy was struggling for his life. Viranna's emotions were uncontrollable. Though we were also very sad and depressed by the situation, we all firmly believed that Amma would definitely save the child.

The cries of sorrow and surrender made Sri Karunamayi open Her eyes. She came briskly down from the five foot high mound on which She had been sitting. Amma, who usually walks slowly and gently, rushed to the child like lightning. We saw an indescribable concentration of brilliant light in front of us. But as She passed by, we were unable to see Her form in that dazzle of light! Viranna and his people were very emotional, hitting their heads, crying aloud and looking to Amma with great hope.

Amma came close to the boy with utmost compassion. She put the toe of Her right foot on the wound made by the snake bite, just below the kneecap. That is all… Incredible!! In just a few seconds, the foam coming out of the boy's mouth stopped. He moved a little. After a minute, he gradually opened his eyes and began looking at everyone.

Viranna and his people were stunned by this incident. All of them fell at Amma's feet and sobbed emotionally with joy.

"O Mother, *Parvati, Jagan Mata,* (Mother of the Universe)," Balarama prayed sincerely, "I beg you, bestow knowledge on us, Devi."

The boy's uncle started dancing and shouting, "*Ma Jagan Mata, jai, jai, jai*! (Glory to the Universal Divine Mother)!"

This land is glowing with the radiance of the holy feet of *Amba* Karunamayi!

Amma, with Her usual child-like, innocent smile, looked at us and came very close. She started wiping our tears with the end of Her *sari*. "What is this? Why? Why are you all crying?" Saying thus, She consoled us.

Ammamma lifted both her hands and prostrated. "*Jagan Mata! Gayatri! Lalitamba! Sitamma! Karunamayi!*

Goda Devi! Sharada Devi! Keep on protecting everyone like this always, always. Mother, O Mother!" she prayed thus as the warm tears were flowing down her face.

The enchanting fragrance emanating from Sri Karunamayi filled the air with sandal perfume and purified all of us. A unique energy flowing from Karunamayi Devi entered all our bodies. We all clearly felt we had been charged by divine *Shakti*. Not only did Mother Karunamayi wipe our tears, but it is certain that She also burnt away our *karma* of *crores* of births as She showered this unique energy upon us. Sri Karunamayi's eyes were shining brilliantly like the bright sun with incomparable, formless, indestructible divinity! She was glowing like a pearl!

Thus Viranna, Chinnodu, who had been bitten by the serpent, Balarama, Ammamma, myself, and countless others, had been frantically searching in our *crores* of previous births really for this Mother only! O Mother, where have you incarnated? For so many births we have all wandered here and there (here, happiness—there, sorrow) scouring all the paths for you. At last, in this birth, our Mother has bestowed exuberant kindness on these fortunate people.

Silently, this ocean of abundant compassion—Amma—had given a turning point to our lives towards Her divine feet, which are the cause for liberation. At least now, those lotus feet were guiding us on the path to reach Divine Mother.

For innumerable lives, we had been roaming in the darkness of ignorance. Today, these divine feet were shining within the inner space of our hearts that had become huge containers of the nectar of immortality!

We had walked all these lives amidst the paths of joy and sorrow, but today these divine lotus feet have descended on Earth for the purpose of guiding the human race in the righteous path. Today these feet have bestowed on those who had not experienced it, the treasure of purna *shanti*, complete and everlasting peace!

Those divine feet, beautifully decorated by anklets made of precious beads and pearls, have come down to uplift many people in this journey of life, knowingly or unknowingly, and to escort people to the shores of peace!

O *Sri Mata*! Karunamayi! *Lalita Parameshwari*! None of us ever thought about You even for a second, as we have all been enticed by *maya*. *Devi Maha Maya*! In innumerable births we have been vanquished by Your *maya*. From Brahma to great sages, and amongst ourselves, none is ever capable of escaping from this powerful *Maha Maya*. We know that it is utterly impossible! O *Dayamayi*, can we ever reach You without Your grace? Just by offering a single prostration, those extremely serene feet have chased death away, silently.

"Please allow me to touch them once, Mother," I thought. Like a heavy downpour, the emotions of my heart were flowing through my eyes as tears.

Amma! Endless one, eternal Karunamayi, please take us all to your real feet and give us shelter. My heart completely surrendered to those lotus feet of Sri Karunamayi which give light to *crores* of suns, and which are the gates to liberation.

This *Brahmamayi*, who is four-faced, is the supporting pillar for the four sects, the four *ashrams*, and the fourteen lokas or worlds. She is the root cause for the four states of *jagrat*, *svapna*, *sushupti* and *turiya*. She is the one who is *Chatur Vedamayi*, the four *Vedas* personified. This Devi Herself is the unique glory of *Brahma Shaktimayi*. She is the subtle form of *mantra* and is eternally worshipped by the sages!

This *Brahma Shakti*, who has abundant glory, is the real mother of even Lord Brahma! This Mother is the one who moves in the inner space, or *hridaya akasham*, of *Brahma jnanis*, the realized ones!

She is *Brahma jnana svarupini*, who can be realized only by extraordinary powers and practice. Not only this,

She is the centralized hidden energy in the unique *Brahma Chaitanya Shakti*!

By worshipping this Devi, who is the embodiment of compassion, by the *darshan* of this *Maha Devi's* lotus feet, *Brahma jnana*, knowledge of the Absolute, will reveal itself in the mind devoid of impurity. One will experience *Ritambharatvam*, the experience of seeing the supreme Divinity in all creation. The darkness of *maya* will be permanently dispelled.

Only by the divine grace of *Sri Mata*, is Self-Realization, or *Atma jnana*, attained. This experience is not possible otherwise, either by reading innumerable texts or by listening to the discourses of many scholars. By *uttama bhakti*, true devotion of the highest order, Mother will reveal Herself in the heart of a sincere devotee. As soon as the radiance of the *jnana* ray, born of the compassionate glance of this Supreme Mother, enters the human heart, in that brilliance, realization of the *satya atma*—the real Self—arises.

Thus, *Jagan Mata* is the bestower of *Brahmananda*—absolute bliss—and the divinity that confers *Atma jnana*. Once the devotee experiences this state, he will realize that all the material things such as fame, honor, wealth and sensual pleasures are tasteless and of the lowest value—meaningless and transient.

That is why, O mind, always praise the glory of Devi's lotus feet! Sincere and humble *pranamas* at Her divine feet.

Mānasa bhajare guru caraṇam
Devī caraṇam praṇamāmyaham
Karuṇāmayī caraṇam praṇamāmyaham

Jai Karunamayi!

SRI KARUNAMAYI - A Biography

SARVA SAKSHINI MOTHER KARUNAMAYI

"Amma! O, Mother!" A male voice was heard from outside the room.

Soon after the call was heard, a second voice replied: "I am coming. Please wait for a minute." Saying so, she placed the garland, which she was beautifully tying, on the darbha mat. She placed a wet cloth on the flowers, covering and protecting them from drying. Then Annapurnamma, Mother of Sri Karunamayi, came out.

A little away from the veranda, an old man stood, with a sixteen-year-old girl and an eighteen-year-old boy behind him.

The old man said, "O Mother! I have come for the sake of *Raja Rajeshwaramma* (Sri Karunamayi), with a mountain of desires! But just now, I came to know that Sri Karunamayi is in penance in the mountains since a week!" His voice was filled with unbearable disappointment.

Though Ammamma was not highly educated, she was able to understand his plight and said, "*Tata* (Grand-father), please come in. Whether Amma is here or anywhere, this is your home. Feel at home. We may feel that She did not appear now, but appeared then, and so on, but this is all Amma's *maya*."

"*Tata*," (for this is how an old man is addressed in Telugu) "Amma plays hide and seek with Her children! Though She is physically far away, Amma already knows the fact that you have come here."

Look at the way Ammamma received a stranger, making him feel comfortable. Further, we will see the way she showered hospitality—generously and lovingly.

"Really, Mother?" *Tata* sounded relieved. "Then Amma

certainly would have seen me coming over here, isn't it?"

"Yes, *Tata*. Without Amma's order and call, can you come this distance? Can you proceed even a step?"

"Yes, Mother, it is true! Yesterday in my dream, *Raja Rajeshwaramma* personally came, conducted my granddaughter's marriage and blessed her. Hence, we have come all this way on foot, but there is no Amma's *darshan*. It is unfortunate," he said sadly.

" *Tata*, even those people well-versed in the *Vedas* can't understand the *maya* of Amma! How can we who are uneducated, understand it? But Amma will never disappoint you! She will certainly make you happy by giving you *darshan*. First, you come in." Saying so, she affectionately called the old man inside, holding his hand.

But the old man, for some reason, was hesitating. "Mother," he said, looking down. "I....I am a *harijan*, so I shall sit outside only..."

Ammamma stopped his words. " *Tata*, you are Amma's son, who has come for Her *darshan*. Who is bothered about your caste or creed? Karunamayi is *Sri Mata*, the inner soul in everyone. Isn't it so? Don't feel bad about such differences. Consider me as your own daughter. Why do you hesitate to get into your daughter's house?"

The old man was visibly moved by Ammamma's words.

"Dear girl, come in," said Ammamma, addressing the young woman. And she took them all inside. She was very happy as they entered at last, and she spread a mat for them to sit on. Feeling very delicate, they sat down.

Two *brahmin* ladies from Hyderabad were making garlands in the same room. One of them said to the old man, " *Tata*, please be relaxed and feel at home. We are all equally eligible to have Sri Karunamayi's *darshan* and to sit at Her lotus feet."

Hearing these kind words, the old man felt a little more comfortable. Ammamma gave them fresh lime juice. "We shall go outside on the veranda and drink this," said the old man.

"No, no, you can drink it here itself. This is not a stranger's house—this is the home of your own Mother, Karunamayi," Ammamma gently insisted.

"Excuse me, but we can't drink in front of you, Amma," he replied. So, in spite of Ammamma's convincing words, the old man went out with his people.

Ammamma felt very bad. As the old man was about to wash the glasses, Ammamma grabbed them from his hand and personally washed them. Caste or creed never came in the way of her hospitality. She loved everyone alike. Truly, this shows the height of humility in Ammamma's heart. Though she had people around to get things done, she personally did everything without reservation.

After the trio returned inside, Ammamma finally said, " *Tata*, tell me, what can I do for you?"

"Mother," he replied a little hesitantly, "these two are poor orphans. I have taken the role of their parents. I have brought them here today to get them wedded in the divine presence of *Raja Rajeshwaramma*, as I already explained to you earlier. We have none in this world other than Amma." The elderly man's eyes were full of tears.

Ammamma was hurt by his feelings. "Why do you feel bad, *Tata*? Karunamayi is the one who responds to all our calls! Your desire never goes unfulfilled. Karunamayi will certainly bless your grandchildren on their wedding day! I swear on Sri Rama and *Sitamma* that She shall certainly come here, not only from the Garudachala Hills, but even if She is out of this world. Believe my words," she added.

Saying so, Ammamma instilled confidence in *Tata's* mind. Ammamma had firm faith in Sri Karunamayi, the one hundred percent confidence, which is what the Divine Mother expects. She also affectionately strengthened the others' beliefs, too.

Earlier, a *pundit* of *Tata's* village had fixed a *muhurta* for the wedding: 12:35 p.m. on the same day. Ammamma looked at the sixteen-year-old bride, who was innocent, helpless and in rags. This bride had only a bindi as an ornament. Even the bridegroom was in the same condition. A marriage takes place only once in a lifetime, she thought. They have come in this pathetic condition for such an auspicious occasion! Ammamma felt sad and compassionate towards them. Her heart was soft like butter and melted at the misery of others. Her heart was always full of kindness toward such people.

"Mother, if you will please give me a piece of turmeric root and a piece of yellow thread, and if our luck favors Sri Karunamayi's arrival, the wedding will take place at 12:30 p.m. in the divine presence of *Raja Rajeshwaramma*. Then we shall leave contented with Her invaluable blessings."

Ammamma prayed to *Sri Mata* for a while. She knew that a prayer to *Sri Mata* before undertaking any task would make the effort fruitful. Great people not only preach, but they also put the teachings into practice.

"Masthanu!" Ammamma said to one helper, "go and get mango leaves to make strings for decoration. Also take *Tata* with you." She then called a few girls to bring different kinds of flowers from the garden. On this occasion, come up so suddenly, everybody accepted their participation with pleasure.

"Penchalaiah," Ammamma requested of another person, "go and get the one who plays clarinet at the temple of Penusila Swami." And she sent someone else to a neighboring village to get a priest. Finally, she went into the kitchen to make arrangements for preparing delicacies. Ammamma was always organizing for every occasion with minute detail, sincerely, willingly and with a personal touch.

Ammamma made the two have an oil bath, all the while singing a folk song about Lord Rama and Sita Devi.

SRI KARUNAMAYI - A Biography

Ammamma was an experienced mother. She considered other's children also as her own. Her heart was vast like the sky, overflowing with compassion.

This Annapurnamma is the Mother of Sri Karunamayi! How else would the heart be of one who has chanted and written Sri Rama nama, the name of her beloved Sri Rama, two crore, that is, twenty million, times?

Ammamma is *Dharma Devata*—the personification of *dharma*—who saw divinity in every creature, and served everybody selflessly with a pure heart, without any expectations—not even fame. She conducted many marriages like this. Ammamma shouldered this responsibility for others, considering it to be more compelling even than her own daughters'.

Ammamma's daughter, Revathamma's wedding was fixed for the following week, but the costly silk *sari* and blouse of Revathamma adorned this other new bride. The *mangalya* ready for Revathamma had been placed in the *puja* room. Ammamma asked someone to bring it. She also got the artificial ornaments, which had decorated the idols in the *ashram*.

She personally decorated the bride with bangles, ear-rings and a necklace of small colored stones. As Ammamma was putting the green glass bangles on the bride's arms, she remarked, "Dear child, these bangles belong to Karunamayi Amma. Look! How fortunate you are! Karunamayi Devi's arms are healthy, plump and golden-complexioned. Amma has worn these bangles. By Her grace, they fit you correctly. As I am looking at your arms with Her bangles, I am seeing Her in you." She took the bride's hands, with reverence, to her eyes. Truly Ammamma saw Sri Karunamayi in one and all and in all the things that She used. Amma teaches us all to reach this high state of seeing Divinity in everything and everywhere.

"Amma, you are responsible for my good fortune

today," said the girl with humility.

"No, not at all, my dear," Ammamma said smilingly. "You are Karunamayi's pet child. All these things are Amma's divine play through us."

While decorating the bride, Ammamma asked for a bottle of red paste that belonged to Amma, to decorate the feet of the bride.

The girl who was helping became scared and confused. "Mother," she asked, "that bottle is used by Amma during *Dashehra* Festival. Do you really want me to bring it?"

"Our Mother Karunamayi is ready to sacrifice Her life itself for others. If the red paste is used to decorate this little bride, She will certainly feel very happy. She does not object, my dear child!" All were pleased to hear Ammamma's words.

"Murugaiah!" Ammamma called me the name by which my family members had addressed me earlier. "Did I speak anything wrong? Karunamayi has a great heart to forgive Her uneducated, dullard mother even if a mistake is committed by me unknowingly."

"Even the great Brahma and the sages are not able to understand Sri Karunamayi, who is *Maha Shakti Svarupini*," I responded. "How can you be an uneducated mother, when you are qualified in the *Atma Vidya* school of Amma, who is *Brahmamayi*? You have brought up that child by feeding, playing with and pampering Her who is the protector of these worlds! You carried that child who carries the entire universe in Her womb as *Brahmanda Bhandodhari*; you played with Her. This fortune and privilege is only yours, and nobody is as fortunate as you." With that, I prostrated to Ammamma's lotus feet.

"Do not say such things, Murugaiah! I feel flattered. *Crores* of galaxies are like dust particles under the divine feet of Karunamayi. People like me are insignificant before that ocean of kindness." Humbly Ammamma said this, with tears and prostrations to the all-pervading Karunamayi, who was not visible to normal eyes.

"What about new clothes for the bridegroom?" said a brahmin lady who had been there all morning.

Immediately, Ammamma said: "Take this key to the almirah in which my son Ravi's clothes are kept. Inside there is a new shirt and a silk dhoti. Bring them for the bridegroom."

The clothes were brought and the bridegroom wore them, but the shirt was large.

"Remove the shirt and give it to me, dear son!" said Ammamma. "I shall sew it for you." So saying, she altered the shirt within minutes, after which it fit the bridegroom well.

Ammamma was happily looking at the bride and bridegroom. "Now," she said, "you both look like Sri Rama and *Sitamma!*"

By now the old man had returned. He was stunned with surprise for a minute, unable to recognize the children.

Ammamma brought water reddened with *kumkum* in a plate and lit some camphor. By chanting *mantras* over it, negativity would be warded off. A mouth-watering aroma was coming from the kitchen. A peaceful and happy wedding atmosphere pervaded the whole place.

Before she went to the kitchen again, Ammamma suggested: "*Tata*, you please go and help them to tie the strings of mango leaves." This time when Ammamma returned, she came out of the kitchen with two glasses full of *payasam*. "A wedding takes time. You young people must be hungry, so drink this."

They both received the glasses gladly. I am unable to describe or write their feelings. They had both lost their parents and, since their births, had not experienced maternal affection. Today, wearing new clothes and being decked with jewels was like a fantasy in a sweet dream. They must have heard about sweets, but could not have afforded to taste them. In fact, they could not afford even bread twice a day or decent clothing. *Tata* himself might not have tasted sweets in his lifetime. They were in such utter poverty. As my thoughts went on, my heart was not ready to accept this.

The bride and the bridegroom were looking at one another happily and eagerly.

Ammamma personally went in search of *Tata* to give him a glass of *payasam*.

Common people do not know absolute bliss, but when they are blessed with unimaginable things, they experience them with the greatest pleasure. The old man, the bride and the bridegroom were in that unimaginable state of bliss.

The bridegroom was looking into the mirror often and was delighted to see himself well-dressed. After some time, however, he came to Ammamma and said, "Ammamma, you gave me the costly silk clothes of your son. Won't he feel bad when he sees me in them?"

"Oh, no, dear one!" Ammamma reassured him. "Ravi's heart is like butter. He is very generous. Here, when anybody is sick, he cares for them by getting Horlicks and medicines. He is even prepared to part with the clothes on his body. He is another *Dharma Raju*. Please consider Ravi as your own brother! I know his nature. He will not mind this at all. Be relaxed and do not feel embarrassed, my dear."

The feeling of wearing a stranger's clothes vanished as Ammamma comforted the bridegroom. The boy convinced himself saying,"I am Ravi's younger brother. There is nothing wrong in wearing one's elder brother's clothes; otherwise why would Ammamma arrange my wedding with such intense affection?" These thoughts made the bridegroom feel very comfortable.

Ammamma made a beautiful string of roses to decorate the bride's plait. She also arranged the rose strings, jasmine and other colored flowers artistically.

The girl, by now, had questioned Ammamma several times as to whether *Raja Rajeshwaramma*, Mother Karunamayi, would certainly come for the wedding.

Without a second thought, Ammama patiently and affectionately replied, "Oh, little girl, Karunamayi's heart is like an ocean of compassion. You are Her child. Every one of us in this world belongs to that Jagan Mata. She has thousands of eyes. She would have seen you long ago when you came here with your *Tata*, miles and miles, for the sake of getting married in Her divine presence. She would have known that Her child has come with a deep desire and full of hope, seeking Her blessings. Do you know who is sitting inside everyone and getting things done? It is Karunamayi only!

"That Divine Mother is present in everyone. She is making the strings of mango leaves, preparing *payasam*, and adorning Her children. This is the real truth, my dear! Lokamata Karunamayi will not disappoint you. She will certainly come and bless you!"

Hearing Ammamma's affectionate words, the little girl, who had never before experienced maternal love in her life, melted like ice. She relaxed, leaning on Ammamma's bosom. Ammamma, who had bought the costliest *sari* for Revathamma's wedding, gave it to this bride. The *mangalya* made for Revathamma was also given to her. The girl recognized all these things. She became dumbstruck due to so much love and kindness. Ammamma never inquired anything about me, not even my name, she thought. If Ammamma can be this affectionate, generous and selfless, how would Sri Karunamayi shower Her affection, she wondered.

"Even if my worldly mother were alive, she would not have done so much for me, Ammamma," the girl said, as her eyes filled with tears.

"Oh, don't cry! Be happy and relaxed now or your

make-up will get spoiled. Your mother is alive, dear child. She is Karunamayi. She has been always showering that motherly affection by Her soothing glance, which even *crores* of mothers can't give," said Ammamma.

All the edibles which had been prepared to be offered to Goddess Gauri during Revathamma's wedding were now to be used for the *Gauri puja* of this wedding. Afterward, they would be packed for the bride on her departure. Ammamma was busy preparing the offering.

Meanwhile, Revathamma herself came there with a packet of a few new *saris*, blouses and petticoats, saying, "Amma, you say this girl has no mother. So, give these also to her." When somebody is hungry or in distress, Revathamma is more generous even than Ammamma in serving them. She is service-minded and gives in plenty to charity. She did not feel even a little bad that all the things which had been meant for her wedding were given away to this poor girl, a total stranger. "This poor girl has never known the love of her parents. If we do not do all this, who else will?" she thought.

Ammamma actively got all the wedding arrangements done. All were lovingly involved in the preparation. Usually in an Indian wedding, male domination, criticism, discontentment, hurt feelings of the people criticized, flowing tears, etc. are common. But the atmosphere here was unusually different.

The venue was Lalita Mandiram. There was *kalasha* in the hall. Musical instruments were being played. *Pundits* had been chanting *vedic mantras* for the welfare of the bride and the bridegroom, and the fragrance of rose flowers and incense sticks filled the atmosphere. Beyond all these was that fragrance of peace which emanated from the dust of the lotus feet of Sri Karunamayi!

As there was a call for me, I went inside. Ammamma was waiting. "I made a prayer offering a gold ring studded with gems, worth 1,116 *rupees*, to the *hundi* of Lord Balaji, at Tirupati, when the marriage of Revathamma was fixed. Hence, I have knotted this in a cloth and kept it in the *puja* room. I shall give this ring to the bridegroom. As a penalty for breaking my promise, can I make another ring with a little more money? Is it wrong? I want your opinion."

Ammamma's love of the poor was so great that she was ready to give away even the offering meant for God to them! She saw God in that poor couple, too. And she took my consent in such a humble manner!

"Ammamma!" I exclaimed, "what can I say to the one who has been showing to others what humanity should be? There will not be the slightest mistake in whatever you do!"

As I said this, Ammamma took the ring with her happily. She kept money twice the value of that ring into that knot and apologized to Lord Venkateshwara.

Puja began in the hall. The bride was very anxious. Softly she said, "Ammamma, Amma has not come."

Ammamma replied gently, "Karunamayi is captured by devotion. Certainly She will fulfill your desire."

Ganesh puja and *Gauri puja* were complete. Suddenly the gathering was spellbound. Karunamayi Vijayeswari Devi had entered the hall through the front of the sanctum of *Lalita Devi*! The bride who sat with bent head did not see Her. All other eyes shone as they had Amma's *darshan*. The *pundits* continued to chant *mantras*. As soon as the divine palm which wore green bangles touched the bride's head, the girl lifted her eyes. The palm was Sri Karunamayi's. There was a wonderful expression on the girl's face. *Tata*, the bride, bridegroom and others had prayed for Amma's *darshan*, but the bride had prayed most sincerely.

Ammamma had been praying to Devi that the girl should not be disappointed, and that her desire should be fulfilled.

The girl devotionally held Amma's hand in both her

hands with tears of joy, "Amma, You are there for me! Truly you are there. This is enough for me. What else do I need?" was her feeling. Her gaze was fixed on Amma.

Then the bride, with her plait decorated with rose flowers, fell at Sri Karunamayi's feet and sobbed, unable to control her joy. Even the bridegroom did so. Ammamma's happiness was indescribable. And my heart and throat choked with emotion. Not just words—even feelings had become still.

"Mother, you are showering so much compassion on these orphans," said *Tata*, joining his hands in a sincere *pranam* to Amma. "The happiness that is obtained by seeing You, nothing in this world can give. When You are with me, even a crore of relatives are nothing to me. The greatest riches seem like dust in your presence. I am happier than an emperor that You are here! O Mother! You have descended for the sake of the poor. My heart is breaking and unable to control this joy." All this was said with many tears.

The most important event in a wedding is the tying of the *mangala sutra*. Musical instruments were playing. For the little girl who had never experienced the love of a mother, Sri Karunamayi—being the mother, father, relative and witness of all acts—conducted the wedding, through everybody.

Ammamma was looking at her daughter Karunamayi. "Who else in this world, other than You, can shower so much compassion on us?" was her expression. "You are *Sarva Sakshi*, witness of all, *Kamakshi*, the thousand-eyed soothing Mother! You alone are *Meenakshi* and *Vishalakshi*!" She could clearly see the glance of infinite compassion in Sri Karunamayi's eyes. She joined her hands together. "O Karunamayi, bestow universal peace," she prayed.

The wedding program was complete. Everybody was fed with delicacies. A brass pot of rice grains, fruits, snacks and a little money were gifted to the bride by Ammamma.

Tata hesitated to take these things. "We have troubled you enough. I cannot repay you in any way. How can I accept all this?"

" *Tata*, consider me as your own daughter." said Ammamma. "Won't you accept it when given by your daughter? Isn't it Karunamayi who feeds all the creatures? Has She not come down from great heights just for the sake of this girl?"

Ammamma praised Sri Karunamayi happily and innocently: "She has the sun and the moon as Her eyes. She is the Absolute, the supreme bliss, Raja Rajeshwari!

Ammamma did not allow the newlyweds to return on foot. She arranged for a decorated bullock cart, pulled by a single bull. She advised the bride: "Run the family efficiently. Take care of your husband. Bring a good name to the old man who has brought you up. And bow to Karunamayi every morning before starting your daily routine."

The bride could not bear this separation. Ammamma gifted the gold ring to the bridegroom. We could not trace the slightest feeling in Ammamma that they were strangers. She consoled the bride and helped her into the cart. To the driver of the cart she said, "Subbu, be careful, son! There is a new bride in the cart. Drive the cart carefully. Take care on the road. I will feed you a delicacy you like when you return!"

All three of them were bowing to Ammamma constantly, with folded hands. The cart moved, leaving the gates of the *ashram* towards the forest. Everybody stopped there, but Ammamma continued to follow the cart with tears.

"Who will meet this girl with *arati*, following the Indian custom of receiving the bride at home?" was her thought. She stood sobbing till the cart disappeared.

So, one poor man in the neighborhood had brought up two orphans. He had thought of conducting a simple wedding, asking for turmeric root and thread—of course, with the blessings of Sri Karunamayi, who is the Mother of everyone. Karunamayi Amma's divine play and compassion are great! He had not come here with any desires. He had wished for Amma's *darshan* and blessing only. Never had he imagined that Ammamma would organize the wedding in this grand manner.

Actually, who was this Ammamma, Annapurnamma? She was the worldly mother of *Omkaramayi, Para Brahmamayi, Daya lahari,* our Mother Karunamayi! As she was the fortunate and revered one who had given birth to Karunamayi Devi, it was but natural that compassion adorned Ammamma as an ornament. Glory to Ammamma, Mother of the Divine Mother!

In fact, let me confess that I was not able to pen even one percent of the feelings that I witnessed during this incident. My heart did understand the compassion in Ammamma, but my hand was incapable of writing about it.

THE SILENT LANGUAGE OF LOVE

Kanva Forest was thickly covered by a snow-white fog in the month of December. The chirping of birds had begun to herald the dawn. The banks of the rivers, mountains, valleys and the entire forest were echoing the sweet music of *bulbuls*, parrots and other birds.

The forest was full of thousands of different kinds of beautiful butterflies. The scene of these butterflies fluttering above the wild flowers was enticing. The soft sound of *Omkara*, like the music of fairyland, was heard continuously in the blowing winds like a flowing river. Now and then the cries of peacocks echoed in the valleys of the Garudachala Mountains. The atmosphere was very peaceful.

The rays of sunlight filtered through the branches of the wild trees. The white clouds seemed to be dancing in the blue sky. The branches of tall trees, covered with wild flowers, were waving in the cool breeze, which touched the clouds. That touch made the clouds drop down a pearl-like drizzle. The bright rays of sunlight refracted through the misted drops, and it looked as though the Gods were showering real pearls on Sri Karunamayi, who was seated somewhere in the forest.

We had our bath in the river Kanvamuki in the wee hours of that winter morning. We ten devotees, along with elderly Sheshaiah, started trekking the peaks of Garudachala with great enthusiasm to have Amma's *darshan*. The range of hills was densely vegetated with different kinds of trees. The colorful wild flowers added fragrance to the atmosphere. This beauty enhanced the sanctity of the presence of Devi Karunamayi. Amma, dressed in saffron robes and seated amidst the greenery, appeared like an eternal flame. As we approached, She was chanting a beautiful *Siva Stotra*. Hearing Her melodious voice in that calm environment, we were filled with an unusually divine feeling. The *stotra* is as follows:

DARIDRYA DUKHA DAHANA STOTRA

1. *Viśveśwarāya narakarṇava tāraṇāya*
   Karṇāmṛtāya śaśi śekhara bhūṣṇāya
   Karpūra kānti dhavalāya jaṭā dharāya
   Dāṛdrya dukha dahanāya namaḥ śivāya

2. *Gaurī priyāya rajanīśa kalādharāya*
   Kālāntakāya bhujagādhipa kankaṇāya
   Gangādharāya gajarāja vimocanāya
   Dāṛdrya dukha dahanāya namaḥ śivāya

3. *Bhakti priyāya bhava roga bhayāpahāya*
   Ugrāya durga bhava sāgara tāraṇāya
   Jyotimayāya punarudbhava vāraṇāya
   Dāṛdrya dukha dahanāya namaḥ śivāya

4. *Carmāmbarāya śava bhasma vilepanāya*
   Bhāleksaṇāya maṇi kuṇḍala manḍitāya
   Manjīra pāda yugalāya jaṭā dharāya
   Dāṛdrya dukha dahanāya namaḥ śivāya

5. *Pancānanāya phanirāja vibhūṣaṇāya*
   Hemāmśukāya bhuvana traya manḍanāya
   Ānandabhūmi varadāya tamoharāya
   Dāṛdrya dukha dahanāya namaḥ śivāya

6. *Bhānu priyāya duritārṇava tāraṇāya*
   Kālāntakāya kamalāsana pūjitāya
   Netra trayāya śubha laksaṇa lakṣitāya
   Dāṛdrya dukha dahanāya namaḥ śivāya

7. *Rāma priyāya raghunātha vara pradāya*

SRI KARUNAMAYI - A Biography

Nāga priyāya nāga rāja niketanāya
Puṇyāya puṇya caritāya surārcitāya
Dārdrya dukha dahanāya namaḥ śivāya

8. *Mukteśwarāya phaladāya gaṇeśwarāya*
   Gīta priyāya vṛsabheśwara vāhanaya
   Mātanga carma vasanāya maheśwarāya
   Dārdrya dukha dahanāya namaḥ śivāya

9. *Gaurī vilāsa bhuvanāya mahodayāya*
   Pancānanāya śaraṇāgata rakṣakāya
   Śarvāya sarva jagatādhipāya
   Tasmai dāridrya dukha dahanāya namaḥ śivāya

Listening to the divine chanting, we all prostrated to Amma, who called us close. But as we were settling down, we suddenly heard the loud sound of a rifle. A peacock had been shot in the wing and wounded. It came running in our direction, screaming in pain, and fell down. We were shocked to see the beautifully feathered bird lying there, bleeding.

We were all still in shock, but Sri Karunamayi walked briskly to the peacock, lying beside a bush. She took the hurt peacock onto her lap with tender mercy. She tore a strip from her *sari* and tied the wound to stop the bleeding. The peacock, which had been moaning with pain, felt relieved of its suffering and sat comfortably on Amma's lap, closing its eyes.

This serene atmosphere had been disturbed by the cruelty of the hunter. "Who shot the peacock?" "The sin will not be forgiven." "Who did this cruel job?" All of us spoke simultaneously.

By then, two hunters armed with long hunting rifles had come there. "I have shot this peacock. It is mine. Give it to me," one of the hunters demanded, looking at Amma.

We all looked at Karunamayi Amma. Holding the bleeding bird, She was shedding tears. She looked as if She Herself were experiencing the pain of the bird. Though wordless, Amma's look was adamant. It was obvious that She had no intention of returning the bird, and She hugged it even more tightly to Her heart. She hid the injured creature by covering it under Her *pallu* so that it was not visible to the hunter.

We all spoke at once, attacking the hunter. "This is not fair on your part. It is an offense to hunt animals and birds in the forest. We shall complain to the police." And, "This peacock belongs to Amma. You go away from here." And, "How dare you think you can take away the bird from Amma? This is really brutal."

"How do you feel, hunting a speechless bird?" shouted Sheshaiah angrily. (Sheshaiah was very devoted to Amma.) Hailing from a nearby village, he would come to the *ashram* and stay for weeks at a time whenever he could.

However, the hunter was arrogant. He said, "Hunting is my profession. I have hunted it, and the peacock belongs to me. You must return it." "Who are you to interfere?" was his expression.

For a very long time, we had a verbal war with the hunters, but they did not budge and kept insisting on their own point of view.

Amma was also adamant that She would never return the bird and sat with eyes closed. Amma loves animals and birds immensely. She handles the infants of Her devotees very delicately as well. Amma never even plucks flowers because she feels the plants would be hurt by doing so. Once Amma stepped on a strand of grass without noticing. She could hear the strand crying in pain. Since then, She has never liked to walk on grass. This is the loving and humble relationship She shares with every living thing in nature.

The peacock, which was hurt and bleeding, caused Amma to shed tears continuously. The hunter, however, was refusing to give up the bird and was bearing all these emotions silently. Meanwhile, Amma's face, which would otherwise be peaceful, had become sad.

The elderly man amongst us, Sri Sheshaiah, and the second hunter finally came to a settlement after a long argument. Sri Sheshaiah told the hunter, "Look here. I shall draw a long line with this twig. We shall place the bird on the line. If the bird, whether knowingly or unknowingly, comes to you, it becomes yours; if it walks towards Amma, it shall be Hers. Is that okay?"

At last, the hunter agreed to this proposal with a frown on his face. But Amma did not agree at all with this settlement! She shook Her head from side to side to indicate her unwillingness.

The hunter was very impatient, the anger visible on his face. "I have hunted this bird, and it is mine. Why are these people interfering and refusing to hand it over to me?" was his feeling.

On the other hand, Sri Karunamayi was in despair. Her determination was visible on Her face—She would not part with the wounded bird, towards which Her heart was full of kindness.

Meanwhile, the people were talking among themselves. Amma was worried because the bird, which was speechless, could not understand the settlement between the humans. By mistake, if it moved one step on the other side, the hunter would kill it. This thought made Amma dislike the settlement.

If the bird had been with any other person, the hunter would have fought over the matter and forcibly snatched it away by this time. There is no doubt about this. He would not have remained patient for so long. But where was the peacock? It was on Amma's lap, who was so kind-hearted —Her very name is Karunamayi! The hunter did not have the guts to take the bird away forcibly. Who would dare!

Those who had pacified the hunters all this time, then

came to Amma and said, "Mother, why quarrel with a rude person? Let us keep the bird on the line. The peacock shall certainly come towards You. It will not go on that side, Amma."

Thus after a long time, they reluctantly convinced Amma. With great hesitation, She handed over the bird with utmost care, so as not to cause pain to its hurt wing. Her feeling was that of a mother handing over her own child to a stranger!

After giving the bird to Sri Sheshaiah, Amma turned away to the other side and started to sob uncontrollably like a child, covering Her face with Her palms.

I was furious about what the 77-year-old Sheshaiah had done. I could not bear to see Amma weep. I do not mind even if anybody beats, hurts or kills me, but I get uncontrollably angry when anyone causes even a little trouble to Amma.

Sri Seshaiah was elderly and a revered person to me, but why, I thought, should he come to such a settlement? Couldn't he convince the hunters somehow and send them away? Why should he make Amma cry so much?

I lost my cool and told Sri Sheshaiah, "Respected Sir, why are you making Amma suffer so much? I myself shall not part with the bird. Let the hunters do what they want!" I tried to take the bird into my hands.

Listening to my words and seeing my response. Sheshaiah got scared. He quickly replied, "Dear, please listen to me. Why must we have a fight with the hunters? Wait for a second. The peacock belongs to Amma and it will most certainly walk towards Her. Look! You can see," and he placed the bird on that line.

Because of its bloodstained, painful wound, the bird had its eyes closed. It had also become very weak from excessive bleeding. With the change of hands, the peacock did not realize where it had been placed. With great difficulty, it raised its eyelids and looked around. First it saw the hunter, then painfully turned to the other side. From there it saw Amma at a distance. It seemed as if the bird was swallowing its pain! With great difficulty and much effort, it stood on the line. All of us were calling the bird by stretching our arms. Slowly, very slowly, the peacock walked in one direction—that is, toward Sri Karunamayi, who had turned Her head to the other side! It gradually came and sat near Amma's feet.

A peacock is not educated in any university. It does not know civilization, manners, knowledge or anything about worldly principles. But the peacock did realize the motherly love expressed by Sri Karunamayi, who had taken the bird onto Her lap and who was crying for its sake. It also understood that the hunters did not love it and that they would kill it. "When I was in distress, She took me onto Her affectionate lap and loved me silently," it thought. Amma's maternal affection was clearly evident to the peacock, which is why, even in great pain, the bird wished to have Mother's affection only. And this is why it took refuge at Amma's lotus feet, which are the abode of peace. Whether or not it understood anything going on around it, the peacock certainly did understand Mother's love towards it. The hunters, without further argument, went away disappointed, muttering something.

Amma saw the peacock which had come near Her. She took the bird into Her arms and kissed it again and again with tears of joy, comforting it on Her lap. The peacock took shelter under Amma's soothing maternal love for quite a long time and tasted real love. The bird enjoyed the kindness and motherly love it had never known so far. "Henceforth I need not be scared, I am safe," was the expression in the peacock's eyes.

We were all delighted to see this scene. Our feelings were beyond words.

BHAVANI IS WON BY DEVOTION

It was *Brahmotsava* celebration time at the Lakshmi Narasimha Swami Temple in Penusila, during May, 1990. The scorching heat of peak summer was unbearable. The devotees, with great love and devotion, after having had *darshan* at the temple, were flocking into the *ashram* for Amma's *darshan* too.

On this occasion, free medical camps are always arranged in the *ashram* and food is distributed to all. The arrangements also include the distribution of pure drinking water, singing of *bhajans*, spiritual discourses, special *pujas* and exquisite floral decorations. Thousands of people from all over the state and from neighboring villages participate in the festivities, which last for five days and are celebrated on a grand scale. The last day is the *Garuda seva*, which is followed by the *kalyanotsavam* for Lord Narasimha.

Today was the *Garuda seva*. The people had occupied all the places on the Garudachala Hills, at the temple, under the trees, on the buses, and at the *ashram* too. As the overcrowded lorries, trucks, buses, tractors and carts entered the arch which was the entrance to the temple, the devotees were shouting and chanting the name of the Lord. "*Govinda....Govinda....Narasimha Govinda.*" Their voices echoed in the hills.

"Glory to Amma!....Glory to Amma!" was also heard as they entered the *ashram* of Sri Karunamayi.

Different varieties of *prasadam* were continuously distributed to all, from 4:00 a.m. until midnight. After drinking cold buttermilk, the people relaxed under huge trees and in the *Annapurna* Hall. An endless swarm of people was thronging to have Amma's *darshan*. Many of them were eagerly waiting for their turn, lining up in the scorching heat of the sun. They included the poor and the old, who stood patiently to have a closer glimpse of Amma. The devotion in their hearts towards Her was extraordinary.

The *darshan* of Sri Karunamayi started at 4:00 a.m. Thousands of people had been waiting eagerly since the previous night for this opportunity to have an early morning *darshan*. Amma blessed the people on all the five days, giving *darshan* from 4:00 a.m. to 11:00 p.m. continuously.

It was noon on the *Garuda seva* day, and Ammamma was feeding everybody sumptuously. By now, thousands of devotees had been blessed with Amma's *darshan*.

Suddenly Amma came to the sanctum of *Sri Lalita Devi*. There all the edibles are offered to Divine Mother. Sri Karunamayi asked me to get some cold water, a few fruits and a little of the offerings. Sri Rama knew only to obey the orders of his father, King Dasharatha. Otherwise there would have been neither Sri Rama, nor the *Ramayana*. It was the same here, too. We simply obeyed Amma's orders. Nobody ever dared to question, "Why?" "For whom?" "Where to?"—or anything else. The fear and respect in our hearts come from our reverence towards Amma, so that we do not talk much to Her.

There was a huge crowd outside. After lunch, the people who were sick, wounded, or who had suffered sun strokes were all moving toward the free medical camp. The hot wind blowing made the heat unbearable.

In this weather, Amma started walking into the garden. "Amma! Please wait for a while," I pleaded. "I shall bring your footwear."

"No, my son!" Amma said. "We have to rush back." Saying so, She walked briskly forward.

This was an unusual incident. Generally Amma was not seen outside on the *ashram* grounds. She was always inward and silent. I did not understand anything that was happening.

And why was it that no one recognized Amma? Had they done so, we could not have moved even an inch! She would have been surrounded by crowds of people. For this reason, She perhaps made Herself invisible by Her *maya*!

After walking a little way, Amma suddenly stopped near a stranded bullock cart without bullocks, went under it, and sat there. According to Amma's instructions, I was carrying a jug of cold water, a few fruits and some snacks in a basket. The three sides of the cart were covered by a jute cloth. A folk song was heard from beneath the cart.

> O.........soothing Mother!
> O.........the brilliant moon of the full moon day!
> O.........Karunamayi!
> Please come here ....
> Bless me with your love ......!

I bent down to look for Amma. A young lady, about twenty years old, was singing the song with closed eyes, as she breast-fed her child. The temperature was a scorching 42 degrees centigrade [107 degrees Fahrenheit] and, on such a hot day, she imagined Amma as the soothing moon, and her own heart as a temple, with pure devotion.

As Amma called me, I also stepped under the cart and sat down. The young lady looked surprised and stopped singing.

"My dear, who composed this song?" asked Amma in Her soft voice.

"It is me," replied the lady. "I keep singing whatever comes to my mind. But who are you?"

"Me....," Amma was silent for some time. "I am your dearest one."

"*Akka*! Elder Sister," she exclaimed. "My name is Gowri. I have come here to have the *darshan* of *Raja Rajeshwaramma*," the lady continued. "But as I was very tired and uncomfortable standing in the hot sun, I came here to relax."

Seeing that the lady was in an advanced stage of pregnancy, Amma said to her. "Younger sister! (said because the lady had addressed Amma as Elder sister) Why have you come in this hot sun? Would you like to drink a little cold water?" Asking so, Amma gave her a tumbler of cold water.

"*Akka*, I am dying of hunger! I understand that there is free feeding in the *ashram*. *Akka*, can you please bring some food for me?" the lady requested without any shyness. Understanding Amma's mind by Her glance at me, I immediately served the food I had carried from Lalita Mandiram.

Gowri's surprise knew no bounds. "How did you bring this? Who told you, *Akka*?"

Amma smiled at her. "The people of this *ashram* never allow anybody to starve. Hence, I brought this food for you personally. Have it comfortably."

Gowri was visibly moved. She put the child down, who began to cry. So Amma started feeding the lady with Her own hand. With the food in her mouth, Gowri leaned on Amma's shoulder and said tearfully, "How kind you are to me!"

"Gowri, dear! Have this sweet, too. Is it nice?" Amma continued feeding the girl. To satiate her hunger, Amma fed this child, Gowri, with Her own hand.

How can I express the kindness in Amma? It is indescribable! In spite of thousands of people waiting in the scorching heat for Amma's *darshan*, Amma had come all the way to this pure-hearted Gowri, sitting beneath the cart, to shower Her motherly love on her.

Jai Karunamayi! Words are insufficient to describe the kindness in You! You are beyond the highest degree of kindness! I felt I was very blessed indeed to have this human birth and witness this delightful sight!

Gowri interrupted my thoughts. "*Akka*! You are feeding me all the food. Please keep a little aside for my husband too," she said.

"Do not worry, my child!" Amma responded reassuringly. "There is enough food for your husband. You eat to your heart's content."

After eating a little more, Gowri suddenly stopped. "*Akka*, it is a nice feeling to be fed by you. I have eaten a lot today. But is it not strange that the quantity of food remains the same as it was before?" The girl seemed really perplexed.

"Gowri, no! You ate very little. Don't feel that you have eaten a lot," Mother said kindly and soothingly.

"*Akka*, I have never eaten a lunch like this! Who will feed me in this way? I have had no mother since I was an infant. My father is a drunkard. He never invites me to his house. Me and my husband do the work of digging the earth, but our daily wages are insufficient to make ends meet. How can we ever afford such a delicious lunch? During my first pregnancy, I had a desire for glass bangles. I wanted to eat *laddus*. But these desires remained unfulfilled as we could not afford such things."

As Gowri was speaking, Amma immediately removed Her green glass bangles and put them on Gowri's arms.

"*Akka*, no!" Gowri scolded Amma. "Don't give away those green glass bangles to me. Don't remove them from your arms. It will be inauspicious for you!"

"My auspiciousness lies in your happiness," Amma replied. And, despite Gowri's resistance, Sri Karunamayi put Her bangles on Gowri's arms, retaining only two on each arm for Herself. "Oh, look! Your arms are so beautiful, now," She added.

"*Akka*, how loving you are towards this poor sister! My husband is in the crowd waiting for Amma's *darshan*. We live thirteen kilometers away, and have been walking for a few days to reach here. We have no desire, but we have come as we were told that the very *darshan* of *Raja Rajeshwaramma*, Sri Karunamayi, would purify us. It seems

She is always in silence. They say it is a great blessing to see Her at least once. During my first pregnancy, my husband wanted to know about my desires. I told him that I desired to eat sweets, to have glass bangles, and to have the *darshan* of Amma at least once.

"'I cannot afford to fulfill all these desires at this time. The money we have is sufficient only to buy the sweets and the bangles. But we do not have money for the bus fare to the *ashram*,' said my husband.

"So," she said, "I decided to forego the sweets and bangles and go for Amma's *darshan*. In the meantime, I fell sick and the money was spent on medicines."

Gowri continued. "I felt disappointed and I cried. How can I come here, I thought, without the Divine Mother's call?

"But that night, Amma appeared in my dream and blessed me! She has also blessed the childless lady, Venkatamma of my village with a healthy son. The pains and sufferings of the people in my village have vanished by applying *kumkum*, Amma's *prasadam*, on their foreheads.

"*Akka*, for a long time I have had a great desire to see Amma. The delivery of this child may be fatal. I do not know. So I requested my husband to take me for Amma's *darshan*. But he had no money. He even tried to borrow from somebody, but failed.

"As I was in advanced pregnancy, the crowded bullock carts which start from my village refused to take me, saying the journey would be tedious and dangerous for me.

"So we decided to walk the distance. At first my husband was not ready to do so as he, too, felt that walking that long distance would be dangerous for me. He was very firm that he was not prepared to take this risk.

"Then I told him, 'You said that it is only Amma who commands the sun and the moon. *That* Mother shall give me strength to walk. It is not I who will walk. And these are the days before the full moon. Many carts and people will be moving along the road. So there is no need to fear. Moreover, Mother is with us.'

"But my coaxing was in vain. He would not agree. I was very disappointed and started to cry. Finally, he agreed.

"My husband carried this child," she said, "and I, the one in the womb. We walked all the way. Look, *Akka*! There are blisters on both my feet."

I felt stunned as I looked at the lady. Had she really walked that long distance in her condition?

Amma was moved, too, and shed tears. She sprinkled the cold water on Gowri's feet, gently touching the blisters to relieve her pain.

I am the witness to this incident, which would melt any heart. I could not have been more surprised had I been Kalidasa when Devi appeared before him! This event was an unimaginable scene in my life. The lotus feet of Divine Mother are worshipped by the Gods, who have taken humble refuge in Her. And to think that that same Divine Mother, *Brahmamayi*, washed the feet of this Gowri?

That Universal Mother, who creates, commands and controls all the galaxies with Her divine finger-tips —that kind-hearted *Annapurna Devi* who satiates the hunger of all beings in the universe, that Mother who is *Nadamayi*, *Vedamayi*, and the Bestower of *Atma Vidya*— was Herself bound by Gowri's devotion! She was showing such sweet tenderness by washing Gowri's feet with Her own hands.

"The pain has disappeared just by your touch, *Akka*!" Gowri marveled.

As for me, I was still so amazed and dazed, I could hardly understand Gowri's words!

"Is it so, Gowri?" Amma said. "It's because I sprinkled cold water."

"*Akka*, what is your name?" Gowri suddenly inquired. "You did not give me your identity."

"Name?" said Amma, smilingly. "....You called me *Akka*, your elder sister."

"No, not that." Gowri insisted. "Your proper name!"

"I have no real name. Call me by any name. I will respond."

"Which is your native place?" Gowri went on.

"Place? ....I belong to all the places in the world," said Amma.

"*Akka*, you have neither given me your name, nor your place. At least give me the address where you stay," she pleaded.

"How can I tell a lie?" Amma said. "I am everywhere."

Gowri looked at Amma for a minute in silence. Then she said, "You are educated. I am just a dullard sister of yours. I am unable to understand anything. But I certainly understood that you love me a lot."

I felt that this conversation was very beautiful. When the heart is devoid of negative qualities and is pure, it is easier for one to come closer to Amma. Not only that, you can become even a younger sister to Her, like Gowri, I thought.

"*Akka*," Gowri said in a confidential tone, "I do not know whether I shall survive the risk of delivering the child this time; hence I am doubtful of coming again. So I shall pray to Mother Karunamayi from here itself."

"Gowri," Mother asked, "what do you pray?"

"For good devotion towards Amma who should always live in me," she replied.

"And will your Mother hear your prayer?" Amma asked her.

"What a question!" Gowri looked incredulous. "Amma notices even the movement of an ant! The priest in my village says that She is the Mother of Lord Brahma. I swear to you, *Akka*! Even our conversation is heard by Her. She even knows that I have come all the way walking. But what can She do? There are so many people who have come here who are in more distress than me.

"Solving our problems is nothing for Amma. She does it even without our knowing it. Whenever I have prayed in my difficult times, immediate help was given in some form or the other."

"Okay, Gowramma! What did you bring for that Mother?" Amma smiled gently at her.

"*Akka*," she said, suddenly remembering. "Thanks for reminding me in time. I have brought this pomegranate fruit, the first of the season, which grew on the tree in front of my hut. I want to give this to Amma. Can you please see that it reaches Her? *Akka*, will She eat it?"

"Gowri, this is the favorite fruit of Devi. And when it is sent by you, She will definitely eat it!" Saying so, Amma stretched Her hand to receive the fruit.

Gowri's eyes glittered with joy! "I am happy now! I have no other desire."

Though Gowri was uneducated and had not heard any spiritual discourse, still she glowed with spiritual culture. What faith she had in Sri Karunamayi! Though she was an ordinary housewife, she was a pure, devoted lady who was free from the bondage of desires.

Divine Mother submits to devotion alone. Gowri had the devotion which made Amma shower her with nectar-like affection.

"Please wish me to have a baby girl," Gowri said suddenly.

"Why a girl in particular?" Mother inquired.

"I want to name the girl with Divine Mother's name, so that I shall always call the name which may bring the Divine Mother to me."

"Okay, Gowri!" replied Amma. "You will have a daughter, and you will name her as you desire."

Turning to me, Amma added, "Babu (Swamiji), give these foods and fruit to Gowri."

"Gowri, don't return by walking. This time, if you walk in the hot sun, your Mother's feet will surely have blisters!

Travel comfortably by bus with your husband. Live happily and peacefully with your family."

So saying, Amma blessed Gowri by placing Her palm on the girl's head. She also blessed her little son. "Shall I take leave of you, Gowri?" Sri Karunamayi asked.

"*Akka*, do you want to leave so soon? No, please don't leave me alone. I feel you should always be with me. Your smile is a treasure. I want to hear you more and more and stay with you forever," she spoke innocently, fearing the separation.

"Don't be afraid. I shall leave only for now," Amma promised, holding Gowri's hand.

The ocean of compassion in Sri Karunamayi's heart was overflowing, breaking all barriers. *Rishis*, and scholars have all praised *Para Brahmamayi* in different ways with overwhelming devotion. But this *Veda Mata*, this *Veda vana vasini*, is beyond the reach all of them! This world is like a toy house to Mother Divine. And all living beings are Her dolls. The doctrine of *Sri Mata* is invisible and incomprehensible even to Lord Brahma. In the play between Divine Mother and devotee, between Mother and child, the victory will always be for the one who is devoted. This truth is clearly emphasized in Gowri's innocent love.

Amma submits to devotion.

She is captured by devotion.

She comes running in search of Her devotee.

Sri Karunamayi is certainly *Ishwari* personified.

O Mother, this life is your divine play!

Sarvantaryami Karunamayi, who resides in everyone as soul, dwells in the hearts of scholars, sages, the learned, the realized ones, the devotees and infants.

The song sung by the devoted Gowri is repeated by all of us in the *ashram* every day.

> O soothing Mother!
> O soothing Mother!
> O Moon on the full moon day!
> O Karunamayi!
> O Mother, come to us!
> Bless us with your love! [3]

Gowramma had called out to her Mother, Divine Mother.

Thereafter, this song found a place in the hearts of all the women-folk. They sang it while they drew water from the wells, planted seedlings in the fields, decorated front yards with designs and colored powders, breast-fed the babies or put the children to sleep. It found a way into those hearts that prayed for the recovery of the sick.

In the villages and among the tribal people, everybody sings this song heartily while engaged in their own occupations. It is very popular with everyone. Ammamma also sang these words with utmost devotion while offering to *Devi Lalitambika* the delicacies she prepared.

Smt. Chandrika Gururaj, who has received a state musician's award from Karnataka, has rendered this song very melodiously. Everyone who listens to it is touched by emotion, and melts into tears. Gowramma, the composer of this song, probably isn't even aware of these things.

A song, though beautifully composed, is not worth anything unless it has devotion and sincere feelings behind it. A song composed with deep feeling and love remains in the hearts of the people forever.

We shall be blessed by *Para Brahmamayi* when we are sincere even for a moment, while we think, praise or surrender to Her.

In the ordinary course of things, a common man cannot understand the inner meanings or feelings that flow like

---

[3] O *Challani Talli* can be found on the cassette entitled *Daya Sagari,* Side A, song 2

nectar in Amma's messages. One cannot understand these teachings just by reading books. These thoughts must be experienced in the inner heart. And to do so, one should have a sincere and intense desire for God. This alone will lead us to the goal of realizing the Absolute.

The divine spiritual treasure, which cannot be acquired by penance or chanting *mantras*, can be had just by the touch of the dust particles from the lotus feet of divine souls. This is divine truth. The effulgent energy that emerges from the Self is *Para Brahmamayi*.

Sri Karunamayi is that light which travels eternally, in all states; it is that which is indestructible in the pure and innocent hearts of devotees. One can own Her and place Omkarini in one's heart only when that heart is purified.

As the sun shines uniformly, without discrimination on good or bad, rich or poor, on a hut or a palace, so does Sri Karunamayi shower Her blessings and love. Amma, the ever-content one—whose language is silence, who is the eternally radiant lamp of *dharma*, whose breath is the fulfillment of unexpressed love, who is full of bliss, who glows with peace, who shines like the sun and soothes like the moon—will bless everyone like She blessed Gowri.

Life is a struggle between darkness and bright sunshine. In our struggle, the light of devotion will be victorious. Eternal, true inner bliss will submit to the devotion of the devotee. Sri Karunamayi has proved that She submits to *bhakti*, for She is *Bhakti vashya*. Amma's abundant motherly love graces the heart with purity. And when that soothing divine love flows into the heart, possessiveness and desires vanish. Not the slightest stain of selfishness remains.

Sri Karunamayi is *Mahishasura Mardini* who kills egoism—the "me" and "I" in us. She is the revered one who induces the realization of the Self in us.

One is graced with endless energy when seated for only a moment in Amma's divine presence. And one's heart is relieved of bondages—silently and peacefully—as Gowramma's was. Those hearts become pure when graced by Amma's divine lotus feet. They become temples that glow with Her effulgence.

Gowramma is like a blossomed and pure *parijata* flower. As Sri Karunamayi was wandering in the world of pure devotion, which is so like a beautiful garden, She stopped for a while to enjoy the fragrance of this Gowri blossom. She showered Gowri with abundant and most tender motherly love. Just as the sun's rays make a lotus' petals open, so did Amma bring to full bloom the heart of Gowri, sittting in her heart as Maha Lakshmi, and the *Bhakti Vashya Bhavani!*

Jai Karunamayi!

SRI KARUNAMAYI - A Biography

SRI DAKSHINAMURTI RUPINI

Countless are those who have come to Amma's lotus feet—and all are Her children. Like the sun, Mother never pours greater light upon either the disciple, the devotee or the innocent seeker. She is the Universal Mother. But our ability to see that light, to open ourselves to its full radiance at the cost of obliterating the often too comfortable darkness, to want that light at any cost, and to be in that light eternally—this is rare. In 1982, one such devotee came to Penusila Kshetram seeking the *darshan* of Amma.

Mr. Durga Prasad Rao was a man in his eighties, but he had always had immense devotion to God and a deep desire for Self-Realization. As he narrated his experience to me in good Telugu, I noted it down in shorthand. After finishing this narration, I felt that I had not done full justice in expressing his feelings completely. Here is his story as narrated by him:

"All my life I had preferred the absolute truth, "I myself am *Atman*," to the feeling that God, the soul and the self are different from one another. But I had not experienced this truth. My heart was desperate to have that divine experience of knowing that my soul is bliss, the Absolute.

"I was in search of a real *Guru*. I was fortunate enough, due to the fruit of the good deeds of previous births, to find a great mendicant as my *Guru*. No one knew his nativity, name, age or origin. He lived in a small village, 276 miles from Pune. I had his first *darshan* under a huge neem tree. Laughing to himself, he signaled me to come closer. I prostrated to that one who looked like an insane person! He kept his palm on my head and thrice repeated, "Om," into my ear. As He was chanting the *mantra*, I felt a burning fire within. I felt as though my sins were being burnt and charred. This experience was very clear.

"Within a short time, my worldly attachments ended. All mental pressures were diminished. The pain and sufferings in me were wiped out. In my home itself, I began my *sadhana* in earnest.

"How can a real *Guru* tread the path of untruth? The true *Guru* always shows the way to absolute truth and leads us on the right path. The mind, being limited, cannot imagine the philosophy of supreme bliss. Only a few, those of great intellect, can understand this philosophy. The true *Guru* does not give a specific worldly form to that divine bliss. He cannot bind the *atman*, the soul.

"The preaching of this mendicant filled my heart with great joy. I could not understand what actually was happening in the depths of my heart, but I was feeling very peaceful. Only the *Guru* has the strength to recognize this secret.

"Thus, ten years passed. I used to visit this renunciant every month, traveling from Hyderabad. I experienced immense peace after his *darshan*, but he did not speak a single word to me even once. He was always in silence. He spent the days laughing and speaking to himself. Whenever anybody offered food or fruits, sometimes he ate them, and sometimes he threw them on the ground, laughing away. He never cared about the seasons. Sitting under the trees, the hot summer, the chill winter, or the pouring rain never disturbed him. He was a person of silence—the scholar of supreme bliss. As the soul is nameless, so was this sage. He enjoyed bliss within himself, silently enduring the passing seasons.

"This *Guru* had no desire, even for fame. I had a wish to feed him with good fruits, and I wanted to serve him in some way. But no, he would not accept anything from me. One day during the winter, I took some fruit and a woolen blanket to him. He threw the fruit on the ground and the blanket into the fire beside him. He laughed, looking at me. I just kept quiet.

"I always got a lot of enthusiasm and strength from him. I had taken invaluable peace from him, as alms. But I deeply regretted that I could not serve this great man in the least way possible.

"'He is very kind,' I thought. 'At least he is allowing me to go to him. This is enough for me.' Useless money and all my worldly possessions were like dust to him. What did I have to give him? I was empty-handed, having nothing to offer this great man! Only later did I realize this!

"Then one day, probably after two years went by, the *Guru* suddenly spoke to me, saying, 'Go to Tiruvannamalai. There you will see the real Kumaraswami—Subramanya, son of Lord Siva. Afterward, *Brahmamayi*, Divine Mother, will incarnate. She will give you *darshan* as Dakshinamurti, amidst a dense forest, under a banyan tree.'

"'The Goddess is coming down to Earth on *Vijaya Dashami* day,' he continued. 'She will bestow motherly love and liberation on all mankind. She alone can cut off the chains of bondage. She will remove the veil of *maya* and take you on the path of divinity. Only She is capable of carrying all your burdens. She is that great complete ocean, from which the incarnations come as waves. Surrender everything into the divine hands of that Mother. She will bestow on you the state of attachment to God and detachment from worldly things. *Para Brahmamayi*,' he added, 'will take you closer to Her by Herself and will bless you with liberation.'

"He did not speak further, but I felt as if my spiritual thirst would be quenched.

"I had listened to the words of the *Guru* with surprise. He had spoken very softly, sweetly and fluently in pure

Hindi that was beyond the caliber of any scholar. I was eagerly looking for some more words, but he went into silence again.

"That night my friend and I slept under the same tree where the *Guru* slept. It was dawn. Tender sunshine came up in the sky. We prostrated to the *Guru*, but he never moved. We kept on calling out to him. We even touched his body in an effort to wake him up. I touched his feet, which were chilled like snow. Now we were very worried.

"For the whole day we waited, along with the other villagers, expecting him to come back to his physical body. But he never did. The next day, his body was cremated under the same tree. The mendicant had played his game of life. Like an old cloth, he had sacrificed his physical body into the fire of the yaga of life. I did not feel sad or depressed. I was peaceful and fearless.

"On the third day my friends left for Hyderabad, but I stayed under the same tree nearly for ten more days. Nothing of 'me' remained in me. I felt that probably a little of the egoism in me was slowly diminishing. I thought, 'Is this all there is to life? Is it for this little that we have hurt so many people's feelings?'

"The strong divine compassion of the mendicant had entangled itself in my life very deeply. He had responded to my prayers and destroyed all the thoughts of a weak mind. This kind-hearted *Guru* had made me his worthy disciple, and day by day, started accepting me. 'O divinely-formed *Gurudeva*, you have not parted from me. You have filled my heart. You are here! O Father!' I cried out, holding the temple of my heart tightly.

"My hands shivered as I flung away the ashes of the last remains of the *Guru* in the sacred flowing river. [A custom in Hindu rituals]. My heart was heavy, and I felt that there was no work in this world left for me to do.

"Yes, this is truth. I had not yet experienced the Absolute.

"After that I wandered across the whole of North India, visiting and calling on many holy persons. I was very depressed, carrying the burden of this long life in which I seemingly had no way of realizing the Self. I had delayed for many lives and wasted my time, forgetting this goal, this truth and this *dharma*. I blamed myself for this.

"Although there was a slight discipline in my regular spiritual practice after the preaching of this great mendicant, still I had neglected the sacred goal of a human. I had done this in many previous births.

"In my lifetime, I had met many scholars and holy persons. If they were to look into my heart, they would have surely rejected me as a person who did not have the supreme goal in view, and who was not in the quest of liberation. Actually, they would have been right in doing so. When had I tried to discover the absolute Truth? What had I kept in view as the supreme goal of life? Never had I followed a life of righteousness that led to that divine Light. Probably I would not have been aware of this had I not met that renunciate mendicant.

"The human race is speeding away in the playground of this world. Unhealthy competition, the troublesome burden of riots, jobs, and other difficulties are a few of the storms that are flooding the lives of people in this world. 'O Divine Mother,' I prayed, 'please save me from being washed away in this flood and make me stand in Your divine presence.'

"After a year or so, I finished the wide tour of North India and reached Chennai. At that time, I had no specific goal in worldly life. I had sold my property and invested the money in a bank deposit, spending it little by little. One day I was standing at a railway station, gazing at the people. Suddenly a man appeared and asked me if I wanted to travel to Tiruvannamalai, as he had a ticket. I asked to see it, and he placed it in my hand. Because I wanted to pay him, I reached for my money, but when I turned in his direction, he had disappeared! I searched for him for some time, but in vain.

"In this way, without any planning, I reached Arunachalam, Tiruvannamalai, the place I had heard of through the renunciant *Guru*. There I visited the shrine of Arunachaleswara, a Siva Temple. Somebody in the temple instructed me to go round the Aruna Hills, which I did. During this circumambulation, I met a man who asked me to visit a holy saint who stayed there, and gave me the address. However, as I was extremely tired from walking that day, I slept at the *sanctorum* of Arunachaleswara.

"The next morning, I started out to have the *darshan* of the saint who sat in silence. It was a vast area. There, near the *goshala*, the cowshed, of the *ashram* stood the saint, wearing a minimal loincloth and leaning upon a stick in his hand. Ah, what calmness! Who was this man? Suddenly I remembered the words of the mendicant *Guru*: 'Go to Tiruvannamalai. You will see Kumaraswami, Siva's son, Himself.' From the depths of my heart, the words came to my mind like a hidden treasure!

"From where had this divine person alighted? I was thinking, "Am I worthy of standing before this great soul? What peace! No flower in this world has this fragrance. What a pleasure!"

"He was watching me silently. 'O *Lokeswara*! What is this fragrance?' I had never experienced anything like this, at any time, anywhere! No, not even with my mendicant *Guru*. 'Who are you? Father? Only if you grace me, can I know you. Have I not been desperately and endlessly searching for you for many births? Give me the strength to drown myself in your boundless silence.'

"I can never forget that soothing, merciful look. It was a great flow of peace, and I was drowning in that divine flood. Such a divine smile in that mysterious silence—one can never imagine! Compared to anything in this world—or even this universe—it is matchless. He is none other than Karttikeya, the one who preached about *Para Brahma* to Brahma Himself. This divine soul was none other than the revered *Guru*, Bhagavan Sri Ramana Maharshi!

"But my heavenly time was short-lived. Bhagavan, too, gave up his physical body, just like an old rag.

"For about six months I stayed on at Ramana Ashram. Then again, I started to tour round the country. I did not waste much time, but spent it in silence and meditation, either on the banks of the holy rivers, on the hills, or in the forests. Twenty-five years passed in this way. Though there had been days spent in laziness and ignorance in my earlier life, now my days were good, spent in searching for the true goal.

"Probably there still remained some deep senseless thoughts in me, of which I was not aware. Is it not the game of the Divine Mother to grace us with water when we ask for fire, and with fire when we ask for water? I did realize many a time that in the path of spirituality, the Divine Mother rejects all our prayers for senseless, meaningless worldly things.

"To receive me completely, the Mother was making me worthy of it day by day. But I had not yet experienced, 'I myself am *Brahman!*' When I thought of this I was totally depressed with sorrow. Day by day, the physical body, which is merely an instrument for spiritual practice, was not cooperating. With old age and unhealthy signs appearing in the body, I was no longer able to sit on the ground. I suffered weakness and indigestion. My eyesight was also very poor. I had a continuous cough, pain, and fever. I was very frightened. Would this body wither away like a dry leaf before I could experience the Self? Then the boon of taking a human birth would be wasted! These thoughts made me sad and restless.

"I had read many books of Indian philosophy. And though I had done *sadhana* for many years and visited many great souls, I had never had the experience of the Self. I had received the dust of the feet of many holy ones, but I had not yet attained the complete peace which is beyond birth and death. And how could I imagine this peace without first getting the experience of the Self and of supreme bliss?

"My feelings were sincere and devout. This birth should not be a waste. I should live till I realized the Absolute, but I did not know how long this would take. There was not much time ahead for me. Would my life span be for a number of days or for merely a few hours? Would the work for which I had come into this world remain incomplete? Would I not be able to complete the drawing of the picture of the beautiful Mother of Nature, *Brahmamayi*, on the palette of my heart?

"I had spent my whole life mixing the colors, but had never succeeded in finishing the picture of Mother Divine. I had not mixed the colors in the right proportions. The very seat of the picture was not yet available. The one ambition in my heart was to complete the picture, but I did not know whether I was eligible for this or merely grasping at an unattainable ambition. My whole heart was burning with the pain of my failure. I wanted to offer my soul to *Brahmamayi*. But I had spent all my life arranging to get the offerings. I was not yet prepared!

"How could I complete the offering? This ambition alone had helped me to live for more time. But the dream was not yet a reality. Seconds seemed like *yugas* in an uncertain life. The only fortunate incident in this meaningless life of mine had been getting a desireless *Guru*. Having the glimpse of Bhagavan Ramana Maharshi had been another great incident. Now my life was stuck—confused and silent.

"I returned to Hyderabad and stayed there for many days. A few of my spiritual friends planned a trip to Tripurantakam, Sri Sailam, Tirumala, and other pilgrimage sites and I, too, reluctantly accompanied them. We visited Tripurantakam, Sri Sailam and finally reached Tirumala. After having the glimpse of Lord Venkateshwara, by evening I came down from the hills to have the *darshan* of Govinda Rajaswami.

"Later, we visited the temple of Sri Alamelu Mangamma, Padmavati. While having the glimpse of Divine Mother, I prayed, "O Mother, won't you speak to me? Won't you speak at least once? I shall fill my heart with Your silence. I shall console myself that the silence is the grace You are showering on me. Amma, when shall I see Your divine form within me, outside and everywhere?" I prayed, bowing down, with patience.

"The car started, and we were on our journey again. This time I did not know the destination. It was dusk and getting dark. Then it started to drizzle, which soon turned into a downpour. We were traveling through a dense forest.

"By the time we reached some place, it was ten o'clock at night. We stayed in a choultry, getting drenched. Everyone went to sleep after eating the food we had carried. But I was awake the whole night calling, "Amma.... Amma!" My heart was throbbing for *Brahmamayi*.

"The sun rose in the east, and soon the darkness disappeared. The golden sun's rays were spreading on Mother Earth, and the flowers had bloomed in plenty. We all went to a temple, where we had the *darshan* of the Lord and offered worship. It was the temple of Sri Lakshmi Narasimha Swami. As usual, everybody went for sightseeing of the surrounding area, but because I was old and weak, I settled under a small shelter in the forest. A river was flowing nearby. On the banks of the river, there were many sacred *udumbara* trees. Many birds and parrots were there, too, chirping cheerfully and eating the fruits.

"After having a wash in the river, a farmer came and sat near me. He started asking me questions.

'Master, from where have you come?' he inquired.

'I am from Hyderabad,' I replied. I felt there was some relation between our souls.

'Did you visit the Temple?' he asked.

'Yes, I did. Is there anything else here for us to visit?'

'This shrine of Narasimha Swami is very powerful. He answers all our prayers,' he said. Then the farmer added, 'But there is something more special here—the Divine Mother Herself in human form! It is not easy to have a glimpse of Her unless one is very fortunate.'

"During my tour all over India, I had had the *darshan* of many great men and women. I did not have a desire to visit any more now. I had not experienced anywhere the peace I had enjoyed in communion with Sri Ramana Maharshi. Peace is not to be found outside. Divine peace is within us. That is the natural state of the *atman*. When I had presented myself before Sri Ramana Maharshi, he had given me that experience.

"So when the farmer began to talk about a female saint of the forest, I was only reluctantly listening to him.

'Sir, whenever people who live in the nearby villages and tribes want to cover their huts with hay roofs, they have to come to these hills for it. So they come with their cattle and all the arrangements for food, and they stay on the hills for ten days at a time.

'The rocks on the hills are sharp and slippery on account of which animals like the cow, deer, bison and others break their legs. Straight away then, they run to Mother with the pain and sit before Her for one or two days. That Divine Mother, *Raja Rajeshwaramma*, takes them into Her refuge, wipes their tears, and treats them with love. People have seen this. When the Mother nurses the wound with Her hands the animals become perfectly healthy the very next day! We do not know whether it is by the grace of Her eyes or the touch of Her hand.

'Oh, dear sir, let me tell you about a true incident which happened.'

"I merely nodded.

"The farmer said, 'We were twelve who came to cut the grass. There were at least two, three or four people from each family. We cut the grass for ten days. Then we gathered and tied it into bundles and carried them to the carts to return to our villages. We were to leave the next day.

'In this forest there are many wild bears. On the tenth day, suddenly one of them attacked a boy in our group and tried to snatch out his eyes! We had lighted a fire to keep ourselves warm in that chill weather, and the boy was alert and strong. He picked up a burning stick, threw it at the beast and escaped into the forest. The bear's thick black fur immediately caught fire and went up in flames. The frightened animal ran towards the dry hay we had stacked over ten days, and the hay burst into flames. It was a horrifying and ghastly scene as the wild fire spread everywhere. Everybody was screaming and crying for help. We were all stunned, not knowing what to do.

'*Raja Rajeshwaramma*, Divine Mother, was sitting near a small pond of water, and we all rushed to Her for refuge. 'Amma! O Divine Mother, save us!' I cried hitting my head emotionally on a huge stone which was in front of Her feet.

'After a little while, She opened Her eyes and looked at me.

'Please save us, Mother!' I cried again. 'My people and cattle are all surrounded by burning flames. Save them, please,' I pleaded.

'However, the Mother remained silent and did not offer any solution. She closed Her eyes for a while and then looked up at the sky.

'Astounding! Suddenly, on a scorching bright sunny day, the sky ornamented itself with dark dense clouds! It drizzled, rained and then flooded us with a heavy downpour! That's all.

'I prostrated before Mother and left the place, intending to come back again after visiting my people. The wild fire had been completely put out. But for the heavy rains, all of us would have been charred to death! We did not know whose good fortune among us had favored us. But we did know that we had been saved from great disaster only by the grace of that Mother!

'After a little while, we all went to the place where Amma had been seated. Strangely, She was not there. We searched for Her all around. She would have had to pass by us because there was no other possible way to leave that place. There was only one way to climb down the hills. Then where was the Mother? Where had She gone? We searched in every nook and corner of the forest, but She was not to be seen.

'We were all very disappointed, as we had come to express our gratitude and take Her blessings. Finally, we applied the dust of Her feet on our foreheads and prostrated to the soil where She had sat.

'After that, I visited the *ashram* with my friends many a time, but Mother would be either in the forest or in the caves. We never had Her *darshan*. I had such a desire to express my gratitude to my Mother, but She never gave me an opportunity to do so.

'And another strange thing had happened, too. On the day of the fire, when I had run for refuge and saw Her so close for the first time, the Mother was glowing with effulgence! On that day suddenly I saw the Mother with three eyes! I swear sir, on the Lord Narasimha Swami, that this is true! Even at that time of fear and panic, I clearly saw this.

'For months, whenever we went into the forests for either cutting grass or for tamarind, our eyes searched for the Divine Mother. We aspired for Her *darshan* at least for a second, but never glimpsed Her form. When I was depressed with this disappointment, my nephew, Ranga, told me, 'Uncle, why do you feel sad at being unable to see Her? How can She come to us if She has gone to help someone who is in the kind of disaster we were in?'

'Ranga,' I admitted, 'I did not think of this at all. You are right. Mother has to do good for everyone. Amma, wherever You are, please save everyone and bless everyone,' I prayed and bowed then and there.

'The three-eyed face of the Mother is still fresh in my memory. I can never forget it, sir! I know a little of the *Ramayana*. I learnt a little philosophy of Virabrahmendra Swami. But sir, my heart tells me that there is something unusual in this Mother. Whether I close my eyes or open them, I can never forget Her face with the three eyes! This is what I have seen for myself. Since then I bow to that Mother daily. Mother knows that I pray to Her. She does hear me. I believe it, sir!

'In this way, one year passed by. My eyes were always searching for the Mother. 'Amma, why don't You appear at least once before me? Do You know how much I long to have Your *darshan*?' I asked these questions in my mind.

'After a year or so, I went to Bhairavakona in search of some medicinal herbs. I climbed the highest peak, where a common man cannot easily reach. It was around six o'clock in the morning. I had risked this challenge not only for the medicines, but because my ambition to see the Mother once more was very strong. The peak does not have a regular path. It is a breathtaking journey. I was prepared to even give up my life, and I continued to climb the hill. How did I get so much adventurous energy, strength and bravery?

'Near the top, I glimpsed Her! Finally, I had the *darshan* of the Mother! The withering flowers and leaves were showering themselves on the body of *Raja Rajeshwaramma*. She Herself was in deep meditation. A big herd of deer, which had migrated from the neighboring hills, was there. Two of them were playing with the *pallu* of Amma's *sari*. Another small one was relaxing in Amma's lap. Others were chewing grass. As I entered the place, all the deer looked at me as though investigating my credentials. I felt, 'How lucky and blessed are these deer!' For one long year, I had been desperate to have Her glimpse for a second, and these deer were enjoying Her company this much! They were sitting, even leaning on Amma. How can I praise their fortune?

'For a very long time, Mother *Raja Rajeshwaramma* never opened Her eyes or looked at me. But as I gazed longingly at the glory of Her form—sir, yet again I witnessed the third eye on Her forehead! The experience had been repeated! I realized that what I had seen the first time was absolutely true, and I was overwhelmed with joy. I sat at a distance of about ten feet from Her.

'Time passed; the deer were active in their own world. Amma did not move even a little bit. I could not even see Her breathe. It was noon, and dusk followed.

'I could not understand how I had borne my hunger for so many hours. I had had no water since sunrise. Usually I could never sit in one place even for a few minutes. But I had been sitting still since morning. Where had this patience come from? But I knew the answer. This patience, without any feeling of hunger or thirst, had come to me only because of Amma's divine presence!

'Many questions came into my mind, 'Is She Herself *Para Brahma*? What would She be seeing? What would She be doing, closing Her eyes?' I was gazing at Amma constantly, without blinking, to my heart's content.

'Around 5:30 in the evening, the golden rays of sunlight were falling on the divine feet of Amma. Slowly, Her eyes opened. And She looked at me.

'I wept loudly with uncontrollable joy. I still don't have words to explain that joy. As I went closer to Her—the one who was sitting with the right foot on a platform and the left foot folded up—I wept like a small baby.

'Amma,' I cried, 'why were You not seen for so long? Had You not saved us that day, I would not be here to have Your *darshan* today!' I showed my happiness in different ways. I expressed my gratitude to Her and prostrated again and again before Her. Amma was silently watching me.

'Amma! I never knew that I could get Your *darshan* today. Had I known it, I would have brought something for You to eat. You are fasting since morning like this. How can I eat my stew of *jowar*, a poor man's food, without feeding you anything? Amma, I am a fool that I have come with empty hands! If I have to fetch some wild fruits in the forest, You may disappear and may not be seen again. So please take the offering of this poor man. It was prepared this morning itself.' So saying, I plucked a leaf and placed the food upon it.

'I knelt down before Her with the food in my hand. Amma, with a smile, stretched Her hand forward and received the food.

'Amma, is it good?' I asked.

'She smiled again as though to say that it was nice. How beautiful is that smile!

'Amma did not speak a word. Silence... silence... silence! That silence was great! The blue sky was leaning down all around. The devadaru tree was standing on the peak as if it were holding an umbrella for Amma. I can't describe the bright and brilliant effulgence around Her!

'It looked as though that silence were gushing towards me like a flood and drenching me in absolute peace.

'The herd of deer was surrounding Her, leaning on Her, embracing Her shoulders. It looked as though they were enjoying the love and affection of the Divine Mother! I thought how nice it would be if Amma would come to a normal stage and say something to me.

'Just then, a parrot came down and sat on Amma's shoulders. The parrot looked at me. It said, 'Sivaiah! Are you happy now? Go home now, peacefully.'

'I was astonished by the way a parrot spoke to me! How did that parrot know my name? I had never been so surprised at any time in my life! Is the Divine Mother speaking, sitting in the parrot's body? How can a bird know about me? I had read the biographies of many great people, but I never expected such an incident to occur in my own life! Sir, how could I imagine that I would see a Mother who could command the clouds just by a glance? A Mother who saved us and our cattle?

'When I expressed my gratitude, there was no reaction of any kind in Amma. Her look said, 'You are my children, and is it not my responsibility to take care of you?'

'Sir, this great Mother is *Maha Shakti* personified! The real Absolute! Silence is Her language! That was what I could understand, sir!

'I have spoken a lot. I do not know much. I am an illiterate. I do not know any spiritual practice. Everybody likes Mother here. During May, there is a *Brahmotsava*, the annual festival of Narasimha Swami. The tribals of the hills bring a lot of things from the forest as offerings, with band instruments and music. They also feel *Raja Rajeshwaramma* is Maha Lakshmi and give plantains, turmeric, kumkum, honey, wild fruits and roots as offerings. Amma smiles in silence seeing their joy. She receives everything to make them happy. Amma's mother, Annapurnamma, feeds all of them, and later they leave.

'You must have visited many great people. Have

darshan of this Divine Mother also. She is like the full moon amidst *crores* of twinkling stars. Her divine smile itself is enough! It is the most precious one! She neither talks nor reacts. It is not easy to have Her *darshan*. But sir, once I saw Her, I could not resist the desire of seeing Her again. Her divine smile keeps haunting me!'

"At that time, I made my decision to also seek the *darshan* of this *Raja Rajeshwaramma*. Thus, after the devoted farmer had explained his experiences to me in his own words with deep feelings, I planned to stay back for a week.

"My friends left, and the farmer took me along with him. He treated me with love and kind hospitality. This farmer was service-minded and truly devoted to God. After a night's sleep at the farmer's house, the very next morning we started out to have the Mother's *darshan*.

"On our journey, we carried some *chapatis*, rice flakes, *jaggery*, plantains and honey. We crossed small hillocks. We searched in the caves of every corner of the forest, and climbed the peaks of the Garudachala Hills for three days.

"Another three days passed in difficulties. We were passing through the dense forest with wild trees. The farmer kept me engaged by some talk so that I should not be disappointed and lose enthusiasm. But *darshan* was not available, and I was very tired.

'Sir, I have troubled you a lot at this old age, yet Amma's *darshan* is not possible!' The poor farmer felt very sorry for me. He was in tears.

"'Dear brother,' I asked him, 'is it so easy to have the *darshan* of great people? These hills are not that hard to climb. When the realized souls come to us, or to our houses, they will still be at a height where we cannot reach them. I can understand this. Please don't feel sorry!' So saying, I consoled him.

"The farmer, with the pain of disappointment, prayed, 'Amma, even if you don't give me *darshan*, it is all right.

This old man has been desperately searching for You, trekking the hard way. Are You not compassionate? Amma, if You appear before me, I shall not talk to You. I will go away from You, angrily. I can't bear this disappointment. I will jump from this peak. Now it is up to You to grace us. Later You shall only weep for my sake.'

"There was so much real feeling in the farmer's prayers and words. I saw in him a small child who was very angry with his mother. I did not have this kind of innocent and pure devotion! I did not have the strength to command that Mother with such purity! The purity of his heart alone had given him that right over Mother.

"That night we slept and relaxed on a huge stone. The stars in the sky were glittering brightly. The farmer picked up sticks and hay and lit a fire. He fetched some drinking water for me. He gave me the food we had packed, sat at a distance and looked at me humbly, as though requesting me to eat.

"'You also please have some,' I said.

'No, sir. I will have it after you finish,' he replied.

"'Why? Why like that?' I asked.

'If I eat along with you, the fruit of my righteous deeds will be lost, and I shall lose my blissful glow and peace,' said the farmer. [According to the scriptures, a guest should be treated as God and served first.]

"'Who told you all this?' I asked.

'Mother Annapurnamma, Ammamma, sir,' replied the farmer.

"'Who is she?' I inquired.

'She is the mother of Divine Mother *Raja Rajeshwaramma*. She has a great heart like Yashodamma, Mother of Lord Krishna,' he answered with conviction.

"'Okay then…. as you wish,' I said.

"The farmer continued, 'Sir, the other day when the Divine Mother had my food, I can't think how I reached the house! It seemed as though the God of Wind was pushing me forward! I don't understand. How did I cover that long distance so fast? I had gone to the peaks to fetch medicinal herbs, but forgot all about them when I had Amma's *darshan*. I narrated the whole incident to my people. I gave the food that remained to everybody as *prasadam*. Sir, whether you believe it or not, it was the most delicious delicacy I have ever eaten. How did this happen?

'I also gave some *prasada* to one of my very sick relatives. I told him that I did not fetch the herbs. I asked him instead to eat the *prasadam*, thinking of the Divine Mother. And this patient, who had been declared near death by the doctors, recovered completely after a month.

'Sir, I am not bothered even if Amma does not give me *darshan*. But till She appears before you, I shall sit and weep here, hitting my head against this tree. Let Her have any opinion about me. I don't care.'

"I realized then the depth of the love that farmer had for me, and asked him not to harm himself. But I really laughed to myself. I thought about the farmer's words. He had an open heart, which was filled and overflowing with devotion towards Mother.

"Soon the seventh night was over. The eighth day, too, passed without any luck.

"I was in the middle of the forest at the peak of Garudadri, gazing at the sky. The farmer's firm belief was that the Mother would definitely give *darshan*. I was just imagining the glory of the sudden appearance of the Divine Mother.

"The ninth day came. Our package of food was slowly dwindling. The search began again. My feet had blisters and they were bleeding. Seeing this, the farmer brought some water, washed my feet and nursed me. I realized that I still had a little attachment left for this worthless body of mine, which could wither away at any moment like an iron rod corroded by rust. I was alive only by the Divine Mother's grace.

"We did not feel sorry either about wandering in the forests, trekking the hills, or sleepless nights. But both of us had the same desire—the longing to have the *darshan* of Divine Mother.

"But the Mother was playing hide and seek with us. '*Brahmamayi*! Is it not the love for You that is making this child of Yours search for You since countless births? Amma, is it not the goal of my life to merge with You—become one with You like a river with the ocean? Amma, is it not the time for that? Is there any job left incomplete by me?' I went on with my thoughts. 'Amma, there have been so many days in my life during which I was neither ready nor prepared. Are You dodging me, keeping all that in mind? O Amma, are You enjoying playing hide and seek with this old man who is like a lamp about to be extinguished?' Warm tears were flowing down my cheeks.

"The farmer said, 'Sir, I have troubled you enough. It is already the ninth day. Mother is not kind. Please excuse me!' He cried loudly like a small boy.

"'No, my younger brother,' I insisted. 'Why are you feeling so sad? Do you think even an ant can move without Mother's command? Probably She is making me wander like this for some inner purity. It looks as though She made us walk every day to save us walking millions of miles in future births. If She has made us walk for these nine days, it is probably to prevent us from walking in the path of hell for many more births to come. This must be the essence, dear one! Our lives follow each other endlessly like dawn and dusk, but the Mother's compassion is with us through them all. Thus, we keep eagerly waiting for Her. Why do you feel sorry? As we keep our eyes open, suddenly, the Mother will grant us the happy moments of *darshan*.'

"But then I felt sure that someone else was speaking

within me with the utmost confidence. Who could it be? The voice said, 'It is Divine Mother. Don't get disappointed. Self-confidence and enthusiasm should never be lost at any cost!' I wiped the farmer's tears.

"The farmer said, 'Sir, you said, 'Even if this Mother comes to us in reality, we can climb the peak of the hill, but not to Her height.' What does this mean?'

"'I will try to explain,' I said. 'The height of the peak can be measured and may be some thousands of feet. So we can climb it. But the Divine Mother *Brahmamayi*, the subtlest one, is above and higher than all these hills, mountains, stars and geographical structures. She is beyond the reach of all these! She is *Omkara*, who is mingled in everything and is all-pervading. When She is in front of us, we can see Her physically, but cannot understand Her all-pervading nature as *Brahmamayi*! This is the peak we can never climb. Only She can help us to climb and cross this hurdle of the highest peak. Hence, Her name, *Durga*.'

"The farmer was very happy with the answer. 'Does it mean so much!' he exclaimed.

"But I was distracted. Suddenly, in the distance, I had heard something new and marvelous. I had the same feeling inside. 'Brother,' I cried, 'don't you hear some jingling footsteps? It is the Divine Mother Maha Lakshmi! Brother, Amma is coming! She is coming! Really, She is coming!'

"My mind was flashing. 'Always, always, She is. Every night, every morning, every day, every minute, every second, Mother is within us. She is with us forever and wherever we go. It is enough if we realize this truth. See, even on these peaks of Garudadri. She was within us, making us trek the range.

"'She will be with us in future! She is with us now! She was with us in the past! Always, forever and eternally She is within us—She can never be separate from us even for a moment! Amma's age is *crores* and *crores* of years! She is not the physical form that you have seen.'

"As I spoke, the breeze was blowing with a strange, soothing fragrance. From where was this coming? Our hearts were flooded with happiness! This pure divine fragrant breeze was very sweet. We were enjoying the divine flow in the wind.

"Suddenly, without even our knowledge, we became silent. In front of us was a large banyan tree. The Mother was seated beneath that tree! Her left foot was folded up, the right foot was resting down, and the lotus-eyed Mother was looking at us! She appeared to me to be the Goddess Maha Lakshmi seated on the full-bloomed lotus in the ocean of blissful effulgence! I stood looking at the Mother, astonished!

"Her divine eyes showered grace and compassion on me. She was sending a message through Her silence. 'Dear one, your search for me was meaningless. The indivisible, the complete, the *Omkara*, I myself, am all-pervading.'

"I clearly heard these words inside me, in Mother's own voice. I swear on this! I felt as if She were lifting me from the dust of *crores* of births just by Her compassionate grace!

"Leaving behind all my rage, my pains and bleeding wounds, my body was enjoying the divine vibrations of Mother's presence. Amma, who had covered my eyes with the mask of *maya* (illusion) for many births, removed it now to save me. She made me visualize the absolute truth. The fragrance of the Self was flowing as sun's rays from the ether.

"From where did this Divine Mother descend? *Wah*! O wonder! What peace! What fragrance! It is a perfume not present in any lotus, rose, jasmine or other flower in Her creation. What a pleasure! What boundless bliss!

"A mysterious, indescribable smile was glowing on the face of Divine Mother, sitting in silence. Probably there is nothing that can match this smile in the whole universe! My heart felt exactly the same as when I had the *darshan* of Sri Ramana Bhagavan! The same experience! The same peace of mind. I had not felt this when I met other great people. No, never did I feel this.

"Suddenly the words of my *Guru*, the mendicant, echoed in my mind: 'That great ocean of supreme bliss from which all the great incarnations scatter like drops, that complete ocean will incarnate on *Vijaya Dashami*, to share love and to give salvation to all humanity! She will give you *darshan* in the middle of the forest under a banyan tree, as Dakshinamurti personified. She is the ultimate goal you have to reach. Surrender yourself completely into Her hands. She alone can release you from the chains of bondage, and She will remove the veil of *maya*. She is the only pilot capable of rowing your boat. She will bestow on you the *samadhi* state.'

"And now I was witnessing the words of the mendicant *Guru* come true. The Divine Mother was seated here. 'O *Gurudeva*, how did you visualize the distant future, years back?'

"*Ambika*, Divine Mother, was flooding us with Her grace—in undisturbed silence, in the highest, indescribable peace! Strange happiness bubbled over from our hearts!

"We sat there for many hours. Amma appeared like Mother Alamelu of Tiruchanur. She was glowing with radiance! Her silence was gushing out like the holy Ganges. That divine peace, for which I had been searching in *crores* of births, was now flowing into me from the right foot of the Divine Mother!

"I have no strength or words to explain this experience. There was no end to the flow of grace. Mother was seated, glowing like an eternal light, on the peaks of the Garudadri Range! The whole atmosphere was lit up with Her radiance and there was fragrance everywhere. The dew drops on the leaves were reflecting that golden radiance.

"This was the light that fills the entire universe—the light you can't see with open eyes. Where was this light coming from: the light which is absent even in sunlight; the light which is beyond any electrical light; the light which can brighten the cave of the dark heart! Ah, what brilliance! I was drowning in an ocean of radiance and the waves of golden glow were carrying me up and down. The compassionate eyes of the Mother were looking at us eye to eye, as though assuring us, 'I am always there for you.'

"My heart was touching Her divine feet. 'Amma,' my mind said, 'every minute and every second, I was eagerly waiting for You. I bore everything in life just for Your sake. Whatever I am, whatever fruits of evil and good deeds I have, whatever liberation I desire my love, my everything is flowing towards Your lotus feet. You are the boundless, great ocean. Neither mountains nor dams can prevent the merging of this stream in the ocean. My life, my breath, are one with Your divine feet.'

"Mother was making the world glow by Her effulgence. The dust touched by the divine feet of the Mother mixed with the wind and dashed against the rocks of my *karmas*, cracking them open and destroying them.

"Words were not coming from my mouth, even if I had wanted to speak. Amma had tied up our hearts with endless peace. We were being sprinkled by showers of serenity, drop by drop. Our hearts were opened wide by Amma's grace.

"I had swum tiresomely in the ocean of births and deaths. At last I had reached the shore! This is true. I had the blessed *darshan* of Mother's divine feet. This *Ahalya* blessed that day. Amma had given the knowledge of wisdom—that Mother is the Absolute. She is the universal Mother. She is the one who gave a vision of the future to the mendicant *Guru*. She had opened the door of salvation and invited me in. In the limited form of *maya*, illusion, She had appeared as Dakshinamurti personified!

"A peaceful glow is still dancing within me. Happiness is overflowing! The joy of knowing that everything is my Self. The darkness in me has been washed away with tears of joy—a happiness which can never be expressed by mere words or expressions. Oh, how I enjoyed that *Brahmanandam!*"

After Amma's divine *darshan*, Durga Prasad Rao remained in absolute silence, without troubling anybody. He laughed to himself, he spoke to himself, and he lived a simple life. Though he returned to his home in Hyderabad, he was a frequent visitor to the *ashram*.

Then one day this fulfilled soul announced, "Oh, dear ones, the time has come for me to depart. I am bowing to you all for the last time. Amma is calling me. I am going far away from this Earth. Amma is drawing the final curtain on this play. She is calling me to take leave of life silently and come to Her."

Durga Prasad Rao left this world for eternal peace on *Vijaya Dashami* day in the year 1987.

Jai Karunamayi!

SRI KARUNAMAYI - A Biography

AMMA AS ANNAPURNESHWARI

It was the night of the 28th in the month of December 1988. The time was exactly 10:10 p.m. There was a heavy downpour, accompanied by thunder and lightning. Many waterfalls were flowing down from the Garudadri Mountains.

I was writing about Amma in my diary. "O mind, take shelter at Sri Karunamayi's lotus feet—like a parrot safe in its nest. Take refuge in those feet which are the root of the *Vedas* and are adorned by the halo of the *Shrutis*; in which the *pundits* and realized souls take refuge; which are eternal and real; which bestow the eternal nectar of *Brahma jnana*, (knowledge of the Absolute); which remove the hunger for material things that leads to suffering; which make all the worlds glow with their ruby luster. Surrender at Sri Karunamayi's feet with absolute, total freedom and pure devotion, conquering the six inner enemies. Always meditate upon Mother Karunamayi, who is described as *Uma Devi* in the *Upanishads*. I worship the divine lotus feet of Sri Karunamayi, which destroyed the ego of the demon *Mahishasura*, which are enriched and beautified by tender and divine qualities, which manifest by *sattva guna*, and to which all the lesser Gods offer *puja*.

She is *Omkaramaya sharirini*, the sound of *Omkara* personified. She is *Maha Devi* who is ever serving and protecting Her devotees. May that *Maha Shakti*, supreme energy, blossom in the lotus of my heart! She is *Arya Devi*, the first and foremost noble one. She is meditated upon by yogis, and is the limitless effulgent one, attainable through the practice of the teachings of the *Vedas*. She is the personification of eternal inner bliss, ever praised by a host of divinities. She is one with, and mingled in, primordial energy. She is the indwelling soul of all beings. My salutations to *Uma Maheshwari*, Sri Vijayeswari, Sri Shambhavi!

She is the *Para Brahmamayi* who pervades the entire universe, Sri Karunamayi—embodiment of compassion—who bestows liberation during one's lifetime. "O *Kaivalya sukha prasadini*, I take refuge and beg for shelter at Your divine feet, which can be searched for and found through *jnana marga*, the path of knowledge.

"Pure devotion protects the devotee, like a mother protecting her child....Amma, Amma, please grant me pure devotion....O *Parameshwari*, there is nothing unattainable for those who worship Your lotus feet!"

As I was writing this, more than eighty-five villagers, getting drenched in the rain, were standing on the verandah of Sri Lalita Mandir. One of them was calling out, "Amma....Amma!"

"All of you please come in!" I invited everyone inside. They were all completely wet. All of them entered the *mandir*, prostrated to *Sri Lalitambika Devi* and sat down humbly.

After three minutes, Devi Karunamayi came out. As soon as they saw Amma, they were immensely pleased. All of them took the liberty of touching Amma's divine feet and prostrated to Her.

"Mother *Raja Rajeshwaramma*, it is the harvest season. As it has started raining heavily, we don't have any place of shelter. We don't have any bus tonight. That is why we came here. We shall stay here, Mother!" The eldest man among them spoke.

"Oh, *Tata* (Grandfather), this is your own house. You can stay without any hesitation." They were pleased by Amma's words.

The devotees who usually stay in the *ashram* had gone

to their native places two days back. They were not due to return until January 1.

For three days, Amma had been in the Garudadri Hills. Meanwhile, Ammamma had left in a van to get some things done, intending to come back before Sri Karunamayi's return. Ravi and Balaram had also accompanied her, along with sacks full of clothes and bed sheets for distribution to the poor in the surrounding villages. Ammamma—Smt. Annapurnamma—and Revathamma (Sri Karunamayi's mother and sister respectively), often visited the poor and the helpless who were lying in their huts. They distributed rice, wheat, fruits, and vegetables grown in the *ashram* kitchen garden, savories prepared with lemon and tamarind, as well as *saris* to ladies, and kerosene oil for all the needy people. Sushilakkaiah (the elder sister of Sri Karunamayi), who distributed medicines for headache, fever, cold, toothache and the like, had also gone to a nearby town.

As Amma was not in the *ashram*, all these people had left in the morning, planning to return by night. Meanwhile, in the evening Sri Karunamayi had unexpectedly returned from Garudadri Hills.

If Ammamma had been present, she would have cooked immediately for all of them. Now, only we gents were in the *ashram*, and none of us knew how to cook!

Amma inquired about the welfare of the assembled group, and went inside after some time.

I thought these people would have to stay hungry that night, so I went in, brought out a huge bunch of ripe plantains and distributed three to each person.

Then I went into the kitchen to get some rice flakes soaked in milk and sugar for the people. How surprising....! Amma was there alone! ....She was putting a huge vessel with washed rice on the stove. She had put dal and tomato to boil on another stove. Sri Karunamayi, who ordinarily covers Herself entirely with a *pallu* around the shoulders in a dignified way, with a pleasant face, had now tucked Her *pallu* in the waist, like an ordinary housewife!

Amma saw me and smilingly said, "How can I allow them to starve just because Ammamma is not here?"

"Amma, I shall assist you,...." I quickly offered.

Amma, laughing, replied, "What will you do?... Get those *papads*. Get me the oil."

I started doing what Amma told me to. The rain intensified.

"Amma, it would have been nice if Ammamma were present. But I had to bother you," I said apologetically.

"I am not cooking for outsiders. It is for my own children I am cooking, isn't it?" Amma said, naturally and sweetly.

Strangely, within half an hour, several varieties of dishes were ready, as if by magic! I can say with certainty that nobody can cook so fast—and without messing up, keeping the kitchen neat and tidy.

I was immersed in amazement as Amma was using the huge heavy vessels with great ease, as if handling small toys.

"After serving, give them more sweet, my dear. When will they eat again? Serve them as many times as they ask. Don't hesitate...."

By the time I placed tumblers in the hall, Amma had brought the heavy vessels to the hall without any effort. I was stunned and stood staring at Amma.

"What happened? Why are you staring at me as if you are seeing a devil?" Amma said.

"No, no Mother!" I did not even know what to say. I was seeing a great force in Amma. I could not understand how Amma had lifted and carried the huge, steaming hot vessels, which were as high as Herself! It is not comprehensible! One has to see it personally to believe it.

What a power is hidden in this form! We should become inward, and with spiritual strength, analyze this Antarayami, who is hidden in everyone in the form of Soul. One should experience Her within. The principle that needs to be understood, the person who understands it, and the act of understanding—everything is inside, attainable through the soul.

This is the wonder of Sri Karunamayi! None can see the supreme *Para Brahmamayi*, who is the indwelling soul in us. And what could be more wonderful than this? This *Divyatmamayi*, this supreme divine Soul, is within, but makes us feel that She is far away! For innumerable births, this spell of *maya* (illusion) has continued. We can stay away from anybody in this world, but we cannot be at the distance of even a millimeter from *Para Brahmamayi*! Being entangled in this net of worldly *maya*, we have forgotten the real form of the Self.

As I served the people, I thought, "It is really very strange to me the way Amma has cooked—the way she has carried all those huge containers!"

It was 10:50 at night. Meanwhile, I could hear a van approaching the temple. When it stopped, Ammamma, along with the others, entered the hall. All of them were very surprised and happy to see Amma there. Ammamma held Karunamayi's hand and felt as though she had got back her lost treasure. The villagers told Ammamma that the Divine Mother was feeding them.

With disbelief on her face, Ammamma proceeded to remove the lids of the giant pots and looked into the containers. The aroma of sweet *kheer* filled the entire hall. Ammamma's surprise had no bounds. "Who cooked so much? Since when?" Her thoughts were clearly visible on her face. "My dear!" she finally exclaimed. "All these?... Who...?" She was really puzzled.

I could not answer a word, but kept looking at the divine lotus feet of Sri Karunamayi.

She spoke to Ammamma: "Amma, these people are very hungry. They are hard-working laborers. Serve them soon."

Coming out of shock, the people who had just returned started serving the food.

"O Divine Mother, *Rajeshwaramma*, by now I have finished a second helping of *kheer*. May I have a little more?" asked one of them.

Sri Karunamayi, who is usually dignified, reserved and pleasant, now laughed aloud. She said, "*Tata*, drink as much as you like and feel at home. Nobody here is a stranger to you. I have prepared all these only for your sake. Feel free and drink to your heart's content."

Through Amma, I was personally witnessing the happiness achieved in serving others. These were simple villagers. They were very pure. But still, they did not accept it if you remained silent. They did not understand silence or spiritual philosophy.

Amma was personally supervising the serving, going around to attend to the needs of everyone. She was making sure that the food reached them all. Amma was mixing freely with them and chatting with them pleasantly. I was very pleased to see Amma in such joyful and informal moments amidst these villagers.

Ammamma, Balaramanna, Ravi, Revathi, Akkaiah and I started serving the food. All of them were very fortunate in eating food prepared by Sri Karunamayi Herself, and we were equally fortunate to be serving it. Ammamma had been so surprised to see the items prepared! For the first time she realized that her daughter Karunamayi could so efficiently prepare such huge quantities of food without anybody's help. You should have seen her expression! She was not able to come out of her amazement.

Actually, where is the necessity for Amma to cook? Usually the ladies of the *ashram* and the devotees who come to the *ashram* help Ammamma in the cooking. Hence, Amma had never entered the kitchen till today. Yet so actively, enthusiastically, and without any fuss had She prepared the food! This was an inspiration to others. We wish our work to be recognized by others, however small it may be. We get so excited unnecessarily.

Just then, delayed by the storm, another thirty-five people arrived by bus from the villages over the mountains. Ammamma fed them too, along with the drivers and the residents of the *ashram*.

Everybody was surprised as to how the huge containers had been brought to the Annapurna Hall! The villagers were all very poor. Finding it difficult to make both ends meet, how could they afford such delicacies? Hence, they freely demanded three and four helpings.

On one such earlier occasion, a devotee, while helping Ammamma serve food, had said angrily, "If you serve these people like this, how about food for the people who will eat later?"

But Ammamma had replied, "Don't be foolish! When the naivedyam is offered to Amma before we begin serving, there can be no chance of lack at all. At no time have we experienced scarcity. This is Her grace." On that same day, food cooked for one hundred people was fed to one thousand!

After serving the people, to the disappointment of the villagers, Sri Karunamayi had left the hall. Upon cleaning up, they had wanted to prostrate to Amma, thank Her for the food and bless Her. What innocence! I very well knew that Amma did not accept such thanks.

Still, one of them said, "Some day we shall definitely do a good favor for Amma."

I smiled and kept silent. "Who can do any favor for Amma? Who is capable of it? If we do not do any disfavor to Amma, knowingly or unknowingly, that itself is the greatest favor we can do," I thought.

The rain was incessant. Later everybody, including Mother, relaxed in the nearby Lalita Temple. The kitchen and granary were getting flooded, and all the other *ashram* rooms had been occupied by the villagers.

The deluge was coming down in all directions, but Mother had come to the mandir to talk to the people. On the way, Balaramanna, Ammamma, Akkaiah and myself–the four of us—held a tarpaulin over Amma, holding it at all the four corners. Amma resisted this, but we did not listen to Her.

That night Amma talked to us all a lot about devotion. We forgot the roar of the storm, the thunder, and the water dripping on us. We were totally involved in listening to Amma's compassionate words.

It was dawn. The rain had slowed down. All our feet were bleached, as they had been continuously drenched in the downpour. But none of us felt this. Why? The saying, "One who has realized the Self is beyond body consciousness," is very true. And staying the whole night next to that *Para Brahmamayi*, we, too, had experienced that.

Jai Karunamayi!

SARASWATI ANSWERS ALL OUR DOUBTS

It was *Brahmi muhurta*, the auspicious wee hours of the morning, in the *yagashala* at Penusila Ashram. The sacrificial hall had been newly constructed, using the sacred darbha grass and the palm leaves of the coconut tree. It was the fifth day of the year 1990, in the most auspicious month of *Magha* (January-February). Having had a holy bath in the nearby river, many scholars of the four *Vedas* had assembled.

Each day, the scholars had formed four rows, twenty-seven scholars in each row, totaling the auspicious number 108. They had commenced meditating on the *Gayatri Mantra* of *Veda Mata*. This meditation had continued for three consecutive days at the *ashram* of Sri Karunamayi. Each day, the chanting of *Sri Rudra mantras*, along with *Sri Rudra abhishekam* had also been performed. Now the chanting of *mantras* and meditation of the *vedic* scholars were over. On this sacred day of *Sri Panchami*, dedicated to Maha Saraswati, special *pujas* and *homas* were to be performed. The Sun, casting his golden rays on the world, was just rising. This Sun, who grants life energy to all living beings of the universe, is indeed God in perceptible form! Those same scholars were carrying water in small pots with red flowers in them. They were chanting *vedic mantras*, such as *Madhu vātā ṛtāyate*

In this great land of Bharata, India, which is sweeter than the sweetest, every atom of dust is, at every second, emitting endless divine sweetness. How sweet is the air blowing throughout the entire world of moving and non-moving things! The air blowing over Bharata has mixed with the sacred dust of the holy feet of saintly persons and acquired even more sweetness! Oh, how sweet is the air!

In the same *stotra*, *Madhu ksharanti sindhavah*, the importance of the rivers in India is beautifully described. For the people of Bharata, over the ages, the life-sustaining rivers have been the Ganges, Yamuna, Godavari and Krishna. They originate in the forests of the high mountains, carrying *Veda nada*, the sound of *vedic* chantings, and energize all living beings. How sacred and pure are the waters flowing in the rivers of India! How sweet are they!

Madhu vātā ṛtāyate
Madhu kṣaranti sindhavaḥ
Madhvīr naḥ santvoṣadhīḥ
Madhu nakta mutośaśo
Madhumat pārthivam rajaḥ
Madhu dyaur astu naḥ pitā
Madhumanno vanaspatir
Madhumān astu sūryāḥ
Madhuvīr gāvo bhavantu naḥ

Raśmi mantam samudyantam
Devāsura namaskṛtam
Pūjayasva vivasvantam
Bhāskaram bhuvaneśvaram
Sarva devātmako hyeṣa
Tejasvi raśmi bhāvanaḥ
Eṣa devāsuragaṇān
Lokān pātu gabhstibhiḥ

The choruses of *mantras* were echoing from the nearby Garudadri Hills like majestic thunderclouds, and flooding the hills like the Ganges flowing down the Himalayas.

Listening with concentration to those *mantras* with closed eyes, one is elevated from the lower plane and carried higher and higher—beyond the *bhuvah* and *suvah lokas*.

SRI KARUNAMAYI - A Biography

We were feeling as though we had unknowingly touched something very valuable and true. That is the great strength inherent in the *vedic mantras*. The Sun is the combined form of all the divinities. By spreading His rays, He performs the three eternal activities of *srishti, sthithi* and *laya*, creation, preservation and re-absorption. Because He grants life, the name *Savita*, by which He is extolled, is fully justified. It is our human duty to salute, in gratitude, the Sun God whose nectar-like rays, while traversing the skies, are instilling the life force into all living beings. This Sun spreads His golden yellow beams—a combination of seven colors—through all the seven worlds.

Divakara—one who causes day, another name for the Sun—is a perceptible God, glowing brilliantly on the *Ratha Saptami* day in the month of *Magha*. It is a festive day, celebrated by the entire population of *Bharata*.

Darkness is totally dispelled by the rising of the Sun God, *Bhaskara*, whom we also worship as *Shambhu*, Lord Siva. The day was *Sri Panchami*, and it was essential to have both the grace of Lord Siva and *Sharadambika*, the bestower of knowledge, *Jnana Dayini*, the one who splits the dark curtain of ignorance threadbare.

The chanting of the *Vedas* and the salutations to *Surya*, the Sun God, were over. All present offered oblations to *Surya Bhagavan*.

Meanwhile, *Rudra abhishekam* was going on in the yagashala. Some were chanting *mantras* after taking three spoonfuls of cow's milk as *achamanam*, an act of inner purification.

Sri Karunamayi had occupied the *Omkara pitha*, and one of the scholars was pointing at the river waters in different pots, explaining to Ammamma: "Look, Mother, this water is from the River Gomukhi, this is from Gangotri, this is from the River Ganga at Haridvara, this is Yamuna water. Look at this specially decorated *kalasham*;

it contains water from all the sacred rivers. Here are waters from the Rivers Reva, Tungabhadra, Brahmaputra, Cauveri, Kalindi, Krishnaveni, Klipta, Vasudhara and Penna!" He was reading out the name on each vessel containing river waters. There was a collection of water from 108 rivers. Water from the oceans had also been collected in huge decorated brass vessels. With great devotion, that ritvik narrated, "Ammamma, I have read somewhere that all the rivers and the seven oceans come down to have the *darshan* of *Brahma jnanis*. Now, by Divine Mother's grace, I have had the great fortune of witnessing the ensemble of all the 108 rivers and the seven oceans at the sacred feet of Sri Karunamayi. All these have come to have Amma's *darshan* in this form." [In India, rivers are considered to be holy mothers.]

He further described the items: "These are pots of earth collected from the various pilgrim centers all over Bharata, and have been so labeled. Look there! That earthen pot is full of cow's *ghee*. All these are medicinal herbs. Here are waistees and *shalyas*, small vessels used in the *pujas*, earthen vessels and wooden spoons, different grains, herbal sticks for *homa*, *palasha*, the herbal sticks that provide *Brahma tejas* (divine radiance), and *bilva* fruits. Holy herbs of holy trees such as *nyagrodha, udambara, ashvattha, bilva, shami, darbha, amra, amrita lata,* etc. have also been gathered." Ammamma was looking at all these things with tear-filled eyes.

Ammamma and other ladies cleaned the *yagashala* with cowdung mixed with water, and decorated the ground with beautiful *rangavalli*. In India, the cow is considered as Divine Mother, and now She was worshipped elaborately. Later, some people offered *kumkum archana puja* to the cow, chanting *Sri Lalita Sahasranama*, where Mother Divine has been praised as:

Gomātā guha janma bhūḥ
"The holy cow is the embodiment of Sri Lakshmi."

SRI KARUNAMAYI - A Biography

While offering *puja*, as Goddess Lakshmi was invoked in Her, the sacred cow was standing still, accepting the honor with half closed eyes and without shaking either this way or that. The *arati* was over.

On one side, they lit a fire by rubbing together sticks of firewood. After some time, the flames began to glow brilliantly in golden hues. Everyone saluted *Agni*, who was in the form of flames. White lotus flowers dipped in pure cow's *ghee* were offered to the sacrificial fire, as well as white sandal sticks, white flowers and sweet *payasam*.

All the *vedic* scholars went near Sri Karunamayi, one by one, and got the blessings and *tilakam* from Amma. Sri *Maha Saraswati homa* was now performed for universal peace.

The Garudadri Hills were resounding with *mantras*. The *yagashala* was another *Satya loka* on Earth, with Sri Karunamayi, the embodiment of Goddess Saraswati, being praised by the scholars as the bestower and mother of knowledge.

It was a pure, divine and fragrant atmosphere, filled with the aroma of white sandal sticks dipped in *ghee*, offered into the *homa* fire. The *yagashala* was decorated with strings of white lotus and jasmine flowers.

At the culmination of the *homa, purnahuti* was offered with a nine-yard white silk *sari* with a green *zari* border, a silk blouse piece, green bangles and *mangala dravyam*. Later, after the completion of the *homa*, the chief priest approached Amma with *yajna raksha* and received the *tilakam* from Her.

Amma was dressed in pure white and was in total peace beyond description. Amma's mind was inward. The *yajniks* offered fragrant white lotuses at the lotus feet of Amma, while chanting *Sri Saraswati Sahasranama*. Auspicious *arati* was offered after the *Sri Pada Puja*.

All these programs ended by 2:30 p.m. Later, lunch was arranged for all on a grand scale. It was 5:30 p.m. by the time the feeding of *prasada* was over. At 6 p.m. there was a music concert, in which nine musicians played on the vina and entertained everyone with unusual ragas. After the music program, the day ended with the chanting of the *Vedas*, *sandhya* salutations and *shanti mantras*.

In the open space of the *ashram*, on a spacious platform, Sri Karunamayi was seated on the *Omkara pitham*. Then—like mothers everywhere calling their children closer to them by musical notes, as though inviting the faraway moon—with a gesture, Amma called everyone closer as She usually did. All the devotees moved nearer. Like a magnet attracting iron particles, Amma's soul attracted all our souls.

Amma asked someone to get sweets from inside, and She distributed them to all. "Have another sweet, dear," Amma said endearingly, but as She was ready to give it, one of the devotees replied, "This sweet is bigger than the ones distributed in Tirupati! I can't eat any more!"

Later, the *pundits* were discussing their problems with Amma in low voices. They had come down to Penusila to seek Amma's blessings on *Sri Panchami*—on this special day honoring Saraswati Devi—from far-off places such as Kanya Kumari, Kumbhakonam, Sri Valliputhur, Tirupati, Madurai, Palghat, Tanjore, Kanchi, Sri Rangam, Trichy, Vijayawada, Rajamundry, Antharvedi, Mysore, Chennai, Shringeri, Bhadravat, Kashi, Badhari, Dwaraka, Nava-dwipam and Kashmir. They had really come from every nook and corner of India!

The real Mother was seated amidst Her children, sharing their joys and sorrows on this fifth day of *Magha*. The fire in the *homa kunda* was still flickering. As the cool breeze was blowing, it carried the fragrance of turmeric and the perfumed smoke of the *homa*. Sri Balaram Reddy removed the stale flowers and strings of dried up mango leaves and decorated the place again with fresh flowers and strings of mango leaves. All rooms in the *ashram* were clean and tidy.

The entire surroundings were filled with the mixed fragrance of turmeric, vermilion, incense sticks, jasmine and roses, thus reminding one of the fragrant *sanctum sanctorum*.

As many of the *pundits* were talking to Amma, to allow them to have privacy, I moved a little away and sat looking at Sri Karunamayi.

After their conversation, Amma called everyone even closer. She inscribed *Sri Saraswati Mantra* on everyone's tongues. She then answered the questions that were raised by several devotees.

"Amma," said one devotee, "because of limited feelings and ignorance, I am unable to come out of this materialistic illusion. Yet I have the desire to get Self-Realization."

"One should control the mind and enter the door of the soul," Amma replied. "When one is firmly established in the knowledge of the Supreme, the curtain or veil of 'I' and 'mine'—which has till then separated one from the Self, but which is actually non-existent—will be rent, resulting in the experience that everything, seen or unseen, is *Atman*."

"But why," the questioner continued, "is the *atman* caught in the net of births and deaths, undergoing so many changes?"

"Manifestation of form is birth," Mother replied. "Mind, intellect and strength are not the same in all bodies. They vary from person to person. Mental sufferings are related to the mind, while physical sufferings are related to the body. The separation of the *atman* from the mortal frame of the five elements is death. All these changes thus pertain to the mind, the intellect and the body. They do not have any bearing on the *atman*.

"Forgetting the true nature of the *atman*, immersed in the thought that the changes occurring in the mental, intellectual and physical planes envelop that *atman*, man has the illusion that the changeless soul is undergoing those changes. But the *atman* is self-effulgent and ever-present. For the realization of the *atman*, one should quell the mind by giving up egoism and crossing the barriers of 'I' and 'mine.'"

"But can I escape from the clutches of *maya*?"

"You are always a liberated soul. You are the pure soul, more effulgent than the fire and the sun. But you have to make an effort to understand your Self." Amma smiled at him.

"Mother, can I attain the knowledge of the Supreme (Self-Realization) by mere reading of the *Vedas*? I am anxious to experience it. What should I do, Amma?"

"The *Atman* is indescribable. It is beyond everything. It can never be thought of. It is fearless and without duality. It is firm, changeless and beyond the there *gunas*. It can be experienced only in deep *samadhi*. Without the help of the eternal *Atman*, one cannot obtain the human form, cannot live, cannot move, cannot grasp or experience anything, and cannot attain any knowledge.

"Dear one, knowledge of the *Atman* will not dawn by the mere reading of books. Meditation is like a ladder to tear the curtain of mind and attain purity. By meditating upon the *Atman* with unwavering mind, the mind itself gets destroyed. Mind is another form of ignorance. Only when the mind is overcome, will the darkness of ignorance vanish.

"You are there as the self-glowing Supreme on the other side of the ocean of ignorance. You are all-pervading, without beginning or end. You are not this body at all, you are the total Supreme, second to none.

"The mud of a broken unbaked pot can be remolded into another pot. But can that earth by itself take the form of a pot? It is only the potter who converts the mud into a pot. Our bodies are like the unbaked earth.

The *atman*, the inner occupant of the body, manifests in the body at birth and disappears from the body at death. In this way, again and again, it changes from body to body. Those who cannot go deep into the *Vedas* and sublimate their minds, cannot attain supreme bliss. One cannot liberate oneself without realizing the vital *brahmic* force.

"Dear one, don't worry! Meditation on 'Who am I,' referring to the Self, will enable you to reach the goal. You will certainly succeed in this very life. You will understand that *sadhana* and detachment are essential for attaining *atma jnana*, the knowledge of Self."

One aged man was sitting and looking at Amma. It seemed he wanted to ask a question, but just couldn't do so. Finally, he said, "Mother, I have practiced *pranayama* along with *Soham Mantra* for some time. I got deep concentration. But, at the time when indescribable peace was approaching me, one of the relatives came to my house to inquire about his son's marriage from the astrological point of view. I could not answer all his questions, so, instead of the approaching peace, commotion took hold of me. In spite of all my efforts, I could not come out of that darkness. Now my suffering has abated after sharing my inner feeling with You, Amma." So saying, he wiped his tears.

I could see clearly that the aspiration for supreme knowledge is latent in everyone. This world is in need of one who can remind us to fulfill that aspiration, just as we kindle a fire by repeated blowing on the sticks. I firmly believe that Amma has descended to the world in this form for this purpose alone. And not only myself; it is the opinion of several spiritual giants!

Amma was very much moved by the old man's predicament. Her kind answer was, "Dear one, search for the root! It is useless to brood over the past. We have to pursue the spiritual path till the very end.

"One can attain the merits of the spiritual path only after the curtain of 'me' and 'mine' has come down. Those who run after fame, money and flattery in this world, will be defamed by the same world later. Dear son, try again to attain that peace which had come close to you."

The old man beseeched Amma, "O Mother! Grant me purity! Lead me to that noble life bereft of dishonesty, attachment to worldly things and aspiration for fame. Bless me with the strength to pursue the path again."

"Dear son! You have understood your drawbacks. That is enough. Forget your sorrow." So saying, Amma wiped his tears with the corner of Her *sari pallu*, as a mother does naturally.

"I am already seventy years old. You are eternal. Please shower your kindness on me," said the man, as he went on sobbing.

"What is there in money and worldly fame? You have grasped this truth. Truth does not co-exist with untruth and pretence. Having understood this truth, your heart is pure, like a pearl washed in milk. Meditate again. Controlling the mind, you will realize that you are *Brahman*, your nature is Truth, you are devoid of materialistic *maya*, you are the light of knowledge."

After listening to this old man's outbursts, all others also opened their minds fully. The very presence of Amma grants freedom. Further, the *vedic* scholar's outpouring of his feelings to Amma, without ridicule by the youngsters there, instilled a sense of greater freedom in all others. They began to speak freely, as if they were in their own homes talking to their mothers.

Amma was seated in the south of the *ashram*, where there was a garden of naturally fragrant pink roses beside a short compound wall. The breeze, blowing from the South, was spreading the fragrance, as though the *ashram* had been sprinkled with rose water.

In the midst of this scene of beauty and incredible awareness, another devotee cried out, "Amma! *Bhavatarini*, destroy all my entanglements. Grant me liberation!" His tears were flowing down.

"Dear one, nobody has bound you," Amma replied softly. "These bonds are created by one's own *karma*. You are indivisible *Brahman*. Nothing in the world has the power to bind you. Don't worry! I will shoulder your responsibility."

"O Amma....*Satyamayi! Sharadambika!* Now, I understand clearly. In this world, I need only one thing. My real mother is *Para Brahmamayi*; nothing else—certainly none other than *Para Brahmamayi!* Let my mind always remember this truth.

"All these years I have wandered, bound by tasteless *maya*, though a *vedic* scholar. O *Shambhavi*, grant me the supreme knowledge of the Self! O *Akhilandeshwari!* Karunamayi! He was sobbing like a child separated from its mother and unable to bear the parting.

Amma would always speak about *Advaita* philosophy. "*Vedanta* is the direct route to reach *Brahman*. There are no shortcuts." Amma was caressing his head, consolingly, wiping his tears.

In everyone's heart, there was strange, unimaginable change. Inner transformation had taken place.

Amma continued. "Since ages, many people have walked this path. But not all of them reached the gamyam, the destination....Many *vedic* scholars, are well-versed in the *Vedas*, but only a few of them have grasped their hidden, inner meanings. Many devotees have traveled the path of music to reach *Brahman*, but Sri Thyagaraja—one of the greatest musician saints of Bharata (India), and a staunch devotee of Sri Rama—was one who realized the truth of the blissful *Sri Ramuni sannidhi seva sukham*....

"Great devotees and poets like Pothana never gave prominence to worldly honors and money. That is why they attained the knowledge of the Absolute.

"This sacred land, which has been the home of great realized souls, such as Sage Shuka or Sri Adi Shankaracharya, is yours! How can *Brahmamayi* desert you, who have taken refuge in *Veda Mata?*"

"Life is not only for earning money. You all know that life is for *Satyanveshana*—the realization of the Absolute. Human life is great. But life becomes purposeful only when one understands the hidden *dharma* in it. My dear, you have realized that you are traveling on the dark path. The light of *Omkara* will guide you like the sun's rays. Dear one, enter the new wonderful world where everything is the Self—the *Atman*, the *Paripurna Brahman*."

Aha! How meaningful were these words! Our old or earlier world is full of selfishness and the darkness of ignorance. It is materialistic, full of differences. Amma had described a totally new world, where everything is only one, pervaded by unique pure energy. Even the uneducated could clearly understand Her words.

All these people were *vedic* scholars with devotion for Divine Mother, too. Many of them were known to Amma in their worldly life. They had brought some other people with them. In this way, a large number of people had assembled here on this auspicious day to be in the divine company of Amma, and to stay here, totally forgetting everything.

Sri Karunamayi peacefully opened the doors of liberation. And the scholars, out of curiosity, casually peeped in, to find out what was inside. What they saw was the true effulgence, which is beyond description! There they recognized their own *dharma*. These *vedic* scholars ranged in age from twenty-six to eighty years. But no matter what their age, can *Veda Mata* ever neglect Her children? No! They realized the ultimate truth and the ultimate *dharma* in Amma's words. Their hearts melted.

Amma's very face and words made crystal clear, and conveyed to the listeners, a mixture of the vital force of the *Atman*, inner vision, and the rare experience of the Supreme. Tears were overflowing from the eyes of all. The real beauty in Amma's exposition is the lack of exhibitionism of scholarship. These things are conspicuous by their absence in Her speeches—unrelated stories, meaningless quotations and roundabout ways of talking. Instead, Her conversations are replete with explanations of the *Atman*, appearing from the innermost shrine of the heart, understood by everyone, and expressed sweetly and clearly, with a personal approach.

Sri Karunamayi's words are filled to the brim with a rare natural sweetness, and this style is neither learned nor practiced.

Like the hidden treasure is in the depths of the ocean, the true and eternal divine wealth is ever sprouting spontaneously from Sri Karunamayi's heart. That depth is the real santripti, complete fulfillment.

When Nachiketas visited the abode of Death, Yama —*dharma* personified—told Nachiketas (the poorest of the poor) to ask for enormous wealth, a kingdom, chariots, horses, elephants, servants, a long life—anything. But though he had not enjoyed any of these things earlier, Nachiketas preferred to continue in the same state. He knew that none of these things could yield total contentment. He knew contentment was in the knowledge of the Self alone. And this is the supreme *dharma* which man has to grasp. The real aspiration is for *dharmic* aspiration, knowledge of the Self, realization of the Self! This aspiration cannot be called desire.

Another person had asked Amma a question. "Why is this mind always wandering?"

Amma replied, "Whenever a desire crops up, people try to fulfill that desire. It is the mind that prompts them to do so. A person who has the quality of *rajas*, acts accordingly. A person filled with *tamoguna*, acts likewise. These *gunas* influence the mind's movements. With the exception of some great people, generally, every human being engages himself in action with an expectation.

"Why can't a person stay in one place? Because some thought or desire is always sprouting in his mind. The mind begins to work for the fulfillment of that thought or desire. It is the mind which makes man wander about hither and thither in an effort to find fulfillment. This movement of

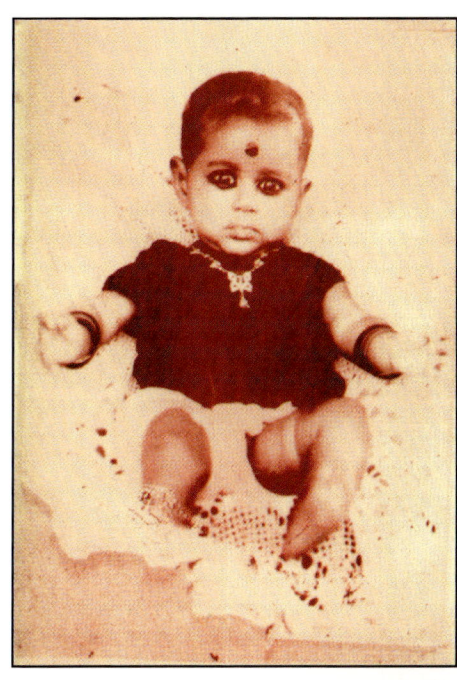

Sri Karunamayi at the age of 3 months.

Sri Karunamayi at the age of 3 years.

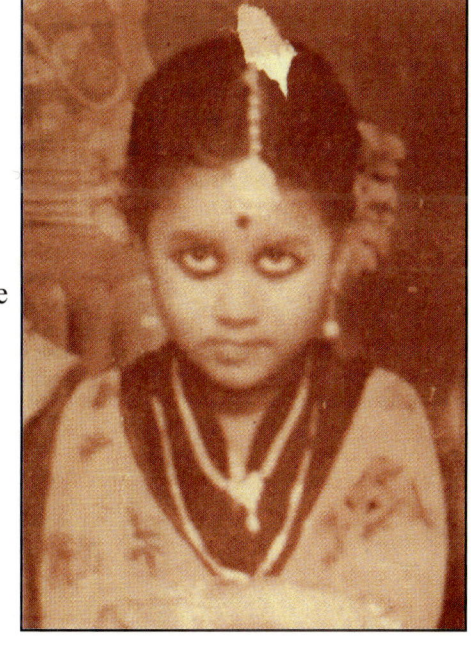

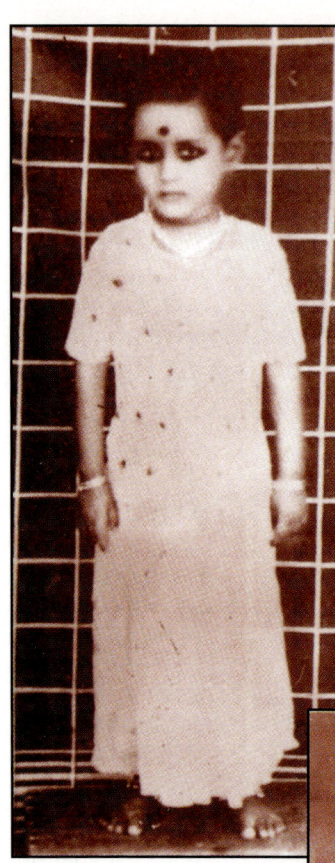

Sri Karunamayi at the age of 5 years.

Sri Karunamayi at the age of 7 years.

Sri Karunamayi
"Amma"

With her sister.

Visiting Europe . . .

and USA . . .

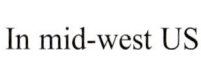

In mid-west US.

In Alaska.

Amma just loves animals . . . .

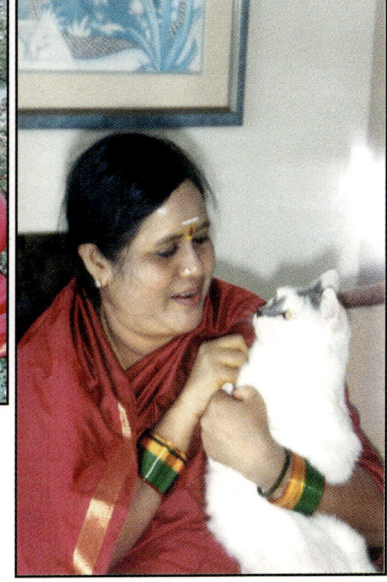

... and they love Her too.

Amma with Her devotees.

Children are most precious.

Pujas

Sri Pada Puja to Amma's Lotus Feet

Homa at the Bangalore ashram.

Sivalingam.

Homa at New York, USA.

Sri Padam.

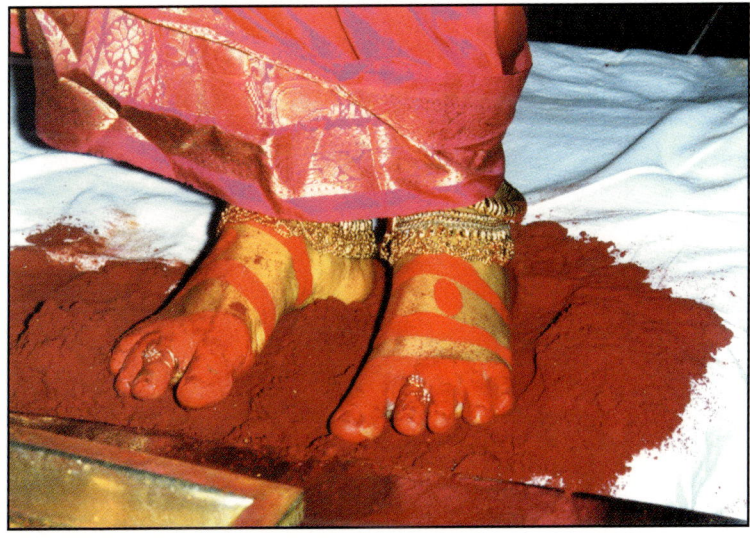

Divya darshan.

Sri Karunamayi Hospital

Architect's concept drawing

Construction as of September 2000

Eye Camp 2000

Free Medical Camp Dec. 2002

Sri Karunamayi School

Amma with the students.

Construction of a new school, November 2002

The students hard at work

They are just adorable!

Penusila Ashram

Bharat Mata Mandir.

Ashram gardens.

Residence hall for sadhakas.

At a retreat.

Peace Village

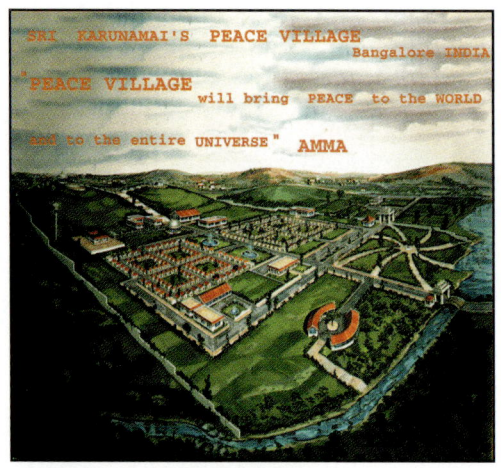

A tour of the construction.

Peace Village near completion.

the mind for any work creates commotion. Desire is the elder sister of commotion. So long as the desires are plentiful, there is no escape from a wandering mind.

"When desires and their root cause—the mind—are annihilated, it is then that the *trigunas*, thoughts, and their consequent results, disappear forever. Only then will the mind become still, and calmness prevail. All of you know these things. We have simply recollected them once again."

"Amma, I do daily *parayanas* of *Sri Rudram* and *Purusha Suktam*. I also meditate regularly upon *Sri Mata* with the *Aham Brahmasmi Mantra*. Then, why am I not able to have the *darshan* of *atma prakasham*, the inner light?"

"Dear son, only when the mind vanishes, does the inner lighting become visible."

Another devotee seemed distraught and called out to Amma, "*Bhavani*! Probing in the darkness of ignorance insanely, I am oblivious of my destination. I feel I am left with nothing!"

"Dear son," Amma reassured him, "let me tell you the truth. Nothing of yours shall remain, not even a little! Everything is the Self only! Only one! Don't worry, my dear! You have spiritual insight. You can certainly experience the Truth in this very birth."

Amma was wearing a white silk *sari*, shining like the moonlight, with a pink border. Amma's hands were decorated with green glass bangles with golden dots on them. Her lotus-like face was glowing with *chandan* and *kumkum*.

Amma's eyes were twinkling with a special radiance. Her divine force, the flow of wisdom in Her words, and the presence of Her divine lotus feet, held everyone spellbound and carried them to a different world of philosophy.

The dust of this materialistic world has never touched Sri Karunamayi since Her childhood, just as Goda Devi, born in a *tulasi* garden, was never the least affected by the world of sensual pleasures. Sri Karunamayi has grown up like the sacred, divine *Lakshmi tulasi*. She was born upon this Earth with supreme divine energy. Sri Karunamayi is the Divine incarnate who has merged in *Brahmi Chaitanyam*—divine Consciousness—effortlessly. Worldly desires never dare to even approach Sri Karunamayi. They shudder to come near.

Sri Karunamayi is the unique, divine *saundarya lahari*. Motherly love, sweet devotion, absolute knowledge—all these supreme attributes have settled in the ever-pure heart of Karunamayi Devi, and have become Her natural dynamic adornments.

Another devotee was unable to speak clearly as he was grieving terribly. He said: "Amma! *Bhagavati*, as I am your son, please forgive me *crores* and *crores* of times! I was boasting in front of people, that without any divine grace, I have realized *Jagan Mata*. I have bragged that, though I am young and have not attained *jnana*, She grants me *darshan*. Please forgive me! Lead me in the right path, *Janani*."

Amma, not in the least disturbed by his words, said, "The heart becomes pure the moment you realize your mistake, committed in ignorance, and repent for it. When you start *sadhana*, a day will come when what you said earlier becomes real. The principle of your origin is beyond everything; it is all-pervading! Henceforth, everything will work right for you, *nanna*!"

Another devotee wished to know: "What can I offer to my *Guru* who, with great mercy, has shown me the right path?"

"Realizing the Self is the best possible honor you can offer to a *Guru*."

"If I meditate with a spiritual bent of mind, '*tattva drishti*,'" one young devotee asked, "can I visualize that *Tattvamayi* (Mother Supreme)?"

"My loving child!" Amma exclaimed. "Though you are very young, how worthy are your words! The *Atman* is the ever-existing embodiment of *purna jnana* and is beyond philosophy. You can't grasp the *Atman* through *tattva*. Only when the mind merges with the One can you realize the *sva svarupa*, your true nature and origin—the *Atman*. By arresting the flow of words, deeds and the mind, the heart fills with silence, like a royal road without traffic. Only then will the wavering nature of the mind be destroyed. He who has realized *Brahman* within—subtler than the subtlest—he is the real yogi. He achieves immortality."

Another longtime devotee beseeched Amma: "My dear mother! O *Ishwari*, please forgive the *crores* of sins committed by me, knowingly or unknowingly, in this life and in my past lives. I have been reading the *Bhagavad Gita* since my childhood, but I have not gained sama drishti, the vision of equanimity. Impatience and anger have not diminished though I have become old. You are *Sri Lalita*, Maha Lakshmi, *Sharada, Tripurasundari*. O *Gayatri Devi*, protect me! Please guide me on the righteous path."

Amma answered him kindly: "Dear son, don't worry! As soon as there is an awakening of the divine energy of *purna Brahma jnana*, you will realize that inside your heart, outside, wherever you see, the indivisible all-pervading *Brahman* is your Self only! Your original birthless state itself is equanimity. Closing the eyes, go inward firmly and deeply.

"You shall see the most brilliant light....exuberant light; and you will realize that this light is the root secret of this world. Then, wherever you look, you will see your Self. In temples, there is often a unique palace of mirrors. As soon as you enter that palace, you can see thousands of images in those mirrors. All of them are your reflections only. You see yourself everywhere! And who is the source of those images? Yourself only."

The same elder continued, "Amma, I have been meditating upon the Gayatri Mantra with great discipline, but I am facing many obstacles in my *sadhana*."

"Son, *sadhana* is done to destroy desires. Mind is the form of desires. Once the mind is subdued, the inner effulgence, that had been dull and weak since many lives, begins to radiate brilliantly. Thereafter, there is no darkness in the mind or heart. Desirelessness leads to *Brahma chaitanya*. This Gayatri, this *chaitanya*, this *Brahman* are one and the same. This *chaitanya* is not transient at all. The sun, moon, stars and the five elements are all transient, but this supreme force, *chaitanya shakti* is indestructible. It is the most wonderful force. *Nanna*, this force is the soul, which is the source and support of all living beings. There is no pleasure greater in this world than *atma jnana*."

"Amma, will I succeed in my efforts?" He wanted to know.

"*Atma jnanam* is the sole aim of life. If you do *sadhana* with such strong determination, you can attain *atma sukham*. If you sow a mango sapling, gradually it will grow into a tree. After some years, it is sure to give sweet mangoes!"

The old man smiled and bowed to Amma.

A man wearing glasses had a doubt. "Mother, I have read the *Brahma Sutras*. I have gone through many great books and have heard many spiritual discourses. But, Mother, I feel that controlling the mind is impossible! Where have I gone wrong?"

"Dear son, you need to do *sadhana*. The curtains should be downed. A magician will never get caught in the spell of magic he has created because he knows the truth. He knows the secret that it is a temporary illusion. Since time unknown, it is the force of the Supreme that is energizing the entire universe. The *Para Brahman* was not accessible even to the great ascetics like Sage Vishvamitra in the beginning stages of their *sadhana*. Wisdom dawns in your heart when you mediate, after subduing the mind that is full of 'me' and 'mine.'"

One aged scholar was shedding tears. Unable to speak anything, he was just listening to Amma. With overflowing compassion, Sri Karunamayi wiped his tears. For a long time he held Amma's hand. His melting heart overflowed in the form of tears, and he could only utter, "Amma, Amma." Their bond of Mother and child, which was sweeter than the sweetest, had to be witnessed personally. It was beyond words.

Finally, Amma said, "Dear children, you are the ever pure *Brahman*, devoid of *maya*. You can experience the absolute truth only with inner sight. You are the all-pervading supreme truth. You all know that in different languages, Mother is addressed differently. She may be called *Mata, Amma, Talli,* Mother, *Janani, Ma*, and many other names. But the principle and meaning are one and the same. Gradually, in the realization of *Brahma tattva*, a *jnani* gets rid of all the *karmas*. Only when the Truth is experienced as Self, will one be liberated. 'Me-myself' is the materialistic application; 'self-me' is *maya*. Observe the merger of the self in the Self—the eternal truth, the Soul, *Brahman*, the original form."

One young man asked, "I can't even close my eyes and sit for meditation. Will I get any experience or peace?"

Mother turned to him. "Son, a lamp is lit by pouring gingelly oil on a wick. If you bring and pour just the seeds, will the light glow? Only by spiritual knowledge attained through meditation, will the bondages of *karma*, which have been binding you tightly so far, wither away by themselves, like grains being gleaned from the husk."

One man at the back spoke up. "My heart is hardened. I am running after desires foolishly in the desert of life. Please call me back, Mother. I am in darkness, struggling to find the way, falling and rising again. Show me Your path. Save me from this abyss! I have stupidly tied myself up in entanglements. Please release me from them. For how many more lives can I bear the burden of these never-ending entanglements?"

Sri Karunamayi was silent. Her heart, overflowing with mercy, started soothing Her son.

The devotee was overwhelmed. "*Janani*! Sri *Chamundeshwari*! *Annapurneshwari*! *Bhiksham dehi!*" he cried.

"Son," Mother said, "will you beg in front of your own house?" Her voice was dripping with mercy.

"Mother, my only search in this world is for the spiritual experience to realize *Jiveshwara*," the devotee replied.

Then Amma said earnestly, "Are you waiting for me? Anticipating me? Then your expectation is meaningless! Because I am always, always forever with you only. This is no exaggeration at all!"

"Amma, don't say 'no' to my wish! I want to do pradakshina, to walk reverently around my Mother and prostrate."

Smilingly, Amma answered, "Dear son, you can circumambulate me if I am a small *Shivalinga* in a temple. I am the all-pervading indivisible supreme effulgence, occupying everything and everywhere. How can you do *pradakshina* to me?"

Though Amma spoke these words softly and casually, everyone was dazed and sat looking at Amma.

Now, what Sri Karunamayi spoke were not mere words. The total supreme truth was flowing from Her heart in the form of deepest silence. Really, they were not just a combination of words—they were Truth, from the depth of the heart. It was *mauna sudha madhuri*, a silent sweet song. This sweetness is very natural to Sri Karunamayi.

The elixir of motherly love, mercy and compassion was flowing brilliantly from Amma's eyes like the combination of the rivers Ganga, Yamuna and Saraswati.

Amma Karunamayi *Sharadamba's* words filled the entire surroundings with purity. The words were so freely flowing, so sweet, extremely soft, and so unusual….

It was getting late. As it was time for supper, everybody offered *pranamas* to Amma and dispersed.

SRI KARUNAMAYI - A Biography

The following day was a misty morning in the month of *Magha* (in February). The sun's new golden rays were awakening the sleepy flowers. In the east the *vedic* chanting of the brahmins could be heard. Later one could hear the chants of the *Purusha Suktam* and the *Sri Suktam*. Then the worship of the sun, the cow, and the *Rudra abhishekam* were all completed.

Everyone finished breakfast hurriedly. Today was the day we would start with Amma for Vasishtha Kundam, the place where Sage Vasishtha had performed his *tapas*.

After a few hours of walking, we reached the place with difficulty, as there was no proper road. Silver clouds were gathered in the sky. The beauty of that place is beyond description. The serene silence, the sound of waterfalls, are heart-stealing.

"Amma," said one devotee, "if you serve us food, we'll feel like staying here forever in meditation." Amma started laughing.

Like children, everyone happily proceeded towards the stream, drank the *tirtham* and sprinkled the holy water on their heads. All resolved to meditate for three hours. Sri Karunamayi applied *tilakam* on everyone's foreheads. Amidst the silent mountains, the *dhyana shloka* of Sri Gayatri echoed in chorus:

> *Om muktā vidruma hema nīla dhavala*
>   *chhāyair mukhai*
> *Strīkṣaṇair yuktām indu nibaddha ratna*
>   *makuṭām tattvārtha varṇātmikām*
> *Gāyatrī varadābhayāṅkuśa kasām śubhram*
>   *kapālam gadām*
> *Śaṅkham cakramadārvinda yugalām hastair*
>   *vahantīm bhaje*

Thus, after praising Goddess Gayatri, all started meditation, inviting Devi from the endless inner worlds.

SRI KARUNAMAYI - A Biography

In that forest, beautiful flowers were swaying back and forth, as though to offer the honey in their different colored containers to the hidden *Jagan Mata* Sri Karunamayi!

On the upper part of that mountain, *Aditya*, the Sun God, had ripened the wild plantains and many other fruits with His bright rays. Many wild fruits were emitting sweet fragrance as though kept in readiness to be offered to Amma.

Keeping my eyes closed, I gazed at the inner space that is boundless and still. Sri Karunamayi's divine sole eye, which is wisdom, was gazing at all of us, inviting us silently into our origin. Nearly four hours passed. Everyone had meditated with deep devotion and concentration.

By 1:00 p.m. we all had received sweet fruits as lunch. Amma inquired, "Shall we leave for the *ashram*?"

"If you permit, we would like to stay back and continue meditation silently for another three hours," a few requested.

Amma said, "Is this the opinion of everyone?"

"Yes," came a chorus of voices. "All of us would like to do so, Amma."

And so, the afternoon round of meditation continued from 1:30 to 4:30 p.m. No one got up in the middle. No one even moved! By 4:45 p.m., the meditation concluded. Everyone prostrated to Amma and to that sacred place. All of us were sitting under a huge tree. Everyone was still in silence. This silence was special. After reading the *Vedas*, the children had sat around their Mother, *Veda Janani*. The scene reminded me of one of the names in *Sri Lalita Sahasranama Stotram:*

Śuddha vidyānkurākāra dvija pankti dvayojjvalā

Finally, one devotee broke the silence. "Amma," he said, "only two questions are pestering my mind. Kindly save me from this ocean of doubts. One is, how does the mind become an enemy, if not conquered?"

Amma started speaking very softly and clearly.

"Endless desires in man's mind are the cause for commotion. It is mind's nature to be entangled in useless worldly matters. The mind is responsible for grief, irritation and restlessness.

"Peace, which is the true nature of the *atman* is hiding behind the thick screen of the *trigunas*. That is why grief occurs on account of even small desires. It is not possible to experience *atma sahaja sthithi*, the natural state of the soul, till the mind is destroyed. That is why the mind becomes an enemy. Is the mind destroyed? Then you shall merge in your natural state in total peace.

"Devotees call that *Para Brahma, Durga, Bhavani, Shambhavi, Shankari* and *Parameshwari*. Those who practice *pranayama* think of this same *Brahma* as *Prana Chetana*. This energy is referred to as *Pranada* and *Pranarupini* in *Sri Lalita Sahasranama*. Those who worship the five elements, call this *Pancha Bhutatmika Shakti, Atman*. Noble or realized souls call it *Atman, Nitya* and *Satya*. Philosophers call it *Tattvadhika*, and *Tattvamayi*. Brahman is extolled by all these names!

"Mind, not conquered, becomes the greatest enemy hidden in man. A seeker will recognize the divinity, *Brahman*, within himself when, with discrimination, he turns the heart completely inward from worldly matters and separates himself from the hold of the body, mind and intellect. Then he will attain that state of *shuddha chetana*—pure Consciousness—that is Truth, Eternity and Soul. In this state, a *Brahma jnani* sees not only this world, but everything in the universe, as *Shuddha Brahma mayam*, pure Consciousness. Dear one, only those who have conquered the mind can experience this divine natural state of soul, *divya sahaja atma sthiti*."

"Mother, my second doubt is, what happens to 'me' when my mind is destroyed? How will 'I' experience the supreme bliss?"

Amma smiled. "In a dream, a person may see himself crowned as an emperor. After waking up from sleep, if he behaves like an emperor, how would it be? Before sleeping, does he have kingship? After waking up also, he does not have the throne. That which was not there in the beginning and at the end, how did it exist in between? So, wise people have recognized mind as illusion, as *maya*. A person who wakes up from deep sleep is on a bed in his own room, not in the palace or on the throne. This is true. Everything that is seen in sleep, in a dream, disappears the moment you wake up.

"A person may feel petrified by a dream of being burnt by fire in a plane accident. When he wakes up, there is neither any fire nor plane accident. So, experiences during the state of sleep and dream are untrue.

"*Jagrat avastha*, the experience when we are awake, is also the same. This is because you are really *Shuddha Brahman*, pure Consciousness, beyond the three states of *jagrat*, *svapna* and *sushupti*—the states of wakefulness, dream and deep sleep. That which is not present in the beginning or at the end, is not present in between, either! Only because of delusion, do the things that are subject to change—such as creatures, humans and plants—though transient and unreal, appear to be permanent and true. But in the state of *atma jnana*, there are no boundaries of mind, intellect and ego.

"In a *Brahma jnani*, there will not be even a drop of *avidya* that overshadows the natural radiance of *atma jnana*.

"As soon as the sun rises in the east, darkness cannot exist. Similarly, once there is the experience of wisdom, ignorance will not stay in the heart, dear one! All doubts will vanish when spiritual practice is coupled with the study of scriptures.

"You asked how one can experience *atmananda* if the mind is destroyed. To realize *jnana*, there is no need of another *jnana*, or knowledge. There is no need to light a matchstick to see the radiance of the sun! Now a curtain is surrounding the natural principle of the soul. The goal of all kinds of spiritual practice is to eliminate this dark screen, this screen of *maya*, the selfish curtain comprised of 'me,' 'mine' and 'for myself.'"

And the devotee answered, "Amma, I am so pleased! All my doubts have disappeared."

All of us were in silence.

"Shall we leave now?" asked Amma finally. Everyone got up. There were *ashramites*, devotees, and scholars numbering more than two hundred. Amma was moving ahead. As She was walking, everyone was looking fondly at Her divine lotus feet with deep reverence and devotion.

Those sacred divine feet had been decorated with *parani*, a red paste, with an added lotus design. Those feet, which are soft and delicate like the *parijata* flower, were walking on the hard stones. Seeing Amma step on such hard stones, everyone felt a pain in their hearts, as though pierced by sharp nails.

But Amma, our hearts are full of the huge stones of selfishness, ego, jealously, arrogance and hatred. How will You step there? Huge boulders, such as ego and selfishness, have occupied the whole heart, not leaving any place for Your divine feet! How will You walk there, O *Janani*?

Mother Earth, *Bhu Devi*, must have performed great penance for Your descent on this Earth! Then only, O *Nirakarini*, O formless One, have You come from Manidwipa, residing in the *bindu* of the *Sri Chakra*, taking form and carrying on this divine play! O Mother! *Patita Pavani!* O Devi, is this how You walked all the way from Kashmir, from the *sarvajna pitham*, the seat of knowledge, when Adi Shankaracharya brought you to South India?

We were unable to have your *darshan* that day, but today, we are all indeed blessed to have the *darshan* of *Maha Vidya, Maha Shakti, Maha Devi* and *Maha Shanta*, dressed in fine white robes with beautifully decorated lotus feet!

As we walked, a devotee who had come just then, was questioning an old scholar thus: "Sir, I have heard many saints' messages. I have also participated in spiritual meetings consisting of good stories, laughter and humor. I have no eligibility to speak, but there is something in Amma which was not present in the saints I met. Sir, who is Amma? Is She a saint, a *yogini* or *Para Brahmamayi* Herself? I want this to be clarified by seniors like you. If I have spoken anything unwarranted, please forgive me."

The old scholar was the only man who had been silent since he had come to Penusila! Hearing the stranger's words, his eyes filled with tears. He was well-built and six feet tall, a great devotee and cool person. He embraced the new devotee, though a stranger. "What....What shall.... What shall I say....dear one!" he began. "Our Karunamayi is that *Para Brahmamayi* only. It is She who has blessed and opened the doors of liberation to saints, *yogis*, realized souls, Agasthya, Gautama, Vishvamitra, Vasishtha and many more sages. What more can I say?" Saying so, he wiped away his own tears. My heart melted completely on hearing their conversation, especially the scholar's.

All of us reached the *ashram*, had our baths, performed our *sandhya* worship, chanted *vedic mantras*, and performed *puja* and *arati*. We then dined and relaxed.

The next day, early in the morning, all of the scholars took leave of Amma and went away in a specially arranged bus. Young and old were all in tears, unable to bear the pain of impending separation—like a calf that does not want to leave the mother cow!

Jai Karunamayi!

Devotees' Experiences

SRI KARUNAMAYI - A Biography

The opinions expressed by the following people upon seeing the Apostle of Mercy, Bhagavati Sri Sri Sri Vijayeswari Devi, are reproduced below

THE MIRACLE OF TRANSFORMATION

—*Sri B. Subbarayudu, Anathayya Garipalli,*
Rajampeta, Cuddappah Taluk

I did not believe in God and, in fact, was first in the rank of atheists. I also indulged in many antisocial activities. The ladies in my village used to run home and shut their doors at the very sight of me. Even my mother would advise me to mend my ways and to live peacefully, as I loved to entangle myself in all village quarrels. I had to travel around carrying lethal weapons for protection. This unruly behavior of mine caused me to have many enemies and to witness repeated instances of enmity, selfishness, and suffering. Thus, I became insensitive and hardhearted.

After some time, my life took a wonderful turn for the better. In 1983, some of my friends journeyed to Penusila Kshetram, and they took me with them by force. My actions had made it difficult for me to gain employment, and being an atheist, I did not hope for any improvement in my situation by going to that divine place. The entire world had identified me as a bad character.

At Penusila, after taking the *darshan* of Sri Narasimha Swami, my friends proceeded towards a second holy place situated half a kilometer away. I had no alternative but to join them. People there had gathered in groups near the main hall of the *ashram*. Some had also thronged on the *verandah*. However, though the entire place was full of people, still there was pin-drop silence. I managed to make my way inside and stood in a corner as an anxious spectator.

In the meantime, Amma came into the hall clad in an ordinary *sari,* with a compassionate look and smiling face. From the very first instant that I saw Mother, I experienced a strange feeling in my heart. She then went up on the dais and took Her seat on a tiger skin placed over a *darbhasana.* Later I learnt that Her name was Sri Vijayeswari Devi. The devotees, who all the while had been sitting with closed eyes in silence, opened their eyes and began chanting *mantras* melodiously in chorus.

After the conclusion of the *mantra* chanting, Amma began Her fluent discourse. Among the people and even the women I knew, I had never heard anyone speaking with such a pure mind and so softly. In my sphere of activity, uttering harsh words and replying to my opponents with my fists was the normal order of events.

As I was listening to Amma's words, without my knowledge, my heart melted and tears started flowing from my eyes. She said that every being in the world was Her child. Mother also advised in very simple and understandable language: "Do not hurt even an ant. Give up selfishness. Discard violence." She explained all this with beautiful illustrations in order to communicate Her teaching to illiterates like myself. If anybody else had uttered these words to me, I would have laughed and would not have left him peacefully. But that day my mind was filled with acute pain. As snow melts under the sun, my unruly attitude vanished on hearing Mother's words.

After the discourse, Mataji was applying *kumkum* to all those who had gathered there. When my turn came, without anybody's persuasion, I hurriedly went and prostrated before the Mother. She placed Her holy hand on my head and blessed me. She also spoke to me with much warmth, as if She knew me well. Never had anybody spoken to me with such tenderness.

Taking the dust of Her feet and Her blessings, I went back to my village. Even after I returned home, however, my mind was constantly urging me to go to Amma. My mind was totally focused on Her regardless of any activity. Her sweet words kept ringing in my ears all the time.

Devotion, love and adoration, never offered by me to anyone, were offered to Sri Vijayeswari Devi at my first *darshan* of Her. Just as ripe leaves fall from the tree, all my bad habits withered away at the feet of the Mother. After listening to Her message, my mind was totally changed. My repulsion for God vanished, and I began prostrating to Him. At the same time, I began withdrawing from my old, bad associations.

Shortly thereafter, I purchased a mango grove and started working long hours. The words of Mother repeated themselves constantly in my mind: "Laziness should be given up. Every man should work hard and earn his livelihood. He should eat and live on his own earnings, give in charity and not beg."

Due to Mother's grace, my personal life improved, too. Earlier, I had had no knowledge of the pleasure to be derived from hard work. However, after a long day's labor, I began to return straight home. I then offered my prayers to God. My desire to return to Mother intensified.

After six long months, I went again to Penusila and heard the Mother's message one evening. I felt that I was coming out of a diamond mine with a diamond in my hand, so valuable were Her words which adorned my heart. The Mother again spoke to me with great affection and tenderness. She inquired after my welfare. I collected the dust from Her feet and, agonizing over the separation, left for my village.

Upon my return, I started getting up early in the

morning, taking a cold bath, meditating, and praying. I also began offering flowers and incense sticks to the photo of Sri Vijayeswari Devi. I have many times felt that someone was waking me up. Since then, if I have not had Mother's *darshan* physically once a month, I feel that I have lost something precious.

The people of my village were surprised at my sudden change. They started wondering how *puja* and devotion had descended on an unruly fellow like me. However, I never followed this path to please anyone. Sri Vijayeswari Devi simply extended Her immortal and protective hand and salvaged a wayward person like me.

Often I prayed to the Mother: "O Mother, I am a very bad fellow! But still, I want to receive initiation from you and do meditation. Will you oblige me?"

"My boy, you are never a bad fellow! The soul that rests in you and me are one and the same. If you are afraid of your past sins, cast all of them at my feet and be free. Instead of you, I will bear them. Tread the path of divine life." This was Mother's advice to a rogue like me.

Since then, whenever any problem confronts me, I pray, and the problem gets solved instantly through the Divine Mother's invisible help. In one instance, I was offered a job to escort workers going to the Gulf countries from my place, Rajampeta, to Mumbai, where they would board the plane. As a result, my financial problems were solved, and I got mental peace.

All of my worst qualities soon died. Earlier, even my mother could not change me. The *darshan* of Mata Sri Vijayeswari Devi and the touch of Her feet alone transformed me. Mother's influence changed my entire outlook—She replaced a dilapidated building with a new one; She changed useless iron into gold by the Midas touch of Her compassion. The moment an atom of the dust of Sri Vijayeswari Devi's feet fell on my body, my old lifestyle changed for the better. The only way to purify myself is to serve Mother throughout my life.

Not too long ago, women of my village used to shut their doors whenever they saw me approaching. These same women now request me to escort them to the bus stand and ask me how to solve their various domestic problems. I now have a respectful relationship with the elders of the village. My prestige as a good man in society too has been enhanced. I can only attribute this sea of change to Mother's grace.

A further proof of Mother's overflowing compassion occurred when everyone in my family had given up hope. My little girl was on her deathbed. Even the doctor who had come to attend on her silently walked away. At that time, I prayed before Amma's photo and lit a stick of incense.

A flower then fell from Her picture, and I gained the utmost confidence that my daughter would survive. I declared to those around me: "Don't be afraid. She will survive. After passing the night peacefully, she will get up in the morning and ask for food."

I then applied *kumkum* to my daughter's forehead while she was lying precariously ill on her cot. Praying all through the night, my wife and I remained awake. When day broke, the child opened her eyes and expressed a wish for food. This was how my faith in Mother got reinforced. And, ever since She answered my prayers by saving my child, my love towards Her has doubled.

I lived in a small house in which I had reserved the bigger room for prayer. I used to prepare the sweet *pongal* rice on full moon day and offer it to Mother with fruits, sugar, sugar-candy and other ingredients. However, one particular full moon night in February of 1985 was really memorable. That evening, after the *puja* and *arati,* we distributed *prasadam* to all present. On the seat bearing Amma's photo, we left betel leaves with nuts and sugar candy. Finally, the door of the *puja* room was closed for the night.

As usual, we all slept soundly. At midnight, however, a neighbor named Papiah tapped at my door and asked me whether anything was burning inside the house as there was a bright light visible from one of the rooms. Papiah and I went near the window of the *puja* room where I found, to my astonishment, that the window I had closed earlier was open. As we came closer, we also clearly heard the jingling of dancing bells. All those who slept outside the house heard the sound as well. Then, a light brilliant as the sun at noon enveloped the entire house! Unable to face the brilliance, we both ran far away. At that time, I was graced with a divine vision of Mother.

After sunrise, my wife and I entered the *puja* room. To our welcome surprise, we found that half of the offerings we had left on the seat bearing Mother's photo were missing! Our joy knew no bounds, and I mentally expressed my gratitude to the Holy Mother for visiting the house of a poor man and accepting his small offerings.

In August of 1985, Amma once again took me from the depths of despair and showered Her omnipotent grace upon me. On the fifteenth of that month, I had left for Mumbai. That same evening, my mother went to sleep after having served everyone with food. Early the next morning, the lady who had given me birth and guided me all my life, breathed her last. Previously when I had taken her to the *ashram*, she had made a special prayer to Amma to bless her with a peaceful death during sleep. The great Mother had agreed to her wish and now She had sanctioned it literally. As I was in Mumbai, I did not know about my mother's demise, but strangely, I began to suffer an untold agony in my heart. That night, Sri Vijayeswari Devi appeared in my dream and said, "Get home fast, my son!" I obeyed Her with a heavy heart..

It was my usual practice to enter my house calling my mother's name. I did the same this time also. Imagine how I felt when I was told: "Your Amma is dead. Thinking that it would take time for the news to reach you, the elders decided to cremate the body and to conduct the obsequies after your return."

This news was an unbearable shock! It made me roll on the ground and weep like a child. I remembered Sri Vijayeswari Devi saying many a time, "There is no heaven greater than the mother and the Motherland, so serve your mother with devotion." I thought back to all the times when my mother had advised me to be good during my younger days. I felt now that it was a tragedy I couldn't have been by my mother's side to offer the sacred *tulasi tirtham* to her at the time of her death. This aggravated my grief.

The next day, however, I had a wonderful dream in which I saw Sri Vijayeswari Devi softly walking towards me from the lofty Himalayas. Compassion was flowing towards me from Her calm and peaceful face. I knelt down and bowed to Her. She said, "O son, I could not bear your agony, and so I have brought your mother with me. Take a look at her." So saying, She showed me my mother, and I spent more than an hour with her. Then Sri Vijayeswari Devi said, "Son, you are happy to see your mother. Is this not true?" When I gratefully prostrated to both and lifted my head, they had disappeared. When I woke up, it was 3:30 a.m.

The next day I went to Sri Penusila Kshetram, although everyone had advised me to go to Kashi. My firm conviction was that all sacred places were at the holy feet of the Mother. As such, I felt that all deities like Vishvanatha and Vishalakshi were residing in the heart of Sri Vijayeswari Mata.

It was noon and one could not get the mother's *darshan* at that time. So I just sat silently in the meditation hall, crying inwardly. Suddenly, I felt a movement of soft feet coming toward me, and when I opened my eyes, I saw the eternal Mother standing before me! She placed Her boon-bestowing hand on my head and consoled me.

"Now that you have seen your mother in your dream, you have to bid goodbye to her," said Sri Vijayeswari Devi in Her soft voice. As I had not told anyone of my dream, there cannot be better evidence of Sri Vijayeswari Devi's omnipotence, omniscience and omnipresence. This experience filled me with deep faith. I stayed in the *ashram* for four days and returned home with a peaceful mind after surrendering all my sorrows at the sacred feet of Mother.

In October of 1986, Sri Vijayeswari Devi blessed me again with the most memorable day of my life. For some time I had a great desire that Amma should visit my house and receive our *pada puja*. However, I could not muster the courage to openly invite Her as I was very poor, and could not even offer Her a suitable seat if She should consent to come. On the other hand, I also felt strongly that She would not refuse my request, as She is the Ocean of Mercy. As a result, I was silently and anxiously looking forward to that great day.

In May of 1988, the devotees of our village could not contain our joy when we discovered that the management of the Pullampeta Maharshi Mallik School had invited Mother to officiate at their inaugural ceremony. We knew that She would have to pass through our village on the way, and all the devotees had written to Mother requesting for an opportunity to meet Her. Therefore one can imagine my immense joy when I received the news from Mother that She would visit my house on Her return journey from Pullampeta. I danced in bliss, read Mother's letter again and again, and rushed about like a mad man. Mother had long before said to me, "Son, you be ready with your lamp of devotion and light it with purity of mind. Will the sun wait for your convenience? Like the blossoming of flowers, be prepared because your Mother will come to you when you least expect Her."

Therefore, in anticipation of Mother's visit, I went around to all the shops and selected the best flowers. I also plucked from our own grove mangoes that were both ripe and semi-ripe, taking care to see that they had not been touched by any bird or other creature. I washed and wiped them carefully. In fact, all of us in the village whitewashed our houses and decorated them with *kumkum* and *turmeric* paste.

At the appointed time, Amma arrived for the inauguration of the school. The students sang an invocation and offered prayers. The principal, too, offered a garland of fresh roses. Holy Mother then spoke to the gathering in Her natural and affectionate way. Afterwards, She went to the poorer sections of people and inquired about their welfare. People were surging forth to meet Mother in a constant stream, and without disappointing anyone, She blessed them all.

Half an hour later, on Her return journey, Mother reached Anathayya Garapalli, my village. At the sight of Mother's car, all of the village residents shouted, "Jai Sri Vijayeswari Devi! Jai Karunamayi!"

My village is a small one, and I am not an important man. I have no merit. Mother has thousands of devotees, but She knew my heart's desire and visited my house. She came walking there, placing Her soft, tender feet on the road smeared with cow dung and decorated with designs drawn with white powder. Tears overflowed from my eyes, and I fell at Mother's lotus feet. As She sat on a small seat covered with a mat, we saw that She seemed very happy to grace our home.

I washed the feet of my visible Goddess and sprinkled the water on my head. I adorned Mother with a garland of flowers grown in my garden. I offered Her a variety of sweet mangoes cut into pieces. When She accepted a few, we felt that we were really blessed. The happiness I felt at this time could not be compared with anything else in this world! Not even *crores* of *rupees* would have made me as happy. I felt that my house had become Manidwipa, the celestial abode of Divine Mother, and was greater than Kailasa or Vaikuntha. By Her visit, Mother showered my family copiously with Her rain of compassion. How can I ever repay that debt?

Mother spoke to all the people gathered outside. She asked me to bring the leftover mangoes, and distributed them to everybody as *prasada*. There were hardly fifty mangoes, and it was a miracle that Mother could satisfy over five hundred people! She spoke to everyone with the affectionate familiarity of a birth Mother.

One year later I was taking a nap in the mango garden at noon. At that time, Mother appeared in my dream and said, "Tomorrow I am visiting the Maharshi School again. Go home and meet me there."

When I reached my house, there was a message from the *ashram* waiting for me, saying that Mother would be attending the second anniversary of the school.

On Her return journey after the Maharshi School function, Mother came to our village and gave *darshan* to all those who could not afford bus fare to the school. She also distributed sweets among all the poor. We got the golden opportunity of posing with Her for a photo, and I was blessed by being able to offer Her a *sari* purchased with my own hard-earned money. It was the greatness of Her compassion that She accepted this poor man's humble offering.

One day in 1990, Mother again showered me with Her loving grace. I had been taking part in the *Dashehra* festivities every year, but at this particular time, I was forced to remain in Mumbai due to my work. Though I was not physically there, my entire mind was at Mother's shrine, and I wandered about absently and restlessly the whole evening.

Suddenly, a big tractor loomed right in front of me and was about to run me over. At that moment, I heard a familiar voice call out, "Subbarayudu, move aside!" I jumped out of the road, and looked around, but could not see anyone—save the back end of the huge vehicle. Nevertheless, I knew the voice of the Holy Mother! If She had not warned me, I would surely have been killed.

That same evening of *Vijaya Dashami*, I spent much of my time in *puja* and meditation. During the early hours, I was blessed with a divine vision. Instead of my usual visualization of Her wearing a white *sari* and casting a merciful glance on me, incredibly I saw Sri Vijayeswari Mata sitting on a big tiger! Her eight hands were holding different weapons, She had three eyes, and Her body was glittering like gold. As I could not go to Her, Mother had come to me, descending from the peak of the *Vedas*, and was giving me *darshan* in the form of Sri Durga! I am really blessed. I remember Sri Vijayeswari Devi as my *Guru* and Goddess. I do not have any other desire than to meditate upon Her lotus feet and to serve Her all my life.

Finally, one day not too long ago, I was in my *puja* room and a man named Potukuru Krishnayya visited me. He had been suffering from constant thirst for the past twelve years and was desperate. He said to me, "Brother, protect me by giving me the *prasadam* of Sri Vijayeswari Devi." Then he began to cry that none other than Sri Vijayeswari Devi could save him.

"Brother," I replied, "I am not that great. I can only give you *prasadam* with all my heartfelt good wishes for a speedy recovery." I gave him *vibhuti* and *prasadam*. Afterwards, he was completely cured. Following his recovery, many sick people and children came to me for *prasadam* and got relief.

My life is dedicated to the service of Mother, Sri Vijayeswari Devi. She is the all-pervasive Divine Mother. She is a moving God in human form. I have not seen in the Mother anything other than kindness, mercy, peace and divine love. I cannot offer anything other than myself at the lotus feet of the Holy Mother, who took mercy on a sinner like me and blessed me.

THE EMBODIMENT OF LOVE AND AFFECTION

—G. Suryanarayana Raju,
Indian Army, Corps of Signals, Jammu

I had completed twenty years of service as a signaler in the Indian Army. However, though my juniors advanced in rank, I did not get the promotion I deserved as per the rules. In fact, in 1987 I suffered for the whole year because my superiors were continually finding fault with me.

In my younger years, I had not studied much, but it had been my desire to join the army and serve the nation. Now, though I still cherished my goal, I could not find job satisfaction. I did not reveal this to anyone in my family, since my home was very far from where I worked. At this time, my professional problems were so distressing that there was no day on which I did not weep. My devotion to the nation was also slackening due to my disturbed mind.

On the 18th of June, 1987, I returned to my village after a long absence. Although I was eager to see my family, the fact that I could not be open about my job situation made me sad.

That first evening in my village, I went for a walk and saw my old friend, Subbarayudu (author of the previous experience). I had heard that he was worshipping a Devi, but did not know much more about it. Subbarayudu embraced me affectionately, in an appealing manner typical of the people of my village. This was quite a change from the cold atmosphere of the military! As I hadn't seen my friend for a long time, we took a long stroll, mainly discussing his new philosophy. I was stunned and surprised at his new attitude and outlook. Later, he invited me to his home.

Subbarayudu went to his *puja* room, completed his evening worship and gave me Devi *prasadam*. I was very curious about his activity, wondering who could this person be who was able to bridle this untamed horse? My curiosity and anxiety to personally meet the Architect of Architects who had moulded and shaped the life of this wayward friend knew no bounds.

At my request, Subbarayudu led me into his *puja* room. There I saw a divine figure resembling Sri Sharadamani Devi in a photo beautifully bedecked with different colored flowers amidst the glow of lamps and the pleasing aroma of incense sticks. Indicating the photo, Subbarayudu introduced the divine figure as his mentor, father, mother, Goddess and everything. Without being conscious of doing so, I knelt and bowed before the picture. Then I told my friend about my career problems. Subbarayudu's reply was: "Narayana, you get Mother's blessings. The moment you get the *darshan* of Her holy feet, all your problems will be solved. If you have faith, I shall take you to Penusila Kshetram."

We reached the retreat of the Mother on the evening of the 20th of June, 1987. I had not heard of this place before. The *ashram* of Devi was situated in the midst of green forests at the foot of a lofty mountain. There was a meditation hall capable of seating about three hundred people with an image of *Lalita Devi*. In front of the meditation hall, there was a rose garden.

By the time we reached the *ashram*, Sri Vijayeswari Devi was giving a religious discourse in the meditation hall. Subbarayudu and I were standing in the *verandah*. With great interest, I had *darshan* of Mother.

"Friend, will the Devi speak to me?" was my question to Subbarayudu.

"No doubt, Amma will speak to everyone, especially those in difficulty," was his reply.

"Can anybody talk to Her?" was my next question. Subbarayudu answered, "Why do you ask? Nobody needs permission to take a bath in the Ganga River. For my Mother's maternal love, there is no distinction of caste, creed or religion. Anybody can get the blessings of the Mother."

"Are we to offer anything to Her?"

"Yes," Subbarayudu replied. "An offer has to be made. We have to submit ourselves wholeheartedly to Her. Mother will accept only that, and She has no concern for other offerings."

He continued, "Amma may look new to you. However, She has the knowledge of *crores* of your births. Therefore, She will speak to you with great receptivity. She will remove all your doubts. The moment you receive Her blessings, all your problems will vanish like darkness at the sight of the Sun."

"Should we present to Mother the fruit we brought?" I added.

"If you offer even a *tulasi* leaf with devotion, She will receive it with great affection," was my friend's concluding reply.

Somehow we managed to get inside the hall. We took our seats and listened to Mother's message with interest. With closed eyes, I took in Her words, flowing like the Ganges water in a soft and sweet voice. When the discourse ended, I opened my eyes. Mother had spoken for over an hour and a half.

All the devotees prostrated before Mother, who, with all Her affection, was talking and giving Her blessings by applying *puja kumkum* on their foreheads. It looked as though She was wiping off the fate written there by Lord Brahma and writing a new chapter. For a man in the Army, She appeared to be a heroic mother applying the victory mark on the forehead of her son before sending him to the battlefield.

My friend and I offered our salutations at the feet of Mother. "Raju, are you okay my son?" She inquired. Hearing these words, I was spellbound. I remembered my younger days when my mother used to take me on her lap. In this very first meeting, my ego crashed like a house of cards. I shed tears of joy at Mother's feet. Being carried away by my emotions, I just nodded, unable to answer Her. Mother was smiling at me. I felt I was sitting near my own mother. I opened my heart and told Her about all my problems—problems I had not discussed with anybody else. Mother gave me a very patient hearing. I then prostrated before Her.

As I was talking to Her, the tears began to flow from Mother's eyes and She wiped them with the corner of Her *sari*. The manner in which She expressed Her compassion to a stranger visiting Her for the first time surprised the onlookers. After listening to me, She said "You have suffered such difficulties—it is very painful even to hear about them. How did you bear them, my son? From now on all your problems are over. People who were hitherto your enemies will become your friends. You will soon be promoted in your official cadre. From now onward, you will be under the protective care of your Mother. You will have nothing to fear." Saying so, She blessed me with good wishes for a long life.

After many years, I had a sound sleep that night in the *ashram*. I enjoyed the sublime peace that I had craved for years during my service. I felt that I would have come here years before, if only I had known that such tranquility existed in Mother's hermitage.

Mother initiated me with a *mantra* at my request. I also wanted to get a rosary from Her, but did not have the courage to say so. Incredibly, She held out Her hand and said, "Raju, take this *japa mala*." I was filled with joy.

When I had to return to Jammu, parting from Mother was very painful due to the intensity of my feelings for Her. The first thing I did after landing at Jammu was to place Mother's photo in my room, adorn it with flowers, light *agarbattis* and perform *puja*. Soon, those who had treated me with enmity turned friendly. That surprised me most. Certain other unbelievable changes started taking place on the career front. Every week I used to write to Mother with all devotion. I had the greatest confidence that Mother would listen to all my prayers without fail.

When I sat for *japa* and meditation, tranquility used to envelop me. The disappointment and desperation I had suffered earlier did not remain when I talked to my colleagues about my Mother in the distant forest.

Like many military men, I also used to drink liquor. After being initiated by Amma, however, this habit vanished. I gave up non-vegetarian food and became a vegetarian. I acquired certain good traits too, such as not speaking foul language, uttering untruths, etc. I started reading sacred books of great men. I followed Mother's advice in my daily life. A striking change occurred in me, and as a result, I developed patience and broad-mindedness. Now and then I used to receive letters from Mother on eternal issues, and these letters reflected Her affection towards me. In them, She used to inquire about the welfare of my colleagues as well. We all started feeling Her presence. The days when we received these letters from Mother were days of great rejoicing. We all felt that we had acquired the strength of a thousand elephants, so much encouragement and enthusiasm did Mother's letters infuse in us.

SRI KARUNAMAYI - A Biography

One November night in 1987, Mother again showered upon us Her miraculous grace. I was in charge of securing rations for my military company that were to be issued the following day. However, due to the pressure of work, I went to the storeroom a day ahead of time around 8:15 p.m., to collect the rations. Another colleague came with me to pick up something else. When we entered the room, the moment the light was switched on, we both heard a loud hissing noise. Immediately, I searched the entire area, but could see nothing amiss. Again, the same hissing sound was heard, but with a louder intensity. Lifting my eyes, I saw right in front of my forehead a huge cobra, hanging from the ceiling, with its hood opened and forked tongue stretched out.

I stood motionless in shock, looking at the cobra rapidly slithering down. Both of us were spellbound. Finally, just as the cobra was preparing to strike my forehead, I cried out in distress, "O Mother Vijayeswari Devi, please protect me!"

In the wink of an eye, the entire room was filled with the aroma of *jasmine* flowers. I saw the cobra being wrapped around someone's hand, and then it was thrown far away in a coiled form. I instinctively knew that Mother had invisibly entered that room just to save me. We noticed that things were strewn in a peculiar manner in that room. On the floor I saw a large, newly blossomed *jasmine* flower. I picked it up, bowed reverentially and put it in my pocket. After collecting what we needed, we left the room.

When I was lying down that night, I could not close my eyes. I could see in front of me the blissful form of Sri Vijayeswari Devi, who had listened to my call of distress and saved me from the jaws of death. Nevertheless, this divine experience was enough evidence of Mother's all-pervasiveness. Ever since She initiated me, I had looked upon Her as my mentor, mother and spiritual advisor. I now did some corrective thinking: In this *Kali yuga*, an ordinary holy person cannot travel thousands of miles just to protect one person. So who could Sri Vijayeswari Devi be?

I realized that She is the Self within, the all-pervasive *Brahman* and the merciful Divine Mother. That is why She had the capability to grant me an extension of life. Before I left for Jammu, She had blessed me with a long life, saying, *"Dirghayushmana bhava."* The significance and truth of Her blessing became crystal clear to me as I reconciled Her blessings with this particular incident. Even to this day, I feel a chill run down my spine when I recollect this incident.

I came to my village on leave during January, 1988. The very next day I went to the *ashram* to have the *darshan* of the Holy Mother. It was around 9:30 p.m. and Mother would be available only at noon the next day. I joined the group of devotees waiting for Her. One of the devotees whom I had seen from time to time, asked me, "Where do you come from?"

"I am from Jammu," I replied.

"From Jammu....Are you Mr. G.S.S. Raju?" the devotee asked.

"Yes," I answered. "But how do you know?"

"Where were you at 8:15 p.m. on the 15th of November?" he continued, ignoring my question.

"Why are you asking me these questions, and who are you?" I replied.

"Do not consider us to be different," continued the devotee. "Like you, we too are Mother's children. I will tell you why I am asking what happened to you that night. We were all in the *ashram* at that time, Amma suddenly fell to one side from Her seat. Only the lady devotees who quickly supported Her prevented Her from falling to the ground. Mother's body became cold. We all became nervous. I had never seen anything like this. Mother was lying like there a corpse. However, after five minutes, She got up and started speaking as usual.

"When we asked Her where She had been, She did not reply at first. But, after repeated requests, She said She had been to Jammu to save Her son Raju who was in distress. She said nothing more. We thought of writing to you, but since we were not sure if our action would be right, we did not venture to do so. This is why I asked you so many questions. Do not misunderstand me. Please let us know what happened to you that night."

Hearing his words, tears flowed from my eyes. Then I explained to them all that had happened that eventful night. They were all dumbfounded. Though Mother was physically present in their midst, She had traveled in Her subtle form thousands of miles away to save me!

At *darshan* time, as I came up for *darshan* and completed my prostration, Mother said to me, "Raju, I am accepting your salute every day!"

Actually, I used to salute before Amma's photo every day with my uniform on, before going on duty. No one knew this. But nothing is veiled from the all-pervading Mother. I prostrated to Her once more.

As I said, "Mother, you have saved my life," She replied in Her soft voice, "Son, you are a lover of peace, so God's blessings are ever with you."

I got promoted to the cadre of a Junior Commissioned Officer, effective the first of October, 1988. Once I had craved for this promotion, but now it did not mean much to me. At the same time, I got a letter from Amma. With that letter, diamond sugar candy, *kumkum* and rose petals were enclosed as *prasada*. Mother wrote that to celebrate my promotion, sweets had been distributed in the *ashram*. I was overjoyed at this demonstration of Mother's boundless love. Sri Vijayeswari Devi is the consolidated embodiment of the love found in *crores* of mothers.

In Jammu, all my comrades used to go to the Vaishnavi Devi Temple. My conviction was that both *Vaishnavi Devi* and Vijayeswari Devi were one and the same. As I entered the *sanctum sanctorum*, and offered prostrations to *Sri Vaishnavi Devi*, I said mentally, *"Sri Vijayeswari Vaishnavi rupa pranamamyaham,"* meaning, "I offer salutations to Sri Vijayeswari Devi, who is in the form of *Sri Vaishnavi Devi.*"

Later, when I scaled the Himalayan Mountains and looked at the eastern side, the golden color of the rising sun appeared to me as the *sindura* on the forehead of Sri Vijayeswari Devi. I imagined the sun, when it turned red, as the *kumkum* on Mother's forehead. Towards evening, the glittering stars appearing in the sky looked like Mother's ornaments. The lush green scenery was Her *sari,* and the snow peaks, Her crown. And the drops of dew were Her compassion.

Sri Vijayeswari Devi is my mentor and mother. She is *Lalita Devi,* who dwells in the celestial Isle of Manidwipa. It is my earnest wish that I should dedicate myself to the service of my fellow men, that I should see Sri Vijayeswari Devi in every being, and that I should make this life, granted to me by my Mother, worth living.

SAVIOR OF THE DISTRESSED

—Dr. C. H. Mallikarjuna Gupta,
Southern Railway Hospital,
Ainavaram, Chennai

My life's desire is to serve the cardiac patients of our country selflessly. Therefore, I rejected the many offers I have received from abroad and am employed by the Southern Railways at Chennai as a cardiac surgeon.

In serving those afflicted by heart disease, I feel I am treating my own self or my family. Whether I work in the hospital or am in the *puja* room, I feel no difference, as the medical profession to me is sacred.

Because of professional pressure, I am not always able to eat or sleep on schedule, but my wife never complains. In fact she encourages me to serve my patients. I am fortunate to have such an understanding wife.

My father was my inspiration. It was from him that I inherited a religious temperament. Sri Ranganatha Sai, Sri Goda Devi, Sri Rama, Sri Sita Devi, Sri Ramanuja and my father are my guiding spirits. Sri Rama has blessed me with a daughter and a son, and has given me a profession in which I can serve Him through service to humanity. Thus I am content and peaceful.

On the day before Christmas, after making my rounds, I felt drawn to return to one particular patient. He was lying on a cot, while his wife sat near him. Both were listening to a tape with single-pointed concentration. On the shelf in front of them was the photo of a person resembling Sri Sharada Devi, the Holy consort of Sri Ramakrishna Paramahamsa. The room was filled with the fragrance of jasmine flowers and the aroma of incense sticks.

I listened silently to the divine message on the tape for over thirty-five minutes. At one point, I wiped my face with my handkerchief. The couple became aware of my presence and offered me a seat.

I sat down asked them, "Is this a photo of the Divine Mother whose message you were listening to?" They nodded in the affirmative, and I bowed to the photo, below which written, "Karunamayi."

I thought that I one day I would have the *darshan* of this Mother who had attracted me. I also hoped that She would visit my house to bless me. As if in answer to my thoughts, a flower placed at the foot of the photo fell down. I was overjoyed.

The divine message of Mother, which left an indelible impression on me, had convinced me that She was a holy person. Her words expressed universal ideas and revealed Her wide vision. She emphasized the responsibility of highly placed members of society toward the less fortunate. In these days of violence, unrest and greed, Mother's cooling words comforted me. Her compassion for the poor overflowed like the River Ganga. I felt that She was telling me to double my spirit of service.

To sum up Mother's views on service:
1. Service to man is service to God. A life led with this motto, even for a second, is good. Without such a motto, a life of even a thousand years is a waste.
2. Spiritual life without kindness to others, without devotion to God, and without love, is fruitless.
3. Selfless service with pure love alone reflects the absolute quality of the Divine.
4. A person rendering service to the poor with a compassionate and sympathetic approach will scale greater heights of spirituality.

Later, I memorized many other teachings of Mother and tried to implement them in my daily life, even though I did not even know Her name. I was simply remembering Her as Amma, the Mother with thousands of names. It was, in fact, my belief that the universal Mother would respond to any name, as She is the all-pervasive *Para Brahma*. I was also confident that She would hear me wherever She was.

One day I received a telephone invitation from a relative, Mr. V. K. Rao, to come for the *darshan* of a holy person who was visiting his home. My wife and I accepted the invitation. The traffic delayed us and when we reached our destination, the whole place was full of devotees. However, we were able to sit in the hall, where devotional music was being sung. Then the guest of honor arrived, and the discourse began.

SRI KARUNAMAYI - A Biography

The voice was familiar, and I looked up in surprise. I immediately realized that the Mother who was speaking so softly and lovingly was the same one I had seen in the photo in the hospital. She glanced at me as She talked, and I experienced supreme bliss. My heart was humming with surprise and joy! An ordinary person could not create so much happiness. We see so many people from dawn to dusk who make no impact on us. Here, I felt, was the divine form of an invisible force.

Mother's discourse was followed by *arati* and the chanting of *shanti shlokas*. After a few moments, the universal Mother, Sri Vijayeswari Devi, walked towards me. With great affection, she inquired, "Oh son Mallikarjuna, are you well?" Her most unexpected concern held me spellbound. I was amazed at the divine vision of Mother and fell at Her lotus feet. Surprisingly, She continued with a natural smile, "Tomorrow night at 8:30 p.m., I am coming to your house."

I sat there dumbfounded while my patient, Sri Rao, came and received Her blessings. Rao was a faithful devotee of Mother. There was a long line of devotees waiting for Her blessings, so we took leave.

That night my wife and I spent the entire night talking about the Divine Mother. We did not even sleep, we were so excited and happy about receiving Mother at our house.
The next day, the 10th of January, 1986, we were eagerly awaiting Mother's arrival. We opened the doors of our hearts and spread the flowers of devotion. We felt as if countless *Rama Navami* festivals were being celebrated at one time! The entire house radiated enthusiasm. As 8:30 drew closer, our hearts beat faster.

When the great Mother finally arrived, my heart blossomed at Her *darshan*. We adorned Sri Karunamayi with a garland of *tulasi* leaves and roses, receiving Her with great joy. Then Mother took Her seat.

Sri Vijayeswari Devi, incarnation of the universal Mother,

was radiating Her natural smile. That evening She spoke to all of us for more than one and a half hours on the *Sri Rama tattva*. My daughter sang a devotional song about Sri Rama, and our home was sanctified by the touch of Mother's divine lotus feet. Tears of joy flowed from our eyes.

As Sri Karunamayi stepped into the *puja* room, I felt that it had become Ayodhya, Mithila City and Villiputtur, the abode of Sri Goda Devi! I felt that by Mother's grace I had achieved liberation and that my mind was moving towards eternal peace. Without Mother's love, life is useless. Mother, the one who bestows knowledge of the Self, blesses all those trapped in ignorance, suffering from the cycle of births and deaths. Until our minds are tamed, we are full of desires and doubts. But just as sunlight melts snow, all of our doubts are cleared after hearing Mother's discourses.

Later, Mother visited the Railway Hospital, where She inquired after the welfare of all the patients. We all took leave of Her with our hearts filled with peace.

Sri Vijayeswari Devi's grace extends to all. Once a poor patient had a heart operation. In spite of all our efforts, his condition was deteriorating rapidly. Our staff lost hope, but I prayed to the Holy Mother, "O Amma, You are the Ocean of Mercy. This patient is very poor. Please take pity on him."

Early the next morning, to everyone's surprise, there was a remarkable improvement in the patient's condition. It is my firm belief that this man survived only on account of Mother's grace.

In this creation every being is one and the same for Mother. I have the strongest faith that in the near future the Divine Mother's message will spread to every corner of the universe. Mother is my mentor. She is my Andal. I am sure that Mother will bless me and make my life worthy.

BESTOWER OF PROGENY

—Mr. K. Gopal,
Graham Road, Bellary

My name is Gopal and my native place is Bellary, in Andhra Pradesh. I was married in 1981 to Gita Saraswati. For some years we had no children, but I did not bother about it.

But five years after our marriage, everyone began to sympathize with us for our childless state. Elders at home also felt sorry for me, and began to show indifference towards my wife. Because my shop was not faring well either, I was plunged into restlessness and depression.

Our neighbors began to conclude that my wife would never bear a child. They made hurting remarks when my wife attended functions, so that she would weep like a child on returning home. In the beginning I used to try and console her, but later I had no words to pacify her. Soon people were showering me with their contemptuous remarks also.

My wife and I consulted various doctors, visited many holy places and made several vows to God, but all in vain. When everything failed, we decided to visit my wife's mother at Chirala for a change of scene. When we were about to return, we came to know that my mother-in-law's neighbor, Sri Mallikarjuna Gupta, had arranged a spiritual function in his home in honor of Bhagavati Sri Sri Sri Vijayeswari Devi. So we postponed our return and went instead to Sri Gupta's house for Mother's *darshan*. We also heard that after Sri Gupta had received Mother's blessings, all his problems had vanished.

The house was beautifully decorated in Mother's honor, and She was given a grand reception. After the discourse, everyone present was fed and now devotional music was in full swing.

With Sri Gupta's permission we entered the private room where Mother was sitting on a tiger skin in an unassuming fashion. She spoke to us in a tender voice as we submitted our petition before Her, taking refuge at Her feet. She simply said, "By the grace of *Jagannatha*, you will be blessed with progeny." We offered our sincere salutations and took leave.

I prayed to Mother to bless me with a son and took a vow that I would name him after Her. I attended Her discourses and prayed for a child. Her occasional compassionate glances at me made me feel that She was listening to my prayers. My wife and I were indeed blessed as we were able to listen to Her discourses full of divine knowledge. Every day Mother met the poor and the distressed, inquired about their welfare and consoled them.
On the third day Mother left for Penusila Kshetram. I had the strongest faith that She would bless me.

In June of 1989, on *Guru Purnima* day, my wife and I joined a group of devotees going to visit the Holy Mother. Thousands of devotees had gathered there to attend the *Guru Purnima* celebrations. Both my wife and I were sitting amidst that huge gathering, offering our constant prayer to Her to at least cast a glance at us, as She could not individually talk to us. As I prostrated before Her, I consciously reinforced in myself the feeling that Mother had the power to remove my suffering and bless me with a son.

The *Guru Puja* commenced with *laksharchana*. The devotees were offering flower by flower at the chanting of each *"Om Hrim Srim avyaja Karunamurtayai namah" mantra*. While I was engaged in doing the worship, to my pleasant surprise, I saw Mother standing before me, radiating Her divine smile. She handed my wife and me a mango fruit with Her blessings. I offered the flowers at Her feet, and we ate the fruit She had given.

That very month, my wife became pregnant. We are forever indebted to the Great Mother, for She gave us something of which we had no hope.

Sri Sri Sri Vijayeswari Devi, the bestower of progeny, is our visible God. She is the Goddess of Goddesses who has given me many divine visions in my dreams. I named my shop "Sri Vijayeswari Devi Provisions Stores." I named my son, who looks like the rising moon, Vijaya Durgesh. The moment I place the baby on the holy feet of the Mother will be the most sacred day of my life.

MOTHER—THE OMNIPRESENT

– Smt. P. B. Lakshmi
M.V. Agraharam, Nellore

I am a small fry in the *crores* of devotees of Sri Vijayeswari Devi. I was born into a religious Brahmin family and, in the pursuit of spirituality, was following the ancient traditions in my family life. However, because I had been suffering from hemophilia for quite a long period, I was unable to do any work for days at a time. At the times when my illness became intense, I would consult many doctors and take various medicines. I also prayed to Janawada Kamakshi. However, nothing seemed to help me.

As time passed, I also began to suffer from anemia, and my husband took me to a number of specialists. Needle marks punctured my whole body. The doctors cautioned that the neglect of my disease would result in cancer, and they recommended blood transfusion and surgery. By that time, much money had been spent, and I didn't have the strength for surgery. Fear had also enveloped me.

Since I could no longer walk into the *puja* room, I resorted to mental worship. At this point, a friend of mine named Sugunamma advised me to go to Penusila Kshetram to seek the blessings of Sri Vijayeswari Devi. Though I was not in a condition to travel, as I could no longer bear my suffering, I sought the permission of my husband to visit the Mother.

It was night when my mother and I reached Sri Penusila Kshetram. We were in a deep forest enveloped by total darkness. The roaring of wild beasts could be heard. By that hour, the night *darshan* was over.

The next morning we awoke to discover that Penusila was like Valmiki's *ashram,* a place bedecked with natural beauty. Mother gave us *darshan* that day in a small hut.
Going before Mother, I told Her about my poor health and prayed for Her blessing. Then Mother, placing Her hand on my head, said, "Lakshmi, your faith will cure you." By Mother's grace, I became totally healthy on that very day! I do not wish even my worst enemy to experience the suffering I had previously endured.

From Mother's divine message, I have learned that through service, charity and cooperation, one can reach new heights in spiritual life. Mother's compassion toward the poor and downtrodden teaches us the principle of kinsmanship and love. Mother's firm conviction is that meaning is greater than language and practice is greater than preaching. Every word of the Mother is invaluable.

Among the nine qualities of humanity, kindness tops the rest. Mother's heart always overflows with compassion. By Her own example of kindness, divine love and service to the poor, Mother has become our beacon light. She teaches people to work toward rebuilding the collapsing humanism in our society. She says this should be done without desire for any selfish gain, but only for the betterment of mankind. Truly, She is divine.

Once an aged woman came to my house at noon and, as she was very hungry, she asked for food. At that time, my *puja* was not yet over, but I had learned from Mother that feeding the hungry is itself a *puja*. Therefore, I spread a leaf and served her a sumptuous meal. I did not tell anyone about this incident, as it seemed unimportant and, in due course, I myself forgot about it.

After some time, I went to visit Mother, and She said: "You have done real worship by giving food to the hungry, and your hospitality has been accepted by the Divine." Hearing these words of the Mother, I realized that She was omnipresent and omnipotent. How can I ever evaluate that all-pervading Mother?

Sri Vijayeswari Devi, who has manifested in the land of the Buddha, preaches that compassion, spirituality, social peace, education and health are important to all classes of society. She prevails on everyone to work relentlessly in keeping with the motto, "Service to humanity is service to God." It is my life's desire that all of us should immerse ourselves in selfless service in order to fulfill the aspirations of the Mother.

WISDOM IS ESSENTIAL FOR HUMAN EVOLUTION

—Pandit Prasanna Padmanabhan,
Palghat

Since it was the month of December, a chilling wind blew all over the forest region of Penusila Kshetram. Inspired by the words of revered Dandapani Swamiji, we journeyed to Penusila to seek *darshan* of Bhagavati Sri Sri Sri Vijayeswari Devi.

Our group consisted of Sri Narayana Menon, the eldest of all of us, not only in age but also in knowledge, as he was a *vedic* scholar, Sri Palani Swami Dikshithar, a Sanskrit lecturer and philosopher, myself, and two foreigners, namely Dr. Robert (an exponent in Sociology) and his wife Dorothy, Doctor of Logic. Guided by the road map, we all reached Penusila Kshetram after a difficult journey.

SRI KARUNAMAYI - A Biography

In front of Sri Narasimha Swami Temple, there were two small pathways. We went down the steps to the west of the temple. Sri Dandapani Swamiji had told us that this area was referred to as "Lopalakona" or "Lokona." We soon came to an elevated *mandapam*. Behind it we saw a nicely white-washed two-room tenement. The first room was decorated with light orange curtains. We had also heard from Sri Dandapani Swamiji that the mother and brother *of Sri Mathru Devi* (Amma) lived there. We went in, introduced ourselves and told them that we had come for the *darshan* of *Sri Mathru Devi*. Both of them extended a hearty welcome to all of us. They served two of us with milk and three of us with good coffee, according to our wish. As we were shivering in the biting cold, they provided us with three hearths (fire pots). This enabled us to recover from the penetrating cold.

After formal conversation, we inquired as to when we could be blessed with the holy *darshan* of Divine Mother.

"Normally She does not come down from the hills. Those who aspire for Her *darshan* have to scale the mountain. Mostly, She will be in deep meditation. Until She opens Her eyes and talks to us, we should not speak. Sometimes one may have to keep waiting for a long time," said Sri Balamurugan Swami (Swami Vijayeswarananda).

I inquired whether Mother takes any food.

"She takes very little food when She comes down from the hills," said Smt. Annapurnamma (Mother of *Sri Mathru Devi*), with tears in her eyes.

I did not pursue the conversation any further, as it had wounded the feelings of that noble lady.

The room in which we were lodged was a big one where cooking was also done. We dumped all our luggage in that room. Without the least hesitation they had provided us with shelter. We all stayed in that room. The adjacent room was smaller, but it was very clean, tidy and filled with a pleasant aroma. There was a life-size photo of *Sri Lalita Devi* and also a *salagrama*. It appeared that *Sri Mathru Devi* lived in that room whenever She descended from the hills. We were told that the Mother would meet the devotees and talk to them with all Her divine love, in that *mandapam* situated in front of our lodging.

Before lunch, we were served with coffee and milk for the second time by Smt. Annapurnamma herself. We remained indoors due to the chilly weather. The hearths provided to us were refueled with more burning charcoal. We waited until 12:30 p.m., but *Sri Mathru Devi* did not return. Meanwhile, the food was ready. The cold weather was intensifying, and even the room where we stayed was filled with fog. Except for the chirping of birds, no other sounds could be heard.

The floor in the room was smeared with cow-dung and artistically adorned with *rangoli*. They placed wooden planks on the floor. In front of these were laid newly washed plantain leaves, cut afresh from the trees in the backyard. They served us with steaming food consisting of rice, *sambar,* pepper *rasam, avial, thuvar chutney, papads, avagai* pickles, etc., ending the hearty meal with a dessert of sweet solid curds. We all remembered our mothers. We had never in the past relished any food so peacefully. After lunch we all offered our salutations to Smt. Annapurnamma, who had fed us so sumptuously.

"You are our guests; guests are God-incarnates. You should not salute me. It is my ordained duty to serve you." So saying, she saluted us back.

At 1:00 p.m., under the guidance of Sri Balamurugan Swami, we started scaling the Garudachala Hills from the western side. Before we started off on our journey from Palghat, our *Guruji* had said, "It is not easy to get *darshan* of Bhagavati Sri Vijayeswari Devi. If you get *darshan* coupled with an opportunity to converse, you are extremely lucky."

These words echoed in our minds as we started trekking the hills. The silence that prevailed over the mountain region in the midst of the forest, far away from human invasion, appealed to us very much. We moved steadily up the lofty mountain.

It was 3:00 p.m. The entire mountain range was covered with such thick fog that we could not see one another. The path ahead was also invisible. Clouds thickly filled with fog was moving above, sprinkling water on us. Our noses, eyes and heads became heavy. The scenery around us, though frightening, had its own grandeur.

Soon the weather changed. The cloudy atmosphere diffused and the sun shone brightly. Looking from the top of the hills, the whole landscape seemed to be a green velvet carpet. The mountain peaks in the distance glittered like gold in the sunshine.

Some time later we reached a beautiful spot after our strenuous adventure, placing every step with great care. We could hear the pleasant sound of a waterfall nearby. The beauty of that spot was indescribable and most enjoyable.

As we moved toward the waterfall, we saw Divine Mother Bhagavati Sri Sri Sri Vijayeswari Devi seated on a raised rock at the base of a large tree. She was in a deep trance. That holy sight was beyond expression. She was wearing an ordinary hand-woven *sari* with its upper end covering Her head. Her face shone with the brilliance of flames coming from the third eye of Maha Deva of Kailasa. The rare brightness enveloping the *sanctum sanctorum* of Jwalamukhi Kshetram could be witnessed in Her face. The glow on the countenance of Sri Vijayeswari Devi was as enchanting as the glittering radiance of Kamakshi Devi's face during the evening *arati* in Kanchi. Was She that Maha Lakshmi who did penance at Kolhapur? She shone with the same divine splendor and grace.

The holy *darshan* of *Maha Devi* is accessible only to the Gods. Only those who have to their credit meritorious deeds in innumerable previous births can be blessed with such a divine *darshan*. We were blessed indeed to have such a rare *darshan* of *Sri Mathru Devi* in meditation in the midst of such an enchanting natural environment. Our lives had become worthy. Our bodies and eyes had been blessed and become meaningful. We enjoyed the *darshan* of Sri Karunamayi to our hearts' content. We cannot remember how many times we offered our grateful obeisance to that Supreme Mother.

The foreigners with us also adapted themselves to this environment and greatly enjoyed the holy atmosphere. Overwhelmed with joy, with tears in their eyes and with perspiring bodies, they also prostrated before the Mother.

We were standing fifty feet away from Sri Karunamayi. We remained there till 6:00 p.m. in the same posture. Then the shining dark eyes of Sri Karunamayi slowly opened like the petals of blossoming flowers. With all humility we went forward and prostrated, one by one, before *Ambal*. The eyes of Mother softly and calmly gazed at us. We offered fruits and sweets. These fruits and sweets were taken away by twenty white monkeys, squirrels and birds. Dr. Dorothy tried to prevent them, but Mother, who was calmly watching the parrots eating *jamuns*, softly gestured to her not to disturb them. The grapes were carried away by squirrels, *jamuns* by parrots, and the *sapotas*, oranges, plantains, apples and sweets by monkeys.

Then Sri Narayana Menon addressed Divine Mother as follows: "Oh, *Jagat Janani*, You are Truth absolute and knowledge absolute. Before coming here, I had neither faith nor devotion. Because of the advice of Sri Dandapani Swamiji, I just came to see You with the simple feeling that it was good to have the *darshan* of a *sadhu Mata*. That was all. *O Sanatani, O Ambal, O Para Shakti, O Sri Chakravasini, Jnanakshi* and *Maha Lakshmi*, can You please pardon this culprit? Had I not been blessed by Your *darshan* in the form of *Meenakshi* who is very dear to me, I would perhaps not have understood You. Forgive me, *Bhavani*. In this dense forest, except Your Supreme Self, who else could perform penance? We could get your rare divine *darshan* only on account of meritorious deeds in our past births. All the sins committed by us in *crores* of previous births have vanished by Your compassionate glance. Till my last breath I will carry this divine experience in my mind."

So saying, he prostrated flat before the Divine Mother, with tears of ecstasy. We were all watching this with folded hands. Mother was looking at us with compassion. Tears ceaselessly flowed from our eyes.

In the meanwhile, a group of about twenty squirrels came and started moving all round Mother, a few on Her lap and some on Her head. Addressing them with great love, Sri Karunamayi said, "It is enough, children. You all go home now. When further fruits arrive, you can take them. You should not disturb, children!"

It was then for the first time, we heard the sweet voice of Mother. But those mischievous squirrels did not yield to the soothing words of Mother. Instead, they started moving all over Her body. Then Mother again said, "Oh, children, get down. You should not do so, my dears!" The caressing of the squirrels by Mother was so beautiful!

Then Sri Balamurugan Swamiji placed before Mother a packet containing roasted green gram *dal* that had been sent by Smt. Annapurnamma, just as if she had anticipated such a situation. Even as Mother was picking up the packet, the squirrels raided it. Mother threw the contents before them and the squirrels ate the gram. We were all just wondering whether this was the same Mother who was in deep meditation a few hours ago! How fortunate these squirrels were to receive *prasadam* from the very hands of Divine Mother! Was all that we saw here true? Had we really come to Penusila Kshetram? Was it a dream or reality that we were seeing the *Dayamayi?* After some time, with folded hands Dr. Robert addressed the Mother as follows:

Robert: "Mother, this is my wife, Dorothy. We were both yearning to see You, and we have been able to come here because You willed it and graced us. We are returning to our country in the next five days. If You can kindly give us some message, we will carry it back to our country as Your blessings."

Hearing these words, Mother smiled. Her calm and serene face with the smile brought to our minds the cool and peaceful moonlight. Then, to avoid wasting Mother's precious time, Dr. Robert put forth only a few questions.

Robert: "How can humanity achieve total evolution?"

Sri Karunamayi: "For development of divine fervor, there should not be any kind of restriction. When restrictions are negated, man gets internal freedom. Acquiring internal freedom means the dawn of total evolution. Wherever there is liberty, there exists peace, prosperity and evolution."

Robert: "Can we get internal freedom if we cross the barriers of the illusive mind?"

Sri Karunamayi: "Certainly one can get internal freedom, if one understands the infirmity of the mind and controls it. Gigantic trees lose their original form when their roots are cut and they are planted in small pots. In the same way, the scope for the evolution of mankind to rise to its free form has been marred by restrictions. Assuming unrealistic and unnecessary responsibilities, man remains at a low level. It is enough if he is given full liberty to advance spiritually and realize his free form, realize his true Self. "

Mother expressed all this in beautiful English.

Robert: "Mother! My prayer to You is to wake up the world. To wake up humanity from the deep slumber of ignorance, perhaps the conch has to be blown."

Sri Karunamayi: "For adventurous and learned people, waking up is not necessary, my dear."

These words were spoken by Divine Mother gently and impressively. Robert kept silent since he had nothing more to say. For some time we all closed our eyes and remained silent. We all felt a powerful current moving around us. When we opened our eyes and looked at Mother, She seemed to be the personification of Truth. She appeared as the embodiment of *Sanatana Dharma*. Her eyes were filled with compassion and motherly love.

The squirrels went into the woods, carrying the remaining grains. Vibrations of tranquility were moving around us. We remained as silent fish in the ocean of peace. The entire atmosphere was overwhelmed with *shanti*.

In the meanwhile an infant deer came towards Mother. It stood very close to Mother, as if it wanted to lean on Her. It started chewing the corner of Sri Karunamayi's *sari*. Mother did not object to it. The little deer moved closer to Mother. Mother started massaging its head with all Her love. Looking at that unusual scene, we remained spellbound. We all enjoyed the waves of the aroma of peace coming from Sri Karunamayi.

Robert: "We will carry Your message of peace to our country. We will carry this in our minds till our last breath. We will walk in Your path and remain Your servants." He prostrated before Mother in the Indian style.

Slowly the entire forest was getting enveloped in darkness. But the area in which we sat, strangely enough, was not dark, and we enjoyed the moonlight.

Keeping in our hearts that reverential form to which we pray every morning and the peaceful environment of the Garudachala Hills, we left the place while repeatedly looking back. The sight of the deer chewing the end of Mother's *sari* passed before our eyes again and again. With the help of a flashlight we started descending the mountain. Time passed quickly and pleasantly.

By the time we returned, it was 12:30 a.m. Smt. Annapurnamma inquired about Mother. We suffered a strange pain when we visualized Mother's presence in that dense dark forest infested with wild animals.

Due to the previous day's strain, we woke up late the next morning. By the time we finished our baths, the food was ready. Smt. Annapurnamma served us a sumptuous meal, and we ate to our hearts' content. We prostrated before her as a token of our gratitude for her immaculate motherly affection. We also placed some money before her as our humble offering. But, however much we pleaded with her, she refused to accept it. She had hosted us without any reservations or anticipation. Only on account of the help rendered by Sri Balamurugan Swamiji, could we have *darshan* of Sri Karunamayi. How unassuming they were! We felt ashamed of our behavior in measuring their love with a commercial outlook and for offering them money. Witnessing total satisfaction in the eyes of Smt. Annapurnamma, we saluted her again and got ready to leave for our destination.

Robert: "How sweet is the compassion and love of Smt. Annapurnamma! Beautiful is the selfless service rendered by her."

Sri Balamurugan Swami: "In our lifetime, we can never forget Her who is the personification of contentment and selfless service. In India, hosting guests is a prime duty. Here guests are treated on par with God. This is a common attitude in India. Whenever Smt. Annapurnamma renders any service to anyone, she does so in the name of Sri Vijayeswari Devi."

Robert: (Raising his arms) "Yes, India is sacred. The rare selfless courtesy extended is not seen anywhere else. Swamiji, please bless us to have our next birth in this holy country, so that we can emulate your faith and serve our guests without anticipating any reward."

Sri Balamurugan Swami: "Sri Karunamayi who is the protector of the entire universe will surely satisfy your aspirations."

Again and again, we saluted. Smt. Annapurnamma, the embodiment of selfless service. We also saluted Balamurugan Swami, who has dedicated himself to the service of his sister (Divine Mother Sri Karunamayi) by serving Her with high devotion.

Remembering Bhagavati Sri Karunamayi, who with all tranquility and steadiness was engrossed in meditation in the dense forest of the Garudachala Hills, forgetting the very existence of the entire world, we also saluted that mountain king who was hosting Her. The environment of Penusila Kshetram, the divine personality of Bhagavati Sri Sri Sri Vijayeswari Devi and the tranquility we enjoyed, all left a deep imprint on our hearts.

> *Garuḍācala śikhare ramye*
> *Deva devīm vijayeśwarīm*
> *Dhyānoparata vāsinīm*
> *Smarāmi prasanna mukha pankajam*

AMMA AND THE FAILED BRAKES: JUST ANOTHER MIRACLE

—*Bob Mataloni, Philadelphia*

During the summer of 1995, I was very fortunate to be able to act as a chauffeur for Amma and Swamiji in the United States. In July of that year, I had the opportunity not only to drive them to New York, but to stay with them for two weeks at a devotee's home in Scarsdale. Other than that, I was not doing much else.

One morning, Dr. Jayalakshmi came up for the day from Philadelphia because she had a noon interview with Amma. It was now about 2 p.m., and the interview had ended. Dr. Jaya planned to take the train home.

Meanwhile, Swamiji had come downstairs and he was speaking to Jayalakshmi in the next room. Shortly, he called me in and asked me if I could drive her to Philadelphia. This meant we would ride in my own car—an old Dodge Colt. I didn't answer immediately. It was not because I didn't want to drive Dr. Jaya, but because I was afraid there was something wrong with my car. We wouldn't be able to take Mother's limousine because I wouldn't be able to get it back in time for Amma's use. A few seconds passed, and still I hesitated. I didn't mind risking myself, but I was afraid to involve someone else. Actually, the car had been fixed, but I felt it remained in a shaky condition.

Swamiji realized my reluctance and didn't press the issue. The next thing I knew, Amma had come downstairs. Looking in my eyes, she asked me directly, "*Nanna,* you take Dr. Jayalakshmi to Philadelphia?"

Right away I replied, "Fine."

We left Scarsdale about 2:30 p.m., gassed up the car and proceeded on the New York Thruway to the Jersey Turnpike without any trouble. We were sort of cruising along, having a nice drive and some good conversation. At about 4 p.m., we saw the signs for exiting the Pennsylvania Turnpike to get onto the Philadelphia Expressway. At that point, the three lanes spread out into ten or twelve, where the different toll booths are located. At the time I was going at about fifty miles per hour. We were five or six hundred yards away from the toll-taker. When I put my foot down on the brake to slow our speed, that's when things began to spin out of control!

As I applied my foot to the pedal, unbelievably, it went right to the floor! We were going pretty fast at that point and, as I slammed my foot on the brake again, the whole thing just collapsed!

At that moment, I felt many sensations. For one thing, there was the feeling that the whole universe had turned around. After thirty years of driving, I naturally expected the car to stop when I put my foot on the brake. It's just like a law of nature. Then, there was a kind of panicky feeling, but not total panic. At the same time, in the back of my mind, I knew that if Amma had asked me to drive Dr. Jayalakshmi, we wouldn't be killed. Finally, I felt as though I was a witness to the whole thing, wondering how things would turn out. All these thoughts were happening simultaneously—panic, certainty, and detachment.

Meanwhile, we were headed into the toll-booth, with a car stopped in front of us at the ticket-taker. I pulled up on the emergency brake as hard as I could, which slowed our momentum somewhat. According to the laws of physics, however, we were definitely slated to smash into the car in front of us—no way out of that. My only hope was that the driver who had already paid his toll would move, and I could just go straight through the toll gate and deal with what happened after that. But no such luck! The car ahead stayed where it was.

We were heading straight for collision! Then, for some unforeseen reason, our car suddenly stopped short—less than one inch short of rear-ending the driver ahead. Actually, from where I was sitting in the driver's seat, it looked as if I had hit the car, but we didn't even bump fenders! That lucky person merely paid his toll and nonchalantly drove on his way, never knowing just how close he had come to oblivion!

I said a prayer, breathed a sigh of relief, paid the toll, and we too, continued our journey. I had no brakes at all, but just knew I would get through. It seemed so natural just to go on. And that's what I did. I drove very cautiously, hobbled the remainder of the drive to Dr. Jaya's house, and then to my own home in Central Philly without incident—just an emergency brake and Amma.

Later, people told me I was crazy for driving with no brakes, that I had put both our lives in jeopardy. This may have been true, but I guess I really believed that Mother was doing the driving. It must have seemed that way to Jaya, too, for we never even mentioned it.

JEWEL OF COMPASSION, MOTHER OF ALL

—Smriti Dudley, New York City

Jai Ma! Although I had heard that Bhagavati Sri Sri Sri Vijayeswari Devi was coming to my city, I missed the first opportunity of having Her *darshan*. However, I was called by excited friends, who said that Sri Karunamayi, as I learned She was also called, was a must to see! I was informed that She was another Saraswati (Goddess of speech, the arts, and music), that She had meditated in a forest for a decade, and that She was both exquisitely sweet and powerful. Intrigued, but somewhat reluctant, I decided to go and see for myself. Little did I know that "see for oneself" would be one of Sri Karunamayi's major motifs.

The path of *karma yoga,* or selfless service, was something that had always appealed to me. Teaching was my chosen profession, and I loved it. A dyed-in-the-wool perfectionist, I also very much enjoyed working on new and creative projects.

Meanwhile, on the second day of Sri Karunamayi's visit, I found myself in an Indian store near my music teacher's home, buying a stainless steel tumbler. That evening I showed up at the program with two fans, a small cooler containing spring-water and this new glass, my harmonium, and a bronze image of Saraswati Devi seated on a throne under an umbrella. Right away a group of us pitched in and set up fans and flowers, a seat of honor and a small table holding incense, fruit and the golden Goddess. Those of us present were also wondering what the protocol was for greeting this spiritual master. I suggested that we sing a few short verses to the Goddess of Creation:

"Jai saraswatī namo namo tava caraṇam."

I began to lead the group in a short rehearsal when, in the middle of the chant, I suddenly realized that I was the only one singing. I turned then to find that Sri Karunamayi had entered the hall and that several admirers were circling Her with a flame of veneration. *"Namo namo tava charanam,"* I continued a little hesitantly, but wanting to complete the song. In a moment, as Sri Vijayeswari Devi glided past where I stood, She murmured, "Now here's someone who likes to do things the proper way!" I blushed, thinking She had really zeroed in on my *modus operandi*.

After sitting down, Sri Karunamayi glanced over at the harmonium and asked, "Who brought this?" One person mentioned my name and looked in my direction. I looked down. Next, Sri Karunamayi noticed the Saraswati statue next to Her and asked, "Who brought this?" and again, my name was mentioned and I looked away. Later, during the program, I passed up the glass of cold spring water and, again, there was the same question and the same response. I was feeling very noticed and not a little embarrassed by then!

After beautifully singing a few Sanskrit *shlokas*, Sri Vijayeswari Devi sat for a moment in silence. Then Swamiji instructed all present to chant the *Saraswati Mantra* and to do *pranayama* (breathing techniques) both before and after it. She briefly explained that because this ancient and divinely revealed *mantra* contained seed syllables from each of the four sacred *Vedas,* it was very powerful. She added that repetition of this *mantra* would rid a person of negative traits and gift them with divine knowledge and creativity. A half hour of meditation followed, closed by a prayer for the welfare of the world.

Next, Sri Karunamayi gave a half-hour discourse in

English. In it She would reiterate the major points expressed throughout Her entire Tour: "Any service performed without the practice of meditation will be motivated by ego. Meditation is the hardest and highest form of spirituality. It purifies us, and it goes beyond religion." Amma continued: "Take what you like, practice that, and leave the rest. Don't see me as your *Guru,* or as your God, but see me only as your Mother who loves you and has come to review your spiritual report card. Meditate, experience and practice silence. Always rise higher and higher. My only wish for you is that you attain Realization." The universality of Her words, delivered in the sweetest imaginable voice, rang true and are indelibly printed in my mind.

At the end of Her discourse, Sri Karunamayi received the devotees one by one, placed holy ash on each one's tongue and, from time to time, said a few words. When my turn came to go up for blessings, She smiled deep into my eyes and said, "Thank you for all that you did for me this evening!"

I was very surprised and humbled. "No, no, it was nothing!" I muttered.

Again, she smiled and said, significantly, "You're in Mother's heart!"

"You're in my heart, too," I echoed politely, never dreaming how prophetic those words would be.

Over the next few weeks I had the opportunity of traveling with Sri Karunamayi, of observing Her closely and absorbing Her teaching. Meanwhile, several transformations occurred in my life. The first big change was that, surprisingly, I was becoming a meditator. Before I met Sri Karunamayi, I had loved to chant, to play music and to work devotedly. However, I had no interest in meditation and had, in fact, prayed for help in this respect. I knew intuitively that without going inward, I would make no further progress in *sadhana*. Now I was being awakened every morning, like clockwork, to the soft jingle of Amma's bracelets. And I was sitting for longer and longer periods. This, to me, was no small miracle!

As time passed, I was becoming more and more attached to Amma, despite Her admonitions not to see Her as the body. I dreaded the time when She would leave the country to return home. Several times, however, Amma asked me when I was coming to India. I replied, "You tell me, Amma," and "Amma, I just missed an incentive for retirement this month. Now the offer is closed." Amma simply smiled.

Later, I had an astonishing dream in which I felt that Mother had appeared to me, lovingly rubbed my forehead with Her hand, and asked me to serve Her. It seemed so true, but things like that never happened to me. Was it real, or only wish fulfillment?

Finally, on the last day of Amma's U.S. Tour , I was begging Her to confirm the dream, to allow me to serve Her, to be close to Her. At last, She smiled enchantingly and said, out loud, "Okay, —," repeating my name.

A day later, back home, on impulse I called the Board of Education. To my astonishment, they had reopened their Retirement Incentive offer—for two more days! On that very day, I rushed to the proper places, filled out the multiple forms and—bingo—I was retired! Or so I thought.

A few days later, I discovered I had overlooked one detail that potentially could have nullified the whole package deal. At one office, I begged, "Isn't there someone I can speak to?" "No," replied the bureaucrat, "there isn't!" But just at that moment, an elegant woman appeared as if from nowhere.

"I'm the Director. May I help you?" she inquired.

"Oh, please, I want to retire and I misunderstood this instruction. Can you help me?" I pleaded, showing her my papers. Meanwhile, I was praying hard for Amma to make my wish come true, if it was Her will.

This woman, this director, looked closely into my eyes. "Okay, —," she said finally, "Okay."

A few days later, happily retired and looking forward to traveling to India, I happened to ask someone the exact meaning of the chant I had been singing the first moment I met Amma: *"Namo namo tava charanam."* Incredibly, the meaning is something like this: "Hail to Your divine name; I worship and serve Your sacred feet!"

DIVINE PRESENCE

—John C Platt, Bloomsbury, *N.J.*

Amma's visit to America was a very special event for me. I know it was a wave of purity and love for the entire country. I feel so fortunate to have been in Her divine presence. Thank you! The names Amma, Sri Karunamayi and Saraswati are now very sweet to my ear and heart. Just as I have read that Sri Ramakrishna used to go into spiritual ecstasy at the mere sound of God's name, I feel surges of devotion and love whenever I hear Mother's name uttered.

One of the things that I have experienced as I continue to meditate is much more clarity as to God's presence in and around nature. I feel a great presence which I have felt since childhood, but was afraid or uncertain how to voice, so that it became something I put in the background. Being near Amma made me realize that She is a manifestation of that presence; She always has been. Now I realize that She must be placed in the foreground of my life—not on the sidelines. Mother Nature now cradles me with protection, love, and guidance. The sound of the wind in the trees is like her voice—God's gentle way of saying, "Hello!" The other night I sat outside and listened to the crickets. The darkness seemed to blanket me with a soft velvet hug.

SRI KARUNAMAYI - A Biography

So many childhood spiritual experiences are now coming back to me. I can remember distinctly looking up at the beautiful autumn clouds on several occasions and receiving the vision of a small girl asking me to come with her to a wonderful place. I was so sad that I could not go and told myself that I would go when I grew up.

Another time I remember walking up a hill filled with raspberry bushes. I realize now that the Divine Mother was at my side at the time. I felt loved, protected, and I was happy. I was only eight years old, but I loved Amma's divine qualities all around me—soft, strong and loving.

One summer when I was eleven, I had to go to a school camp. I was not a good student and I had no confidence. Each day I would go into the forest to this beautiful, wooded glen. I would sit there quietly and feel so much better after a while. I was alone, yet I was not alone. In my own way I was talking to the Divine Mother. I was talking to Sri Karunamayi.

Perhaps these are silly childhood fantasies, but something about these experiences and dozens more have left me with a feeling that something very wondrous was happening in each case, and I feel the need to write (to Amma) about them.

My meditations are sometimes hard and filled with thoughts, but I would not stop for anything. In activity I feel closer to the Divine myself. It is becoming palpable, and my devotion to Sri Vijayeswari Devi, to the wondrous Divine Mother, grows with each passing day.

Recently I experienced yet another, perhaps more miraculous, present from Amma. It all began one day in August when I went to a New York apartment to receive the blessings and healing of Mother. At that time I had a chance to discuss with Her privately my experiences and my life situation. I told Her that I had to commute a long distance by car to work and back each day, and that I didn't enjoy this ride. Car travel, in fact, disturbs me, and I never feel comfortable behind the wheel. I expressed all of this to Amma, who told me to play the healing tape while driving. I did this whenever I could.

One day I played the tape while driving to a shopping mall. Upon returning to my car after my errands, however, I found a beautiful piece of classical music playing, and I decided to listen to it on the way home. It was raining and the roads were slick. As I was attempting to drive through one intersection, a car in the oncoming lane waited for me to pass and turn left. I continued on, but the car behind the waiting vehicle swerved and slid right into my lane. It all happened so quickly that I didn't have time either to brake or to stop. Within a few seconds, my worst nightmare came true and a head-on collision occurred. The impact was so sharp that the front end of my car folded like an accordion—right up to the driver's compartment. The engine actually began to slide under the car, as it is designed to do on a Volvo. On impact a second thing occurred, the healing tape engaged and began to play. Calmly, I began to check my body for injuries, blood, etc. Even though I had my seat belt on, my head had hit the windshield, and I suffered a minor concussion.

I stumbled out of the car, ascertained that the other driver was okay, and surveyed the shocking damage. I immediately realized that I had survived a bad accident. At that moment I said a thank you prayer to Amma—and made a note to thank the guy who had sold me my Volvo.

During the aftermath of the accident, I came to the conclusion that I had paid a large *karmic* debt, but that Amma's grace had allowed me to suffer it with lessened consequence. I still feel to this day that God was with me, and that had I not met Amma this summer, I would be unconscious or hospital-bound even now.

Sri Karunamayi is always in my heart, and I am always

at Her service. I thank Her for all the gifts She has given me, I miss Her physical presence, and I await Her return.

Jai Karunamayi!

ALL PATHS LEAD TO THE ONE

For me, it was kind of a cosmic thing, even just getting there. Three of us Americans were staying at the *ashram* of Shivabalayogi in Bangalore. One day my friend Kathleen from London and I decided to go shopping in Bangalore, while my companions, Tom and Sally, made plans to try to visit Sri Karunamayi. They had just an address and stories that She was building an *ashram* in Bangalore, but they had no idea whether it had been started or completed, or even whether She was in this part of India—much less in Bangalore. So, they were starting out on a kind of wild-goose chase. They had no phone number—just an address.

That morning, while taking a shower, I realized that even if there was a two percent chance that Tom and Sally were going to run into a saint, that was the "bus" I wanted to be on. Pure and simple. I didn't want to miss it. Something, perhaps my inner voice, just kind of turned on in me and said, "Start, this is a good opportunity." So, I just talked myself out of going with Kathleen—which was fine with her.

Tom, Sally and I piled into an auto-rickshaw which took us to the other side of BangaloreThe *ashram* had been completed, but it didn't look as though anyone was around. Then we saw a side gate open, went around, and Tom discovered a man inside.

Shortly, we found out that Sri Karunamayi had returned just the previous night, that the *ashram* had just been finished about two months prior, and that Mother was resting. However, because She had stayed with Tom and his wife, Pat, who had sponsored Her in Seattle, Amma remembered him quite well. She seemed very fond of him and, though she was a bit tired, was willing to disturb Her rest period and receive us.

At that point, the three of us had a private *darshan*. It was just quite lovely. I was amazed at how human Sri Vijayeswari Devi seemed. She was, to all intents and purposes, from casual observation, just a wonderful, sweet and gentle, friendly person. We had a great time sitting around chatting, basically. We were there for about forty-five minutes. Mother did a great job of receiving us, and Tom, Sally and She shared a lot of stories about how it had been when She came to visit Seattle. I thought it was unique, but I didn't have much of a reaction. I simply felt it was great to be in the presence of someone who was so special.

Amma was sitting on a chair in a small enclosure upstairs, and the three of us were sitting on a carpet, just behind where devotees come for the lectures. Amma told us, that the *Sivaratri* which was coming up in two weeks would be the most special observance in one hundred years. She added that it would be wise for us to do some fasting and meditation to take advantage of the very special energies that were available. At the very end when we were leaving Mother gave us Her blessings. At that time, She just very, very lightly touched our foreheads with red powder—*kumkum*—and we directly got into our auto-rickshaw and returned to where we had been staying.

By the time I got back to the Shivabalayogi *ashram,* I was in the middle of a very intense spiritual experience. I was so moved that I could barely see. I felt as if I were in a pretty serious trance of some sort, a meditative state.

Indeed, I felt compelled to meditate, (which went on for nearly six hours). I was really quite amazed at the state of grace which that one little, tiny touch to my third eye had bestowed. I'd been a meditator for fifteen years, a serious meditator for about six, and I'd been around spiritual people; but nothing or no one had just so effortlessly put me into an altered state.

The second amazing experience I had was that evening. Sally and I chose to return, even though the evening lecture was in Telugu, Amma's mother tongue. It was very clear to Sally and me, however, that the language didn't matter. We felt that there was only one Truth and, if we listened, we would hear it.

We were sitting there waiting for Amma to come out but, right before the discourse began, Sally and I were summoned again into the chamber right behind the meditation hall, where we had previously met Amma, and again we were invited to have a private *darshan* with Amma for about ten minutes. We were astounded! We spoke some more of *Sivaratri* and of Mother's work at Her main *ashram* north of Chennai. It was a very special energy and, again, She gave us Her blessings, and then went out to the evening's program.

As we sat there and Mother was speaking in Telugu, I had a most wonderful vision. The only thing I can liken it to is an experience I had in the Virgin Islands when I was in a gift shop looking at either watercolors of marine life or at various stuffed fish. The colors were all luminous, and I thought that some artist had a really creative, bright and colorful imagination. Then, a few hours later, I went snorkeling and there, down under the water, were exactly those same fish. They are that color! They are luminous, phosphorescent and iridescent, and the artist didn't have a creative imagination at all.

My vision of Sri Vijayeswari Devi was very much the same. I can only compare it to the very stylized pictures we've all seen of the Goddess, which are sort of luminescent with many bright colors. They aren't quite burning, but they are brilliant and shining. And, indeed, as I kind of saw into

SRI KARUNAMAYI - A Biography

Sri Karunamayi, saw Her as She is, or saw my own projection of Her—who's to say—the vision was very much like those stylized portraits. She was dazzling white. She was luminous. She was golden. She was vibrant. And I felt there to be no conflict at all with my own spiritual past. It felt absolutely parallel and, in fact, just at that same time, I saw Shivabalayogi—smiling and laughing. Obviously, there was no conflict for Him! Yes, I had this miraculous image of the Mother while I was in Her Presence.

The next day, I was eagerly looking forward to returning to see Sri Karunamayi. Earlier She had invited the three of us to come for lunch. We really were getting the royal treatment! That same morning I was downtown, but I got stuck doing an errand. Then my auto-rickshaw got lost, took a wrong turn and got a ticket—which is almost unheard of in India. Therefore, I was about forty minutes late for my appointment with Mother. Ordinarily in India I wasn't that concerned with time, but this was a very special invitation. How in the world could I be late to meet the Divine? I felt embarrassed, ashamed, and slightly angry at the cab driver.

So, forty minutes late, I kind of sheepishly walked into the *ashram* and explained my predicament to the secretary. I said that I was so sorry, etc. Then, I was shortly joined by Tom and Sally who had been waiting for forty minutes because Mother hadn't summoned them. And, after about three minutes, She received us all. I just sat back in amazement and, lo and behold, there was the most immaculate lunch feast I have ever witnessed. I am speaking of immaculate! There were probably fifteen different items on each of our plates, each one absolutely and perfectly prepared and displayed. Even the tangerine sections had been double-peeled. It was a feast for the eyes simply to observe. Literally, I sat there ten minutes in awe, just staring at the perfection. I just felt I had been given the greatest blessing—that it couldn't get any nicer.

Mother sat with us for about ten or fifteen minutes, and again we talked about some of Her plans in India. She explained that She was just beginning Her mission in Bangalore, but that at Her main *ashram* in the forest, thousands came to meditate. It was very clear to all of us that this *darshan* was an amazing and rare opportunity.

Though we stuffed ourselves several times over, there was no way we could finish the sumptuous food. It was a lunch I will never forget in my entire life! It was truly a lunch from heaven!

DOUBLE DARSHAN

—Karen, Seattle

On Sunday nights at the Seattle Shivabalayogi Center for Meditation, we follow the schedule He established—an hour of meditation, followed by an hour of *bhajans* and *prasad.* There are two of us, Sally and myself, who regularly receive Swamiji's[4] *bhava* and, when Sri Karunamayi visited Seattle last summer, during Her programs we also experienced His presence. There was a slightly different quality to the *bhava,* however, that we relished, and we smiled in wonder when Amma told us privately during Her *darshan* that She had especially blessed us that night.

On the next to last evening Sri Karunamayi was in Seattle, other seekers present said that after the *bhajans,* when Amma finished the *darshan* line and stood up to leave, instead of walking to Her left as before, and blessing people on Her way out, She picked up two apples and walked toward the right where Sally and I sat. I had no awareness that the program was finishing and my eyes were closed. However, I am told that Amma stood over me and began to speak softly. I came to sense then a most powerful sweet presence standing near me. I felt Her hand lightly resting on my head and Her voice, the most beautiful imaginable sound to my ears, repeated, "Take

---

[4] Ed.'s note: "Swamiji," in this story refers to Sri Sri Sri Shivabalayogi.

this from Devi," until I finally could take the apple from Her hands. I knew She'd moved on to Sally, but remained immersed in Her love and the *bhava* from Swamiji. My hands continued to show an aspect of Swamiji's *bhava*—fingers locked as His became during *tapas*.

In January, four months after Sri Karunamayi had returned to Bangalore, our meditation programs continued as usual in Seattle. Meanwhile Sally and my good friend Tom Palotas, both strong devotees of Swami Shivabalayogi, had also gone to Bangalore to our *Guru's ashram*.

On one particular night, Tom's wife, Pat Templeman, had finished the *bhajans* and was ready to start the *arati* when a devotee asked for a specific *bhajan*. On those rare occasions when he'd done this before, I'd felt from my state of *bhava* that he had been sensitive to some energy about to appear. On this one night in the middle of winter, right after Pat began playing—and without a hint beforehand—Amma came forward to me. This time, however, She was an even fuller presence that I'd known since She had been here in August. Her brilliance made me ache! She first covered me with light, placing Her hand on my head as She had done that night at the Arboretum with Sally and me.

After all these months, I again could feel Her unlimited power and love. Then She appeared just where She had sat that summer and, from there, leaning forward, radiated through Her wonderful smile, Her blessings to everyone. She was magnificent in Her gift of sweetness and fullness of this blessing from Devi. Once again, I felt that Swami Shivabalayogi had opened the door for Amma to come to us. I shared this with our group, since the blessings were for us all.

The next morning, on Monday, I emailed an account of this story to Tom and Sally in Bangalore. I said I hoped they would be able to visit Sri Karunamayi. An hour later, Pat forwarded Tom's reply to me. From it, we know that a few hours after Amma had appeared to me, he and Sally had spontaneously left Swamiji's *ashram* in Bangalore for a delightful visit with Sri Karunamayi.

I was glad that ice kept the staff away from my office that day, for I found myself overcome by the wonder of this manifestation of Amma's blessings and Swamiji's love.

LONG-DISTANCE HEALING FROM SRI SRI SRI VIJAYESWARI DEVI

—Ishwari, Seattle

On May 13, 1994, I slipped and fell off my deck. I felt something snap; my leg was broken and my ankle shattered. Before this accident, I had been very active. Although I was fifty two, I rode my mountain bicycle, skied in the mountains of Washington, and loved to roller-blade on the many nearby trails. I taught hypnotherapy classes to people all over the United States as well as in other countries. People always commented that I had the energy of a twenty-year-old. Generally, after others were exhausted, I would be going strong.

After the accident, I was in a wheelchair for over a month and on crutches for four months. Even though I did not miss teaching a single class, I had to do so from a wheelchair. I could no longer exercise, roller-blade, run, bike or ski. I couldn't even work in my garden that whole summer. Even though I continued to teach my seminars, as soon as the class was over, I was exhausted. I would go right to bed and stay there as long as I could.

My seminars are usually six consecutive days. Each day, I would have to drag myself out of bed to get there. Most of the students did not know how I was feeling inside. On breaks, instead of socializing, I would go and lie down until it was time to return. During the weeks that I was not teaching, instead of preparing for the next seminar, I spent most of the time lying on the couch. I had no interest in seeing any of my friends and I basically made every effort to avoid people, which is not like me at all.

By the summer of 1995, I was fifty pounds heavier, my ankle was still swollen and painful, and I was unable and unmotivated to exercise. Then in August, I had just called a friend from New York who told me about a "Divine Mother" who was here from India and was doing incredible healing in my friend's living-room in New York City. She said Her name was Sri Karunamayi and urged me to see Her when She came to Seattle. When she told me the dates, they were the exact dates that I was scheduled to teach a seminar in Houston, Texas. I couldn't believe that I wouldn't be here! I was extremely disappointed.

My husband David and our son Jesse (age sixteen) were home in Seattle. They arranged to meet Amma in Seattle and called me in Texas to tell me how wonderful She is. I was very happy for them as they told of Her wonderful healing gifts. They also spoke of Her divine nature and that She embodies Saraswati, the aspect of divine wisdom. I could tell they were "falling in love" with Her.

After speaking with them, I began to feel Her presence in my heart and I could not sleep. I ended up meditating nearly all night, feeling so filled with the presence of Sri Karunamayi, the loving, compassionate Mother. In meditation I received a message suggesting that I call David and have him request a long-distance healing by Mother.

I did that and couldn't wait to speak with him that evening. He said that Mother had requested my picture, which he brought to Her. She rubbed holy ash on it and said the healing chant with her sweet, sweet voice. She sent her picture, some ash, a tape of the chants, and instructions. I followed Her instructions and expected to be healed that very day. When I wasn't instantly healed, I felt disappointed and began to think it hadn't worked. So I sort of forgot about it, even though I did continue the practice which She had suggested.

A few weeks later, a clear message came in my

meditation from Sri Karunamayi. The words were, "Remove the metal." At first I didn't understand; then suddenly I realized She was referring to the twelve metal pins and the metal plate which were still in my ankle to hold it together. I had not wanted to have them removed because I feared going through another operation. I was afraid that I would be re-traumatized and actually have even worse depression. Suddenly, I realized that Amma had removed my fear and I found myself calling my doctor to request the operation. I brought Amma's healing tape and my tape player into the operating room and felt Her presence with me during the entire operation.

As soon as I came out of the operation, I felt as if a huge weight had been lifted from me. I felt so much lighter, I could hardly believe it. And the healing has continued ever since. This, together with other physical treatments, turned around my physical condition. I began to lose weight, lower my cholesterol, and felt like exercising. Each day I felt better.

The most important part of the healing has just become more evident to me: it is the return of my energy. I didn't realize how depressed I was until it actually began to lift. I actually have more energy than I used to have even before I broke my ankle. I need much less sleep and I am excited to arise each day. I teach my seminar all day, dance for hours at night, and still am not sleepy to go to bed.

I am so grateful to Sri Karunamayi. I can't wait to see Her in person, although I realize that I have always known Her and I feel Her presence always. I am looking forward to Her visit to Seattle and hope that many others will be able to receive the healing that they are wanting. Just being able to be in the presence of the embodiment of The Divine Mother feels like an overwhelming blessing.

Jai Karunamayi!

*Blessed Messages
of
Sri Karunamayi*

PRACTICE OF MEDITATION IN DAILY LIFE

Divine Souls,
One can definitely conquer the inner negative feelings of lust, hatred, anger and desires by getting up daily before sunrise, bathing and dressing simply, and with a quiet mind, meditating on *Pranava, Om.*

Seekers with steady minds can become victorious over the uncontrollable disturbances of the mind according to their individual capacity. Our thoughts and imaginary feelings are actually responsible for our failure to control our mind.

One can obtain the power to suppress both good and evil thoughts through regular meditation—not breaking the practice for a single day. When the seeker meditates regularly for a few years, he can certainly attain victory over the mind, leading to Self-Enlightenment.

When one meditates on *Pranavam*, one sees the supreme, eternal and indivisible Light within, and experiences that he himself is that vital force. There is nothing to be compared with the experience of this state of the Self. Nothing else is equal to it or comes anywhere near it. There is no experience like it, none at all!

The cage of this inert body is like a chariot—the five sense organs and the five organs of action are the ten horses, the mind is the reins, and the Self is the charioteer, pleasantly travelling the entire cosmos.

This whole world is a playground for the Self-Realized soul. Such a state comes only through *sadhana*, regular spiritual practice, and not by any other method. Therefore, become thinkers, meditating on *Pranavam* by hearing spiritual discourses, contemplating on them inwardly; understanding them and cultivating true detachment and pure, intense devotion. You should give up all worldly objects and desires and relentlessly pursue the path of self-inquiry to experience the Truth.

Pranavam will reveal its form and open its secrets to all seekers who continuously and single-mindedly practice self-search—meditating according to scriptural dictates, and as instructed by the preceptor, the spiritual teacher.

Those who want to live a spiritual life should not allow themselves to be influenced by the praises and bouquets or by the criticism of worldly people. They should not over-attach themselves to religious rites or social functions. They should only depend on the Self in *Pranavam*. They should be content with what comes their way to satisfy their hunger and thirst and to sustain their physical body. Real devotees should not waste their sacred words and strength by engaging in useless conversations, needless arguments or remembering and worrying over past incidents.

A person's words are the real cause for everything good or bad that happens in his life. Most of the sins we commit are sins of words. Negative words are like arrows that leave the bow, and can never be taken back. Useless, meaningless talk about others causes us great harm. If we cannot give up the bad habit of excessive conversation, not only do we waste our time and our life, our spiritual progress is blocked. A true seeker should free himself of the slavery to useless and meaningless conversations, which cause so many problems. If everyone did this, peace would soon prevail everywhere in the world.

The practice of observing silence together with regular meditation on *Pranavam* prevents us from committing the great sins of the tongue. Restrained and well-thought over talk in the presence of older people brings us spiritual blessings. If we refrain from giving unsolicited advice, it will help us greatly.

The extreme beauty of Sita created problems for Her as She was kidnapped by Ravana. Bali, who was too proud of his extaordinary strength, was vanquished by Sri Rama. So also, Ravana, who was extremely proud and arrogant, was destroyed. Therefore, avoid excess in all actions—nothing should be taken to extremes.

Excessive conversation is not at all good. Excessive eating affects the health. Excessive friendship starting with very frequent visits should not end in a break up. A friend in need is a true friend, and one or two such friends are enough. Even relationships should not be cultivated in excess. By keeping every phase of life within limits, one obtains mental peace.

Silence is the key to open the door of the Self. Live in silence. Observing silence, attain the higher values of life and occupy the throne of the great *Sanatana Dharma* of Bharata. Merge yourselves in the effulgent light of Self-Realization.

Righteousness and self-sacrifice should be the two feet of humanity. If these two great qualities are given up, one's walk will not be steady or balanced; nor can one progress fast in spirituality. Bad habits affect a person like serious diseases and lead his life into utter darkness. One should practise living a divine life in a spirit of self-sacrifice.

Concentrate inwardly on Divinity, *Om, Pranavam* never gives undue importance to small issues. Weaklings speak about minor problems repeatedly, as though they were serious life and death issues. They pass on their mental agony and anxiety to others and destroy their peace of mind. Meditators should never do so. They should live a balanced life recognizing the value of time. They should be in silence as realized souls and awaken their organizing ability. The weak qualities should be discarded with discrimination, not compulsion.

Nothing in this world is as unstable as the three *gunas*. For stability, the noble spirit of self-sacrifice is the only medicine. If everyone in the world possessed wealth and fame, and all their worldly desires were fulfilled, all of mankind in this world would be enveloped in darkness. For the regeneration of people as real sons of Bharata, many social service programs must be undertaken. Amma is praying that all of you become such egoless, self-sacrificing persons and come forward to fulfil the great task of bringing peace and light to the world.

We are all divine souls, identical with the Supreme. We have come from the eternal *Om* and have entered this physical cage of the body. Our soul is beginningless, endless, eternal, complete, omnipotent, omnipresent, and omniscient! Let us meditate on this, experience the Self, and live in this world peacefully. Give up all negative attitudes—disappointment, submissiveness, afflictions and attachments—that weaken your mind. If you cannot do so, put them in my lap and I will burn them all.

Meditate on the vital force of *Pranavam* with a pure and strong diamond-like mind. When you do so, physical consciousness and the sense of time will vanish. You will feel the subtle body gently rising and floating. One who wants to end the grief of imprisonment in this body-sheath, and to end the cycle of birth and death filled with disappointments and fear, must merge in *Pranavam*.

Pranavam, the all-comprising vital force is all-knowing, all-powerful and entirely whole. Disappointments, sighs, grief and mental disturbances cannot enter the kingdom of peace that is *Om*. That is the state of liberation. Those who experience this *Pranavam* attain the Supreme. Human life is more precious than all the riches in this entire world. Human life will lose its sanctity the day it is bereft of morality. Every human must cultivate inner purity and moral strength. Every word of those who possess the supreme power and wealth of self-sacrifice can transform human beings into moral entities. Purity and righteousness are the vital nerves that nourish and strengthen this world. If the true well being of humanity is desired, unity must develop in all of us. We should become one in *dharma*, moral behavior, and *tyaga*, sacrifice. We should walk with the two blessed feet of righteousness and self-sacrifice. Our souls and minds should become one. Our thoughts, words and deeds must be in harmony. All humans can be united in the divine path only when they realize that everyone is an inseparable part of the same supreme Self. Only then can they live as one soul with a single mind, travelling on the same divine path. That is the real divine life. We can achieve nothing by quarrels, differences, desires and hatred. If dwelling only on small issues becomes our goal, nothing can be achieved in this world, and peace will ever remain an unattainable dream—a Utopia beyond our reach. The key to renaissance is hidden in unity only.

The peace and purity obtained by meditating on *Pranavam* take the seeker to the outer boundary of the dark realms of ignorance. That boundary glows with the self-effulgent knowledge of the Supreme. This knowledge of the Supreme, this Self, this glow of *Om*, cannot be imagined. It cannot be expressed in words. It is peace and tranquility supreme, a pleasant effulgent flame of light that makes one fearless. It is known and experienced in deep *samadhi*. The glow of *Om* is pure eternal bliss, the eternal total knowledge of the Self.

We do not need a lamp to see the sun. It is enough to remove the curtain between the sun and our eyes. The sun will immediately appear to us in all its glory.

If the curtains of the mind—the ego, the intellect, and all the good and bad thoughts—are removed, then only will the natural self-effulgent glow of *Pranava*, the soul, be revealed like the radiant glow of the sun. Just as the soul is not confined to the Earth, the sun or the moon, so also is the glow of *Om* the same within us and without—in all names and forms. It is Truth—it is non-dual, constant, motionless, fearless and effulgent—it is the Supreme. It is changeless, firm and eternal.

At the moment of Self-Realization, man leaves the human plane and merges with the limitless center of divine force, like a river merging in the ocean. He then experiences the infinite, formless state. That state is known as *nirvikalpa*, without any movement of the mind. In that state, there is no creation, existence or dissolution. It is the highest state, far beyond everything. No words can explain or describe it. None at all! This is absolutely true.

Earth, water, fire, air and space—all these five elements—all moving and non-moving things in creation may come to an end one day, but the soul is eternal. It is never destroyed, it never ends. There is no death for the soul.

Dear Children,

The foundations of spiritual life in our ancient country, Bharata, are very strongly constructed, having the strength of diamond-like righteousness. The valuable axioms of life laid down in *Sanatana Dharma* very clearly give you complete freedom. Do not accept the thoughts expressed by Amma, do not follow the concepts Amma has put before you. Use your own discretion and discrimination, open your mind fully and completely. Open the eye of wisdom. Do not act in blind faith, but go forward with self-confidence and self-conviction.

Remove all the inner impurities with meditation on *Pranavam*; immerse yourself in that great effulgent light. Be perfect and let the Soul shine brightly. Give fullness to the most important objective—the spiritual advancement of human life.

Dear children, go forward with discrimination. You *have* to go forward. Do not worry about what is past. Move ahead without looking or turning back. You have to blossom into the completely knowledgeable, well-disciplined children of Bharata. Your Mother wishes that you move forward in this world, attain the knowledge of the Self and live in eternal bliss!

There is nothing that you cannot achieve in this world if you practise *sadhana* with patience, strong discipline, and undeterred determination. Bhagiratha, by his untiring efforts, brought the holy Ganga from Heaven to the Earth.

Vishvamitra, by his great penance, attained victory over his anger and other negative qualities and finally experienced *Brahmattva sthiti*, oneness with cosmic Consciousness. If you work with your right hand, you will most naturally hold victory with your left. Of all the victories in life, victory over ignorance is the real victory. You all have to attain this victory. You *must* attain it!

- ❖ Ignorant people argue too much.
- ❖ Intelligent people converse.
- ❖ Seers, the wise ones, live in the power of silence.

You should all become such powerful, self-knowledgeable, self-realized souls!

Hari Om Tat Sat!

DIVINE MESSAGE

Message given by Bhagavati Sri Sri Sri Vijayeshwari Devi on 26th April 1990, at Ravindra Bharati, Hyderabad.(abb.)

Blessed Children of the Divine,
My heartfelt blessings and motherly love to you all.

Bharata, India, is a land that the ancient *rishis* sanctified with their *tapas*, penance. It is a sacred land from which the nectar of the *Upanishads* originated. The divine principle, "Service to humanity is service to God" has been put into practice by the people of Bharata. Divine incarnations have appeared in this sacred land of peace.

We are indeed fortunate to have taken birth in this country where women of the highest spiritual caliber manifested. Only souls with merits accumulated through millions of past births are born on this sacred soil.

This land of peace now faces many intricate problems due to the ways of modern life. Misunderstandings, intolerance, non-cooperation etc. are prevalent. We cannot go back to the lifestyle of the ancients—living in forests on roots and herbs. However, we *can* attain peace in our lives by practicing spiritual disciplines such as prayer, meditation, performance of good deeds, and leading a life of selfless service.

Anger, abusive words and excitement are signs of inner weakness. Negative feelings reveal weak moral values. Quarrels are examples of cultural bankruptcy. Lack of unity is the root cause of all miseries. Absence of mutual cooperation leads to failure in all endeavors.

A country is the integration of many millions of families. Without wisdom, misunderstandings develop. Men of wisdom do not take part in quarrels. Even a small family disintegrates due to lack of unity. If we cannot achieve cooperation in our families, how can we bring about unity and cooperation in the nation? The country whose *vedic* culture is the foundation of world culture; the country that laid down, ages ago, the principles of peaceful coexistence; the sacred land where the holy *rishis* inspired nectar-like human relations, themselves leading a simple and cooperative life—this country is now like a broken necklace, all of its priceless pearls of wisdom scattered. My wish is to re-integrate all the discarded and scattered spiritual traditions. We should all work hard for the creation of a new world where every human is equal, and move towards a new society infused with the spirit of universal brotherhood and peaceful coexistence.

The Lord, *Paramatma*, is the personification of divine love—a love beyond description. The foundations of divine love are purity and selflessness. Giving unconditional love to all is perfection. The eternal Self is the very embodiment of impartial, natural, boundless divine love. Such unbiased unconditional love is, in fact, hidden deep inside every created being. It has been covered by the ego. Divine love is a ray of the Supreme—it is eternal peace.

If we cultivate impartial love towards all living beings, develop compassion, service-mindedness and self-sacrifice, we can soften our heart and purify ourselves. This will lead us to absolute bliss. For the heart that opens to divine love becomes the temple of God. *Paramatma* manifests and resides in the pure heart full of love.

Humanity will perish when people start proclaiming the superiority of *their* God and religion over others, because such discrimination will lead to disturbances, enmity and intolerance. Such consequences wound my heart very deeply. Wars, which cause untold destruction in the world, should be avoided at all costs. Everyone should work for peace and the welfare of all beings. Real religion is not enshrined in rituals, formalities, traditions or beliefs.

The aim of true religion is to cross the barriers of the senses and, with divine love, see the *Para Brahma* in every atom of the universe. Such a vision leads to feelings of universal brotherhood. Then we see the down-trodden and the uplifted, the distressed and the happy, the educated and the uneducated, as also all dumb creatures like reptiles, cheetahs, cattle—the whole animal kingdom—as forms of the same *Para Brahma*. Realization of the Supreme in all beings is the essence of real religion. That essence also recognizes that all names and forms emanate from *Para Brahma* alone. The religion we need today is one that preaches the oneness of all, and enables us to work together towards universal brotherhood and the welfare of mankind.

Committing sins, seeking shelter from the Divine for protection, and repeating one's mistakes is not religion. Every true child of God should have a strong will, indomitable self-confidence, tranquility of mind, an interest in spirituality and a deep longing for Self-Realization.

Those who have taken ultimate refuge in God, unmindful of their worldly problems, will attain eternal peace and absolute bliss. Most hypocritical are those who are unable to see their own weaknesses, yet are always ready to criticize others. A seeker must avoid this tendency.

The first and foremost duty of human beings is to use all their energies to serve the afflicted with love. God dwells in the heart of every human being. One should surrender all one's problems at the feet of the Lord. By lighting the eternal lamp of love in the heart, and by developing complete faith in the lotus feet of God—the Absolute, the blissful Supreme Self—one can scale the ultimate peak of Self-Realization!

Life is a mixture of happiness and pain. A seeker who faces all problems resolutely and calmly, utilizing his time in the quest of the Divine, is a hero. Do not be overcome by minor problems. A piece of cotton will be carried far away by a small gust of wind. But a great mountain will not budge an inch when lashed by a storm. A true devotee of God remains unmoved under all circumstances.

You will face many difficult situations and tests. Through constant remembrance of God, the heart will get stabilized and problems will cease to bother you. A heart that remembers God constantly becomes steady and begins to overflow with divine love. A person with such a heart weeps when he sees others in pain.

When equanimity develops in a seeker, he is filled with divine love. Even if the entire world abuses or tortures him, like an immobile mountain, he pardons all his opponents with compassion and continues to help others. A person with equality of vision, even if he belongs to one's own family, should be regarded as a holy man. Such pure ones are the embodiments of the glory and tranquillity of the Divine! A mother experiences immense joy when she loves her child, because she gave him birth. Similarly, an illumined soul enjoys even greater happiness when he sees all beings as reflections of his own Self; and loves them as his own Self. In such a state not even an atom of selfishness exists. There is no perception of differences—there is no place for "me" and "mine."

Love for one's family is defined as attachment. But when we see all beings as God and love them, such love is transformed into love for Divine Mother.

❖ Attachment to the body leads to bondage.
❖ Universal love is the sign of liberation.

The greatness of a person does not depend upon his wealth, high position, name or fame. It lies in the nature of his heart. A man is really great when his heart has been sanctified and purified, and he has become the sacred confluence of forgiveness, mercy and humility. Such persons love and serve society as doctors, lawyers, judges, peasants, political leaders and spiritual people. They never create problems for others—they are always involved in solving others' problems.

There are two kinds of people in the world. The first suffer from hard-heartedness, impatience, discontent and lack of peace. The second are full of compassion, patience and selflessness. The former cause quarrels, disturbances and sorrow in society. The latter spread tolerance, tranquillity and happiness everywhere. Those who have attained liberation and eternal bliss impart happiness to others—they are truly great. I pray that each and every one of you attains that greatness.

Realization of the Truth depends on living a righteous life. There can be no compromise between truth and untruth —they are like light and darkness. One must have absolute purity in order to attain Self-Realization and merge with the Supreme.

When the mind becomes as clean as a polished mirror, the refection of God shines in it very naturally. Just as the sun is clearly visible in a cloudless sky, the light of the Divine radiates from the purified heart.

You may be a great scholar of the scriptures; you may have performed years of *tapas* in solitary places; you may have visited holy places and taken baths in many sacred rivers—you may even be able to perform miracles. But if you have no compassion for the poor, the sick and the suffering, all your achievements are useless.

The real abode of God is in the heart that radiates equal love for all. God exists in everyone, and the devotee with a pure heart loves and respects everyone as God. The face of such a pure person glows with a golden luster. Such people live only to serve others without any expectation for worldly gains. They are the saviors and protectors of the world. My earnest desire is that every one of you should become such a savior. My meditation and my prayers are for this purpose only.

Selfless service soothes the heart and fills it with peace. We should not even remember that we have helped anyone. Just as the sun very naturally gives light to the world, it should be the natural duty of every individual to serve society. There should be no pride in our heart because we have helped others. We should feel happy that we have been able to discharge our duty as human beings.

If we serve others seeing them as forms of God, the river of divine love will flow uninterruptedly and effortlessly from our hearts without our knowledge. We will be filled with indescribable peace, eternal satisfaction and bliss.

For some time in this modern age, the messages of great sages were neglected. The *rishis* who wrote the *Upanishads* conducted research in order to understand the basics of science relating to the universe. They realized that God was the root cause of all creation. They conversed with God in meditation in the subtle form. By following the teachings of the holy *rishis* we can understand the eternal Truth; we can achieve the ultimate aim of life. They taught humanity how to live in this world in harmony. They laid down guidelines for the training of the mind. They also pointed out that the true aim of life is the achievement of tranquillity and wisdom—knowledge of the Self. If we follow the teachings of the ancient sages we can tread the path of Truth and attain Self-Realization.

You should be humble and selfless. Frustrations and problems will upset you and fear will disturb your peace of mind. God alone has the power to free you from these obstacles. The whole world may reject you, but the God in whom you have faith will never let you down. The moment you think about God's love and compassion, your mind will become tranquil. Man's strongest shield during difficult times is God.

God is not far from us—He rests eternally in the hearts of all creatures. Those who do not recognize this truth suffer many difficulties. Those who want liberation from worldly bondage must meditate constantly upon the supreme Spirit. Then only will they have peace and bliss in their lives. They will also realize *Para Brahma*.

Sadhana, regular spiritual practice, purifies both body and mind and makes the ego vanish. The seeker feels that he is not the doer, he is only an instrument in the hands of God. This feeling fills his heart with love. Life without divine love is like a beautiful flower without fragrance, a pond without water or the sky without the sun. The one power that binds all of creation together is divine love. Divine love is the embodiment of Divine Mother Herself.

A devotee must have two important qualities—mercy and forgiveness. His heart should weep for another's pain. Helping anyone in distress—with no thought of caste, creed or religion—is true worship of the Almighty.

When the negative qualities such as hard-heartedness and selfishness etc. die due to *sadhana*, divine bliss moves into the purified heart very fast. The hard heart withers like a tender leaf, unable to withstand the speed of incoming divine qualities, and divinity shines in it like the glowing rays of precious gems.

We may consider something to be important today, but it may seem unimportant the next day. In this wonderful world we observe that the images of yesterday are replaced by the new images of today. In this strange world-play nothing is permanent except the Truth.

While everything revolves and undergoes fast changes, the Truth remains calm, undaunted and peaceful—at a lofty height which cannot be challenged. Truth alone is the basis of the entire universe.

- ❖ Truth is the state of a pure mind.
- ❖ Truth is bliss and peace.
- ❖ Truth is knowledge and power.
- ❖ Truth is divine love.
- ❖ Truth is God.

Therefore, when Truth, in the form of divine love, enters all creatures in this world, everyone is filled with peace and happiness. Every being is in bliss. Then everything attains a universal character and we experience a close affinity with all existence.

We should never lose faith in the deity we worship. We should maintain our faith throughout life. This is real religion. Is there a better religion than peace and love? When we cultivate these divine qualities we change from imperfect to perfect. From being incomplete, we become complete.

We need perfect purity of body and mind. Purity is the same for both men and women. A pure heart is the abode of eternal peace. The heart filled with love and compassion shines like moonlight and envelops the entire universe with its cooling rays. The human body is a wonderful instrument in the hands of Divine Mother. Through it She displays Her power. She transforms it into Her own temple. By maintaining purity and living with the motto, "Service to man is Service to God," let us all make our lives truly worthy.

Om Shanti!

Sri Karunamayi's Mission

SRI KARUNAMAYI - A Biography

SRI KARUNAMAYI'S WISH

Mother has devoted Her life to promoting individual and international peace, along with the universality of religion. Mother has also dedicated Herself to preserving and sharing *Bharatiya Adhyatmika Samskriti* or Indian Spiritual Culture, and the eradication of human suffering and illiteracy.

In Her native land, Mother's greatest aspiration is that everyone should be made to realize their responsibility in maintaining the sanctity of the spiritual life of the country and protecting its rich heritage. This includes the molding of children to make them worthy of this great tradition.

In this modern age, where there has been a deterioration in the cultural values followed in ancient times, Mother strongly advocates the deep study of those scriptures of *Bharata Mata,* Mother India, expounded by the great *rishis,* whose only aim was the welfare of all living beings in the universe. She feels that this inherent treasure of India should be explored and learned, so as to develop a tranquil society of peaceful coexistence. It is Her wish to spread these teachings from the Himalayas to Kanya Kumari, the length and breadth of India, as well as to the far reaches of the globe, in ways that can easily be understood by every man, woman and child.

Concerning education, Amma has great sympathy for those poor and helpless children who are not getting proper schooling. She therefore calls upon all women's and youth organizations to create special cells in their centers to reach such unfortunate souls and to provide them with educational facilities. In fact, She says that all leaders of Bharata, India, should dedicate themselves to serve this cause. Those who have already started on this path are obviously service-minded and show their commitment to the welfare of the nation.

In any society, achievement is possible through training coupled with sacrifice and love. The axle of life in India is its spirituality, and its vision of unity and eternal peace. Sri Vijayeswari Devi ceaselessly calls for a society based on these ideals.

The heart of Sri Karunamayi is a golden temple of peace. She is a treasure-trove of universal love regardless of caste, creed, nationality or religion, working untiringly for universal peace and prosperity. Life without peace is a hell. Every human being needs peace, and many people in quest of such peace come to Mother.

The main wishes of Mother are that:

❖ The heart of every person should become the seat of God.
❖ Each person should strive to maintain peaceful coexistence.
❖ A war mentality should be discarded.
❖ *Ashrams* should conduct collective welfare activities.
❖ Liberal-minded philanthropists should come forward to offer their help.
❖ There should be increased emphasis on the spiritual heritage of India, and on spreading its precepts throughout the country and the world.
❖ Medical centers must be established to extend free health services to the needy.
❖ Shelters must be constructed for orphan girls.
❖ Leprosy rehabilitation camps must be set up.
❖ A refugee camp for women must be established.
❖ Schools and colleges are to be opened.
❖ Human values are to be protected.
❖ Spiritual discourses will inspire a peaceful daily life.

- ❖ Spiritual literature will be published to preserve Indian culture, and to share its essence with the world.
- ❖ Collective training branches are to be created for teaching the doctrine of love.
- ❖ Good people all over the world should cooperate to implement these aspirations.

SRI KARUNAMAYI - A Biography

AMMA'S CHARITABLE PROJECTS

Sri Mathrudevi Viswashanti Ashram (SMVA Trust):

Sri Mathrudevi Viswashanti Ashram Trust was established to advance the cause of peace on Earth by making the divine blessings and teachings of Sri Karunamayi available to the world. SMVA Trust promotes and supports activities that enable the spiritual, charitable and educational aspects of Sri Karunamayi's mission. Contributions to the Trust in the U.S. are tax deductible.

Sri Vijayeswari Devi Rural Institutions for Education and Medicine (SRIEM Foundation):

The mission of this Foundation is to construct and operate a hospital in the area of Penusila Kshetram where Sri Karunamayi performed Her *tapas*. There is an urgent need for hospital-based medical services for the impoverished people of this remote region.

This need became tragically apparent a few years ago, when a large number of people had assembled at Penusila for a religious festival. There, one of the attendees accidentally lit a large quantity of camphor, causing a fire that quickly spread through the entire area. Hundreds of people were caught in the flames. The intensity of the fire was such that even the temple idols melted. The cries of the victims were heard for a half-mile!

Those who were critically burned and suffering unbearably could receive no help.[5] The nearest town was

---

[5] See also "Bull–The Symbol of Forbearance," p. 36, and "Sri Dakshinamurti Rupini," p. 99.

fifty miles away, there was no phone to contact anyone, and even basic first aid care was not available nearby.

Local primary health centers are not equipped to handle the daily needs of the people, let alone emergencies. Presently, the population of over 300 villages must travel over fifty miles to the nearest hospital at Nellore. During times of crises and medical emergencies, this journey is impossible.

To rectify this unfortunate lack of medical care, the SRIEM Foundation has assumed responsibility for constructing a 100-bed hospital at Rapur Town, Nellore District, about 15 miles from Penusila Kshetram. Seventeen acres of land adjacent to the main road connecting Rapur to Gudur has been acquired for this purpose.

The hospital will have medical services such as operation theaters for General Surgery, Pathology and Microbiology Laboratories, basic diagnostic equipment and facilities for dental treatment and ophthalmology. Such a hospital facility will act as a referral resource for primary health care centers in the region. It will provide a setting for complementary health care treatment and train indigenous health care paraprofessionals. These local recruits can, in turn, provide counseling to the village population in basic sanitation, nutrition, maternity and childcare. The hospital also proposes to have a mobile medical facility to cater to the needs of remote villages. For more information regarding the hospital project, please visit our website.

Sri Karunamayi Free School:

From its inception in the 1980's, Amma's Free School, Karunamayi Vidyalayam, was founded on Amma's vision that knowledge is the door to freedom and that educating children is the key to the upliftment of the whole village.

In the early years, Amma's School was located on the Penusila Ashram grounds and run by Ammamma, Amma's mother, with the assistance of a few devotees. Local tribal children from several surrounding villages attended and classes were held out of doors, weather permitting. However, as the school gained a reputation for its scholastic discipline, achievement and value-based teaching, more parents wanted to enroll their children.

In the 1990's, land containing a small three-sided structure was purchased only a few kilometers from the Ashram. This became the site of Amma's Free School. As the school's attendance and population grew, another vacant but small building was lent to SMVA Trust by the Andhra Forest Department. Today the student population stands at about 250. It has doubled from last year when a student from the school stood first in the district in the year-end annual statewide exams. Students range in age from five to thirteen years, from the first to seventh standard (grade), and Amma plans each year to add another level of instruction. All are offered a curriculum which features classes in math, science, reading, world affairs, social skills, English, Telugu and Hindi languages, alongside Sanskrit chanting and the spiritual disciplines of meditation, *japa* and *yoga*. The school provides free tuition, uniforms and books.

Currently the growing school has many needs. One of these is a new, larger and enclosed school building to ensure protection from theft and from the intense heat in the summer and the twice-yearly monsoons. A dining room is also very much a priority. Presently, students either bring their lunches or leave to go home for their meals if they live close by. Watchman's quarters and a dormitory for teachers are also needed. Most of the faculty now live in Gudur, the nearest town, and due to the bad condition of the roads, travel time on the bus takes them up to four hours daily.

The good news is that in order to serve the children and to facilitate the growth of Karunamayi Vidyalayam—its buildings, books and supplies, and teachers' salaries—SMVA Trust has set up a program whereby interested people can, through donation, sponsor a child's education for a year. This project is especially dear to the heart of Amma's elder sister, Sushilakkaiah. Please check our website for specific information about Amma's Free School.

Peace Village:

After visiting the West, Sri Karunamayi resolved that an oasis with powerful and pure vibrations would be created to facilitate the elevation of sincere spiritual seekers. Thus, the concept of the Peace Village was born.

The Peace Village is located approximately 15 miles south of Bangalore in a serene and idyllic environment free from the pollution, noise and stress of modern urban life. It provides a harmonious and intimate setting from which Amma can conduct Her teachings. It will be, above all, a place for people to deepen their meditation practice in a powerful, spiritually charged atmosphere. Amma will also maintain a residence at the Peace Village.

The Peace Village will be a community of people enlivened by the spirit of *karuna,* compassion. Residents will have the opportunity to expand and enrich their lives through a variety of programs, including meditation courses with Sri Karunamayi, an *ayurvedic* center, a *yoga* training center and Sanskrit classes, as well as workshops on *vastu,* the Indian science of architecture and space, and *jyotish,* or *vedic* astrology. All these will be offered on a registration basis after the Peace Village opens in early 2003. Check our website for more information.

Internet Website & Bookstore:

For your convenience, SMVA Trust has produced a beautiful and interactive website. Our website presents the latest information regarding Amma's mission and teachings, details regarding her annual tours to the West, and includes regular updates on all the inspiring projects mentioned here. Our website address is **www.karunamayi.org**. We invite you to browse through the many exciting selections there.

One section of the website is the SMVA Bookstore. Here you can find an easy way to review our bookstore inventory and to place an order for any item listed there. The Bookstore contains books and their reviews, CDs, audio and videotapes, and pictures of Sri Karunamayi.

Purna Prajna:

Purna Prajna is the Ashram's quarterly magazine, published by Swami Vijayeswarananda. Every issue has a special message from Sri Karunamayi, along with an inspirational article written by Mother. Each one is a jewel, revealing new facets of spirituality. The magazine also features articles on the spiritual history of India, scriptures, sages, and devotees' experiences, accompanied by many new and beautiful colored photographs. Reading *Purna Prajna* is a wonderful way to stay in touch, as it includes Amma's itinerary and upcoming tour schedules, Ashram news, and a calendar of events. For subscription information, please visit our website.

Retreats:

Sri Karunamayi counsels us to achieve higher levels of consciousness through the regular practice of meditation, and suggests one to two hours' daily practice. It is meditation, She says, which gives peace of mind, concentration, self-confidence and self-control. It liberates us from worldly concerns and bestows divine wisdom.

So that we might refine our inner experience and progress rapidly along the path to Self-Realization, Amma offers us the opportunity to attend meditation retreats with Her. Mother welcomes all Her children who are interested in meditation. Please visit our website for the latest announcements regarding Sri Karunamayi Meditation Retreats in India and the United States.

SRI KARUNAMAYI - A Biography

SRI KARUNAMAYI'S ASHRAMS

Bangalore, the garden city of the South Indian state of Karnataka, has been blessed by Mother, to be the location of Her second *ashram,* Karunamayi Shanti Dhama. This new *ashram* of Amma's, located in Ashoknagar, near N. R. Colony, a southern section of the city, has been constructed on a site generously donated by one of Amma's philanthropic devotees. It includes a large sanctuary, with a prayer hall and *homa kunda.* In this hall, Amma gives Her spiritual discourses. Daily *pujas* and special programs are also conducted here. Apart from the residential area on the upper floor, are offices and a bookstore.

The Bangalore Ashram has also undertaken the humanitarian project of providing free medical services to the poor and needy at Pavamanapura, a small village south of Bangalore. Free medical camps are held there every Sunday, where medicines are distributed free of cost. The large number of people taking advantage of the medical camps stands as a testimony to the success of this project.

Her Holiness Bhagavathi Sri Sri Sri Vijayeswari Devi's first *ashram*, Sri Mathrudevi Viswashanti Ashram, was established in the sylvan surroundings of Penusila Kshetram, Nellore District, Andhra Pradesh, in 1980.

"Feed the poor, hungry and helpless," is the call given by Amma in every message. In 1978, in Ahobala, Sri Karibasappa and other devotees distributed food to over a *lakh* of people and in this program, Amma took the initiative to serve the meal. Right from the inception of Her Penusila Ashram in 1980, daily feeding has been one of its essential programs. From that time, a devotee named Sister Prashanti has been a steady contributor from her hard earnings toward food to serve those coming for the *darshan* of Mother.

During *Navaratri* celebrations in 1985, Sri Vijayeswari Devi expressed Her wish that Ashram feeding should be done in such quantity that the water filtered out of cooked rice should flow like the water of the Kanva River. As a result, the Sri Vijayeswari Devi Nitya Annadana Padaka was created.

The responsibility for this permanent program for daily meals is shouldered by many selfless devotees. Begun under the direction of the late Smt. Annapurnammagaru, the blessed mother of Sri Vijayeswari Devi, today Smt. Revathamma, Amma's younger sister, is selflessly continuing the tradition by providing food as needed for any and all villagers and pilgrims. For all-round improvement in this activity, the members of Sri Vijayeswari Universal Integration Women's Organization have also been especially diligent.

Yet another major venture embarked upon in the Penusila Ashram is the magnificent Bharata Mata Mandir. In Her discourses, Amma lays special emphasis on *Bharatiya Adhyatmika Samskriti* and, in order to highlight and rejuvenate India's great cultural heritage, a *mandir* is being constructed. This temple, dedicated to Bharata Mata, Mother India, built in a place where the *sapta rishis,* the seven great sages, meditated, is the only one of its kind in the country. The *mandir* offers many unique sculptures, over 5,000 rare *salagramas* and, at ground level, a capacious, soundproof marble meditation hall. Its foundation is built upon *crores* of writings of the sacred *mantra, "Om Sri Lalitamba"* by devotees from around the world, mixed with sacred *kumkum* and *vibhuti* from *Sri Lalita pujas.* The work on this *mandir,* by Mother's grace, is nearly complete.

Currently, the Penusila Ashram is utilized for meditation retreats and special functions for local residents. Please visit our website for further information.

CONTACT INFORMATION

Please contact the following for more information about Sri Karunamayi:

India
Karunamayi Shanti Dhama
14/5, 6th Cross, Ashok Nagar,
B.S.K. 1st Stage, Bangalore 560050.
Email: smvaindia@karunamayi.org
Ph: 80 650-9588   Fax: 80 660-0518

United Kingdom
SMVA Trust (UK),
22 Lingwell Road,
London SW17 7NJ.
Email: smvauk@karunamayi.org

United States
SMVA Trust
21 Baldwin Hills Road
Millwood, NY 10546.
Email: smvaus@karunamayi.org
Ph: (914) 923-8327   Fax: (914) 923-8329

Appendix

APPENDIX

The Spiritual Tradition of India

The holy land of India has a great and ancient tradition, the beginning of which is not even conceivable. The great incarnations Sri Rama and Sri Krishna, whose gospels of *Ramayana* and *Mahabharata* have become guiding lights for the entire world, chose to take birth in this land. Lord Krishna pronounced in the *Bhagavad Gita* that He would manifest time and again to protect the good and to punish the evil. This same promise of eternal return is made by Divine Mother in the *Markandeya Purana*.

Indian heritage is beautifully bedecked with innumerable holy personalities who worshipped Divine Mother, such as Ramakrishna Paramahamsa, Sharada Devi, Swami Vivekananda, Ramana Maharshi, Sri Aurobindo, Sainath of Shirdi, Radhakrishna Swamiji, and others. There are also *lakhs* of illumined souls who are dedicated to seclusion. Their silent penance has contributed magnificently to the spiritual acumen of India.

The Significance of Navaratri

All over India, beginning in the brighter half of the seventh month of the Hindu calendar, (September-October), known as *Ashwayuja masa,* the people thankfully remember God's promise—to conquer evil and protect the good—with prayers of sincere supplication and devotion. This celebration is known in South India as *Navaratri,* or the Festival of Nine Nights. Three days are dedicated to the worship of Durga, three to Lakshmi, and three to Saraswati.

It culminates on the tenth day, or *Dashehra*, commonly celebrated as *Vijaya Dashami*, "the victory of good over evil on the tenth *(dasha)* day." Though in North India Sri Rama often assumes more importance for the first eight days, in South India, *Sri Devi,* Divine Mother, is honored throughout.

According to the scriptures, long, long ago evil in the form of demons threatened the stability and even the existence of the Gods. The *Markandeya Purana* mentions two such seemingly invincible and evil creatures called Chanda and Munda. In desperation, the *Devas* appealed to the Goddess who, in Her fierce form, after a long battle, destroyed the evil which had threatened to engulf creation. Following Her victory on the tenth day Mother Divine, Devi, Herself assumed a form that combined both the demons' names. From then on She is thankfully propitiated as *Chamundeshwari.*

The Greatness of Divine Mother as Lalita Devi

It is very difficult to imagine Divine Mother for She is the formless One. However, because She is One, it is true that She is also everything. Thus She has many *rupas* or forms. The ancient scriptures which espouse the *Sanatana Dharma* of India are permeated with the assurance that Divine Mother in the form of *Lalita Devi* is solely responsible for the creation, preservation, and destruction of the universe. This process continues endlessly like the rise and fall of the waves in the ocean. The ten incarnations, or *dashavataras* of Lord Vishnu were themselves created from *Lalita Devi's* ten fingernails. In fact, She has entrusted the creation, preservation and destruction of the universe to the *Trimurti*—Brahma, Vishnu and Maheshwara, (Siva). *Sri Lalita* is the all-pervasive witness of the universe, which is totally dependent on Her.

Serving the holy feet of *Sri Lalitamba* is a path to salvation. It is only after taking *crores* of precious human births with records of good deeds that one even gets the desire to worship Her. It is after reading philosophic literature that one is able to serve the Divine Mother. Such a person will not be in any kind of bondage. The Mother blesses such a seeker. She takes Her abode on the tongues of Her devotees in the form of Saraswati Devi. Lakshmi Devi remains forever in the houses of ascetics who are devoted to Mother *Lalita*.

The worship of Divine Mother bestows longevity, strength, courage, wealth, food, progeny and happiness. Poverty and untimely death will not be suffered. Success also will knock at one's doorstep, bringing with it awards and rewards. One will be blessed with the *darshan* of Mother Divine—so difficult to obtain. The scriptures declare that serving the Great Mother will lead the devotee to a state of total desirelessness and freedom from birth and death—Self-Realization, the ultimate goal of human life.

PRONUNCIATION KEY

This pronunciation key applies only to the *"Stotra, Shloka and Kirtana"* section. In the Glossary only the long ā and ū marks have been used.

Letter	Sounds Like	Letter	Sounds Like
a	u in s**u**n	ḍ	d in **d**ove
ā	a in f**a**ther	ḍh	dh in Go**dh**ead
i	i in f**i**ll	t *	soft t as in French '*tu*'
ī	ee in f**ee**l	th	th in **th**umb
u	u in f**u**ll	d	th in **th**e
ū	oo in f**oo**d	dh	theh in brea**the h**ard
ṛ *	ri in **ri**g, *or*	n	n in **n**umber
	roo in b**roo**k	p	p in **p**un
e	ay in m**ay**	ph	ph in u**ph**ill
ai	ai in **ai**sle	b	b in **b**ird
o	o in r**o**se	bh	bh as in jo**b h**unt
ow	ow in c**ow**	m	m in **m**other
ung	ung in s**ung**	y	y in **y**earn
ḥ *	ha in a**ha**	r	r in **r**un
k	k in **k**ite	l	l in **l**ove
kh	kh in sil**k h**at	v	v in **v**ove *or*
g	g in **g**um		w in **w**orld
gh	gh in lo**g h**ut	ś *	sh in **sh**un - Amma often pronounces this as "sa" or "sya"
c	ch in **ch**urn		
ch	chh in cat**ch** her		
j	j in **j**ug	ṣ *	sh in mar**sh**
jh	dgeh in he**dgeh**og	s	s in **s**un
ṭ	t in **t**on	h	h in **h**oney
ṭh	th in an**t h**ill	jn *	ngy in si**ng y**our

* For details regarding correct pronunciation of these and other letters, see "Guide to Sanskrit Pronunciation" in the book *"Sanskrit Mantras, Verses and Hymns"* pages v, vi and vii.

Stotra, Shloka and Kirtana

STOTRA, SHLOKA AND KIRTANA

The following are listed alphabetically by the first word. Unless indicated otherwise, all verses are in Sanskrit. The International Standard of Sanskrit Transliteration has been used. Please refer to the Pronunciation Key.

Aruṇa bīja pūrṇa padmāsana samsthite
Hé svarṇāmbarāvṛte manohara manju gate
Udyana manojna smita pankaja manjulasye
Sampat pradāyini śrī vijayeśwarī lakshmī naumi nityam

I offer my eternal salutations to You, O Mother Vijayeswari Devi, the embodiment of Lakshmi Devi, who bestows all kinds of wealth on Her devotees. O Mother Divine, clad in golden raiment, You are seated in padmasana on a lovely red lotus. Your movements are enchanting, gentle and graceful, Mother, and Your soft smile is like the delicate lotus blooming at dawn.

Dāṛdrya Dahana Śiva Stotram

1. *Viśveśwarāya narakaṭnava tāraṇāya*
   Karṇāmṛtāya śaśi śekhara bhūṣṇāya
   Karpūra kānti dhavalāya jatā dharāya
   Dāṛdrya dukha dahanāya namaḥ śivāya

   Salutations to the great Lord Siva, who burns to ashes all our poverties and negativities. He is the sovereign ruler of the whole universe; His name is nectar to the ears; His complexion is fair and luminous as camphor, and His matted locks glow with the radiance of the crescent moon.

2. *Gaurī priyāya rajaniśa kalādharāya*
   Kālāntakāya bhujagādhipa kankaṇāya
   Gangā dharāya gaja rāja vimocanāya
   Dāṛdrya dukha dahanāya namaḥ śivāya

   Salutations to the great Lord Siva, who burns to ashes all our poverties and negativities. He is the beloved consort of Gauri, the golden-limbed divinity Parvati Devi. The delicate rays of the moon, king of the night, adorn His hair. He is known as Kalantaka, Lord of Time and Death, who wears the king of serpents as a bracelet, and the sacred Ganga in His matted locks. He is the merciful Lord who gave salvation to the King of Elephants.

3. Bhakti priyāya bhava roga bhayāpahāya
   Ugrāya durga bhava sāgara tāraṇāya
   Jyotirmayāya punarudbhava vāraṇāya
   Dāṛdrya dukha dahanāya namaḥ śivāya

Salutations to the great Lord Siva, who burns to ashes all our poverties and negativities. He loves pure devotion and removes all fear of samsara, the dreadful disease of worldliness. The fierce and terrible Lord takes His devotees safely across the ocean of samsara. The effulgent Lord Siva saves us from rebirth.

4. Carmāmbarāya śava bhasma vilepanāya
   Bhālekṣaṇāya maṇi kuṇḍala maṇḍitāya
   Mañjīra pāda yugalāya jaṭā dharāya
   Dāṛdrya dukha dahanāya namaḥ śivāya

Salutations to the great Lord Siva, who burns to ashes all our poverties and negativities. He wears garments of skin. He wears His hair in a topknot and His whole body is smeared with ashes of burnt corpses. His ear ornaments sparkle with precious gems, and the divine dancer wears tinkling bells on His ankles.

5. Pañcānanāya phanirāji vibhūṣaṇāya
   Hemāṁśu kāya bhuvana traya maṇḍanāya
   Ānanda bhūmi varadāya tamo harāya
   Dāṛdrya dukha dahanāya namaḥ śivāya

Salutations to the great Lord Siva, who burns to ashes all our poverties and negativities. The Lord with five divine faces is adorned with ornaments of snakes. He protects the three worlds with His golden trident. Lord Siva removes the darkness of ignorance and leads His devotees to the land of bliss—eternal liberation!

6. Bhānu priyāya duritārṇava tāraṇāya
   Kālāntakāya kamalāsana pūjitāya
   Netra trayāya śubha lakṣaṇa lakṣitāya
   Dāṛdrya dukha dahanāya namaḥ śivāya

Salutations to the great Lord Siva, who burns to ashes all our poverties and negativities. The beloved and luminous adorable Lord —who carries us safely across the fearsome ocean of this world—is seated on a lotus. The embodiment of Time and Death, Lord Siva has

SRI KARUNAMAYI - A Biography

7. *Rāma priyāya raghunātha vara pradāya*
Nāga priyāya nāga rāja niketanāya
Puṇyāya puṇya caritāya surārcitāya
Dāṛdrya dukha dahanāya namaḥ śivāya

three divine eyes and His beautiful body bears all the auspicious signs.

Salutations to the great Lord Siva, who burns to ashes all our poverties and negativities. Sri Rama loves Him dearly, and was blessed by Him with a boon. His divine form is the home of the king of serpents and He is the beloved of all snakes. Worshipped by all the Gods, He is the very embodiment of sanctity and purity—all His actions are supremely pure.

8. *Mukteśwarāya phaladāya gaṇeśwarāya*
Gīta priyāya vṛṣabheśwara vāhanaya
Mātanga carma vasanāya maheśwarāya
Dāṛdrya dukha dahanāya namaḥ śivāya

Salutations to the great Lord Siva, who burns to ashes all our poverties and negativities. The supremely free Master of all beings, He grants the fruits of our actions. Lord Siva rides the divine bull, and wears an elephant skin. The great Lord loves song and music.

9. *Gaurī vilāsa bhuvanāya mahodayāya*
Pancānanāya śaraṇāgata rakṣakāya
Śarvāya sarva jagatādhipāya
Tasmai dāridrya dukha dahanāya namaḥ śivāya

—*Vasiṣṭha Muni*

The greatest of all beings, Lord Siva, is the joy of Gauri Devi's heart. The five-faced Lord is the compassionate protector of all who take refuge at His divine lotus feet. To that supreme sovereign of the world known as Sharva we offer our humble salutations and pray for the complete destruction of all our poverties and negativities.

Dīrghāyuṣmāna bhava

—*Sanskrit blessing*

May you be blessed with long life.

Garuḍācala śikhare ramye

I meditate on the gently smiling face of Sri Vijayeswari Devi, lovely

SRI KARUNAMAYI - A Biography

Deva devīm vijayeśwarīm *Dhyānoparata vāsinīm* *Smarāmi prasanna mukha pankajam*	as a lotus blossom. Though She is seated on the enchanting peak of the Garudachala Hills—deeply immersed in meditation—She pervades the whole cosmos!
Gomātā guha janma bhūḥ —*Sri Lalitā Sahāsranāma Stotra, shl.121*	Lalita Devi is the Mother of Speech and also the Mother of Lord Guha, Swami Karttikeya, Commander of the army of the Gods.
Jai saraswati namo namo tava caraṇam	Victory to You, and salutations again and again to Your divine lotus feet, O Mother Saraswati Devi!
Madhu vātā ṛtāyate *Madhu kṣaranti sindhavaḥ* *Madhvīr naḥ santvoṣadhīḥ* *Madhu nakta mutośaśo* *Madhumat pārthivam rajaḥ* *Madhu dyaur astu naḥ pitā* *Madhumanno vanaspatir* *Madhumān astu sūryāḥ* *Madhuvīr gāvo bhavantu naḥ* —*Ṛg Veda I: 90, 69*	May the breeze be as pleasant and sweet as honey; May the waters be as life-giving and sweet as honey; May the herbs be as palatable and sweet as honey; May the days and nights be as soothing and sweet as honey; May all earthly things be as enjoyable and sweet as honey; May heaven, the abode of our Father, be comforting and sweet as honey; May plants and trees be as fruitful and sweet as honey; May the sun be as invigorating and sweet as honey; May the cows produce milk as nourishing and sweet as honey
Mānasa bhajare guru caraṇam *Devī caraṇam praṇamāmyaham* *Karuṇāmayī caraṇam praṇamāmyaham* —*Śrī Karuṇāmayī bhajan*	O my mind, constantly remember and sing the praises of Sri Guru's feet. Offering my salutations at the divine lotus feet of Sri Vijayeswari Devi, the embodiment of Mother Divine, I place them in my heart, which She has purified

Mandāra kusuma priyā
—*Sri Lalitā Sahasranāma Stotra, shl.148*

Mother Sri Lalita Devi loves mandara blossoms, the fragrant flowers of the coral trees that grow in the celestial gardens of Indra, King of the Gods

Om hrīm srīm avyāja karuṇāmūrtayai namaḥ

Om Hrim, Srim! Salutations to the Mother who is the embodiment of compassion and whose love is most naturally boundless and unconditional!

Om muktā vidruma hema nīla dhavala chhāyair mukhai
Strīkṣaṇair yuktām indu nibaddha ratna makuṭām tattvārtha varṇātmikām
Gāyatrī varadābhayāṅkuśa kaśām śubhram kapālam gadām
Śaṅkham cakramadārvinda yugalām hastair vahantīm bhaje

—*Dhyāna śloka: Śrī Gāyatrī*

Om. Sri Gayatri Devi has five lovely faces that glow with the radiance of pearls, coral, gold, blue sapphires and diamonds. She has three divine eyes and wears the young crescent moon on Her crown, which sparkles with the nine precious gems. Sri Gayatri reveals the principle of supreme Consciousness and is the embodiment of the 24 syllables of the sacred Gayatri Mantra. The Divine Mother has ten hands, two of which are held in the varada and abhaya hasta mudras, hand gestures bestowing boons and freedom from fear. The others hold the spear, whip, skull, mace, conch, discus and two lotuses. I offer my deepest salutations to Mother Gayatri Devi.

Raśmi mantam samudyantam
Devāsura namaskṛtam
Pūjayasva vivasvantam
Bhāskaram bhuvaneśvaram

O most glorious and adorable rising Sun with millions of luminoush rays! All the Gods and demons worship You, O giver of light, as the eternal sovereign of the universe. You manifest in the form of all the divinities with Your countless, shining rays. Kindly protect all the

SRI KARUNAMAYI - A Biography

Sarva devātmako hyeṣa
Tejasvi raśmi bhāvanaḥ
Eṣa devāsuragaṇān
Lokān pātu gabhstibhiḥ
—*Āditya Hṛdayam, verses 67*

worlds, the Gods, the demons and all living creatures with Your divine rays of light!

Śrī rāma rāma rāmeti
Rame rāme manorame
Sahasra nāma tattulyam
Rāma nāma varānane

Lord Siva said, "O beautiful Parvati Devi! One should constantly and ceaselessly repeat the sacred name 'Rama, Rama, Rama....' One should lose oneself in this divine name. Repeating this great name just once is equal to chanting all the thousand names of Lord Vishnu."

Śrī rāma nāmalu śata koṭi
Oka oka peru bahutepi
—*Popular saying in Telugu*

Chanting "Rama" just once gives the merit of chanting any other divine name thousands of times

Śuddha vidyāṅkurākāra, dvija paṅkti dvayojjvala
—*Śrī Lalitā Sahāsranāma Stotra, shl.10*

Salutations to Sri Lalita Devi, whose beauty is enhanced by Her two rows of teeth, which resemble the sprouting of shuddha vidya, pure knowledge.

Glossary

SRI KARUNAMAYI - A Biography

GLOSSARY

Wherever possible, the etymology of the Sanskrit words has been given in parentheses. Meanings explained elsewhere in the glossary have been omitted. Telugu is the language of Andhra Pradesh and Amma's mother-tongue. Tamil is the language of Tamil Nadu.

abhaya hasta mudrā: (abhaya: fearless + hasta: hand + mudra) Symbolic gesture of sacred protection, in which the right palm of a deity or holy person is held up, facing outward. See: mudra.

abhishekam: Bathing or anointing a sacred image or symbol with panchamrita (five auspicious liquids) as a form of puja, worship.

āchamanam: Sipping water as an act of purification.

Ādi: The very first, primal.

Ādi Parā Shakti: (adi + para + Shakti) The primal energy, conceived of as feminine, beyond which there is no other power.

Advaita: (a: without + dvaita: duality. One without a second) The school of thought which believes that there is only one Reality— Brahman, the Absolute—and everything in the universe is a manifestation of this Reality. See: Vedanta.

Ahalyā: The wife of the sage Gautama, who was turned into a stone due to a curse. When Sri Rama touched this stone with His toe, she came to life again and was liberated. See: Rama.

Aham Brahmāsmi: (aham: I + Brahma + asmi: am) "I am verily Brahman!" One of the four maha vakyas, the great truths of the *Vedas*, stating that the individual soul and the supreme Soul are one and the same. This knowledge arises in the seeker at the time of Self-Realization.

ahimsā: (a: without + himsa: violence) Non-injury in thought, word and deed. Personified as the wife of Dharma. See: dharma.

AIIMS: All India Institute of Medical Sciences, a renowned teaching and medical hospital located in New Delhi.

Akhilāndeshwari: (akhila: the whole + anda: the egg of universe + Ishwari: supreme sovereign) Divine Mother, the supreme sovereign of the entire universe.

akkā: (Telugu) Elder sister.

akkāiāh: (Telugu) Respected older sister.

Alamelu Mangammā: (Telugu) Name for Divine Mother Lakshmi Devi (Padmavati), consort of Lord Venkateshwara at Tirupati (Tiruchanur). See: Padmavati

SRI KARUNAMAYI - A Biography

Ambā: Affectionate term for mother; Divine Mother.
Ambal: (Tamil) Amba.
Āmbikā: (Amba + ika: little) Little Mother: An intimate and endearing way of addressing Divine Mother.
Ammā: 1. "Mother" in many Indian languages. 2. Divine Mother. 3. Affectionate name for Sri Karunamayi.
Ammammā: (Telugu) Grandmother; Sri Karunamayi's mother.
āmra: Mango fruit; mango tree.
amrita(m): Nectar.
amrita putra: (amrita: eternal + putra: son) Immortal, divine son.
ānanda: Spiritual bliss. The bliss of the realized Self, which lies beyond all duality. Joy, happiness.
Āndāl: Great devotee poet saint of Sri Villiputur (near Madurai), found under a tulasi plant in the garden of a Vishnu devotee, Periyalvar, who reared her as his daughter. From childhood, she only longed to be one with Her beloved Lord Krishna, a wish that was fulfilled when she merged with His idol in Sri Ranganatha Temple (Tamil Nadu). See: Ranganatha Sai, Villiputur, Thiruppavai.
Annapūrnā, Annapūrneshwari: (anna: grain or food + purna: full; Ishwari: supreme ruler) Devi, who nourishes all beings.
Annapurnammā: Name of Sri Karunamayi's mother.
Antarayāmi: (Antara: inner, of the heart + yami: knower) The Lord who knows all the innermost thoughts of all beings.
Aprameyā: (a: without + prameya: measure) Boundless, inscrutable. Divinity or divine Consciousness which can never be measured.
ārati: Devotional waving of lights before a deity or holy person in which the deity represents the light of divine Consciousness and each lamp the individual soul seeking oneness with the Divine. This ritual is accompanied by songs of praise, offerings of flowers, camphor, incense and the ringing of bells.
archanā: Worship, respect paid to deities.
Arunāchala: (aruna: red + achala: mountain) Name of a sacred mountain in Tamil Nadu, said to be a form of Lord Siva Himself.
Ārya Devi: (Arya: revered, noble + Devi) Most revered Goddess.
Ashta Lakshmi: The eight auspicious forms of Lakshmi, (which vary according to different scriptures) are Adi: material happiness and spiritual bliss, Dhana: gold and material wealth, Dhanya: plentiful food grains, Gaja: animal wealth, Santana: progeny, Vara: courage and longevity, Vidya: wisdom and knowledge, and Vijaya: victory and success. She is also called Samudra Lakshmi because She emerged from the ocean. See: Lakshmi Devi.
ashtami: The eighth day in a lunar fortnight.

SRI KARUNAMAYI - A Biography

ashtottara: (ashta: eight + uttara: after + shat: 100). The ashtottara is a hymn consisting of 108 names glorifying a deity or holy person. Here "shat," signifying "one hundred," is understood.
ashvattha: Sanskrit name for the sacred pipal tree. See: pipal.
Āshvayuja māsa: (Ashwayuja + masa: month) Name of the first constellation, or the month of Ashwin. The month October/November in the Hindu lunar calendar.
ātmā: The individual soul.
Ātma(n): The supreme Soul, the Absolute.
ātma: (adj.) Of the soul.
ātma mādhuryam: (atma + madhuryam: sweetness) The divine sweetness of the soul.
ātma prakāsham: (atma + prakasham: light) The inner light, knowledge, of the soul.
ātma sahaja sthiti: (atma + sahaja: natural + sthiti) The original, pure and natural state of the soul.
Ātma Vidyā: (atma + vidya) Highest spiritual wisdom or knowledge of the Soul, leading to atma jnana.
Ātma jnāna: (atma + jnana) The supreme knowledge that everything is Soul, divine Consciousness.
ātmānanda: (atma + ananda) The supreme bliss of the soul experienced in samadhi, the state of Self-Realization. See: samadhi
āttā: Flour.
Aurobindo, Ghose Sri: (1872-1950) Freedom fighter who became a renowned spiritual leader; prodigious writer on yoga and founder of Pondicherry Ashram in South East India.
avagai: (Telugu) A special mango pickle.
avial: South Indian dish made with mixed vegetables and coconut sauce.
avidyā: (a: without + vidya: intelligence) Ignorance of the Truth due to illusion.
avyāja: Natural and unconditional.
Ayodhyā: Name of the capital city of the kingdom of Sri Rama, located in Uttar Pradesh. See: Rama.

Bādarāyana: Name of Vyasa, especially used for him as the reputed author of the Vedanta philosophy. See: Vedanta.
Badri(nath): Pilgrimage site near Rishikesh 10,000 ft. up in the Himalayas. There a jyoti, light, burns without ghee.
bāla: Child, young.
Bālamurugan Swāmi: Swami Vijayeswarananda. See: Murugan, Vijayeswarananda.
Bāli: A character in the Ramayana, also known as Vali who was the

SRI KARUNAMAYI - A Biography

monkey chieftain of Kishkindha.

Bāneshwara lingam: (< bana: elliptical) Elliptical polished lingam formed from natural white stone and considered most auspicious. See: Narmada Baneshwara lingam.

banyan: A huge Indian tree sacred to the Hindus. Its branches send down new roots to the ground.

Bhadrāchalam: The site of the famed Sri Rama temple in Andhra Pradesh built by Ramadas on the East bank of the Godavari River. The deity in the temple uniquely holds Lord Rama's bow and Lord Vishnu's conch and discus. See: Ramadas.

Bhagavad Gitā: (Song of the Lord) Important and revered Sanskrit epic poem of eighteen chapters, which contains the essence of the *Upanishads*. It is an exposition by Lord Krishna of the basic precepts of Hinduism or Sanatana Dharma, in response to questions posed by Arjuna, one of the Pandavas, on the battlefield at Kurukshetra. Centuries later, it is still an inspiration to seekers of Truth. See: *Mahabharata*, Sanatana Dharma.

Bhagavān: (< bhaj: to worship) 1. One who is worshipped as the supreme Lord. 2. The personal form of God possessed of the six qualities: full supremacy, righteousness, fame, prosperity, wisdom and discrimination.

Bhagavati: Glorious Goddess possessed of the six auspicious qualities. See: Bhagavan

Bhāgiratha: An ancient king of the solar dynasty, and the great-grandson of Sagara. By practicing severe austerities for thousands of years, he brought down the celestial river, Ganga, from heaven to Earth. His purpose was to purify the ashes of his 60,000 ancestors, the sons of King Sagara. Another name of the Ganga is Bhagirathi.

bhajan(s): Devotional hymn(s).

bhakta(s): Devotee(s).

bhakti: Devotion.

bhakti rasa: (bhakti: devotion + rasa: taste, essence) The sweet essence of devotion.

Bhakti vashyā: (bhakti: devotion + vashya: controlled) Divine Mother, who is captured by the true and deep love of the devotee.

Bharadwāja: A rishi to whom many vedic hymns are attributed. He was the son of Brihaspati, the purohita (family priest) of the Gods.

Bhārata: India, named Bharata varsha—today often called Bharat—after the brave and famous king, Bharata, who ruled the country in ancient times. He was a prince of the Puru branch of the Lunar dynasty and his descendants were the famous Kauravas and Pandavas whose exploits are described in the *Mahabharata*. See: *Mahabharata*.

SRI KARUNAMAYI - A Biography

Bhāratiya ādhyātmica samskriti: (Bharatiya: of Bharata, Indian + adhyatmic: pertaining to the Self + samskriti: culture). Indian spiritual culture. The precepts of Indian thought which believe that the universe and all that is in it is the Atman.
Bhāskara: (bhasa: light + kara: one who gives or makes) The Sun God, who gives light to the entire solar system.
bhava: The transitory world, which causes bondage for humans and is said to be an illusion.
bhāva: Feeling, mood or trance.
bhava roga: (bhava: illusion + roga: illness) The disease of worldliness.
Bhavāni: A name for Parvati Devi, consort of Siva or Bhava. She is the one who creates and dispels illusion.
Bhavatārini: (bhava + tarini: one who saves) Divine Mother, who saves us from the ocean of worldly existence.
bhikshām dehi: (bhiksham: alms + dehi: give) Please bless me/us with the alms of Your grace!
Bhima Shankari: (Bhima: formidable + Shankari: Siva's consort) The combined powerful form of Siva-Shakti. The Himachal Pradesh shrine of Sri Bhima Shankari is situated on a mountain in the Himalayas.
Bhū Devi: (Bhu: the Earth + Devi) The Goddess Mother Earth.
Bhuvah loka: (Bhuvah: the area between the Earth and Heaven + loka: world) One of the three worlds. See: loka.
bijākshara(s): (bija: seed + aksharas: letters or syllables) Mystical letters or syllables with special powers, which form the essential part of all mantras.
bijākshara mantra: (bijakshara + mantra) See: bijakshara.
bilva: A wood apple tree sacred to Lord Siva. Its leaves have three petals, signifying the three gunas. Offering the leaves in worship symbolizes offering one's sattvic, rajasic and tamasic qualities to the Lord. See: guna.
bindi: (drop: particle, spot) A decorative mark put between the eyebrows for beautification.
bindu: (drop: particle, spot) A symbol of highly concentrated divine energy. In the Sri Chakra, this central dot in the inmost triangle is the abode of bliss, symbolizing Siva-Shakti in union before manifestation.
Brahma(n): The Absolute, the one, self-existent Spirit without beginning or end, eternal, all-pervading and all-powerful. The Truth behind all manifestation.
Brahma Chaitanya Shakti: (Brahma + Chaitanya: Consciousness + Shakti) The conscious energy of Brahman, the Absolute.
Brahma Sūtras: (Brahma: the Absolute + sutras: aphorisms) A collection of aphorisms on the philosophy of Vedanta, also known

as *The Vedanta Sutras*, by Badarayana or Vyasa. See: Vedanta.
Brahma tattva: (Brahma: the Absolute + tattva: essence) The essence of the One, the Absolute.
Brahma tejas: (Brahma + tejas: radiance) The supreme and eternal effulgence of Brahman.
Brahma jñāna: (Brahma + jnana) Knowledge of the Absolute, Self-Realization.
Brahma jñāna svarūpini: (Brahma + jnana + svarupini: embodiment in female form) Devi, the personification of supreme knowledge.
Brahma jñāni(s): (Brahma + jnani) A knower of the Absolute, a self-realized being.
Brahmamayi: (Brahma + mayi: One who pervades) The supreme Self visualized in feminine form as divine Consciousness. Amma as the Absolute, not the physical form.
Brahmānanda: (Brahma + ananda) The bliss of supreme Consciousness.
Brahmānda Bhāndodari: (Brahmanda: the universe + bhanda: a vessel + odari: in the stomach) Divine Mother, who holds the whole universe within Her.
Brahma shakti: The vital energy of the supreme Self in feminine form.
Brahma shaktimayi: (Brahma + shakti + mayi: one who pervades) Devi is the embodiment of the divine Consciousness of Brahman.
Brahmatva sthiti: (Brahmatva: the essence of Brahman + sthiti: state, being established in) Being established in the essence of Brahman —the state of Self-Realization.
Brāhmi Chaitanyam: (Brahmi: Saraswati Devi, consort of Brahma, creative cosmic energy + chaitanyam: consciousness) Divine Mother as cosmic Consciousness.
Brāhmi/Brahma muhūrta: (Brahmi: Creative cosmic energy visualized as Divine Mother / Brahma: the Creator + muhurta: a period of time, according to Indian calculations, equal to 48 minutes) The early morning hour between 3:30-4:30 a.m., which is the best time for meditation. At this time, all the planets are divinely recharged with cosmic energy. The environment is peaceful and the body and mind are rested and revitalized after sleep. See: Brahmi Chaitanyam
brāhmic: Adj. for Brahman.
brāhmin: (A knower of Brahman) One who belongs to the learned class of priests or teachers, who know and teach sacred knowledge. They perform yajnas, daily pujas in temples as well as rituals for householders (e.g. marriage, sacred thread ceremony, last rites etc.).
Brihaspati Shāstra: (Brihaspati: the preceptor of the Gods + shastra) A treatise expounded by Brihaspati, the Guru and purohita or family priest of the Gods.

 **camphor:** (kapur) A natural aromatic compound from a tree that grows in Nepal. The product of this plant is used in religious ceremonies (where it burns, leaving no residue) and for medicinal purposes.

chaitanya: Consciousness.

chakra: (wheel; circle) The chakras are centers of the subtle energy, kundalini, in the subtle body of human beings. There are actually seven major chakras, but traditionally they are enumerated as the "shad chakras," referring to the six which are situated in the sushumna nadi. These are precisely described in tantric texts (scriptures of Shakti worship and kundalini yoga). They are envisioned as lotuses, with the number of petals and colors corresponding to the rate of vibration of each. The chakras are: the muladhara, svadhishthana, manipura, anahata, vishuddhi and ajna, respectively. 1) The muladhara or root chakra is situated at the base of the spine in the sushumna nadi. It is a bright red lotus of four petals and its bijakshara is "lam." 2) The svadhishthana chakra lies in the sushumna nadi near the reproductive organs and has six saffron orange petals. Its bijakshara is "vam." 3) The manipura chakra is situated in the navel region and is a golden yellow lotus with ten petals. Its bijakshara is "ram." 4) The anahata chakra lies in the region of the heart and has twelve leafy green petals. Its bijakshara is "yam." 5) The vishuddhi chakra lies at the base of the throat in the sushumna nadi. It is a sixteen-petalled lotus of a specially lovely blue. Its bijakshara is "ham." 6) The ajna chakra is situated between the eyebrows in the region of the third eye and is known as the Guru pitham, (seat of Consciousness). It is a blue two-petalled lotus, and its bijakshara is "Om." 7) The sahasrara energy center is envisioned as a thousand-petalled lotus. It lies just above the crown of the head—and is the abode of Siva, the inner Mt. Kailasa. Here kundalini shakti unites with Siva after her ascent through the other six centers. At this blissful union, the yogi attains Self-Realization. See: kundalini, sushumna, nadi, Kailasa, Siva.

Chakra vāsini: (chakra: center of spiritual energy + vasini: one who dwells in) Devi, who dwells in the Sri Chakra and the six chakras in the human body.

Challani Talli: (Telugu) Soothing and cooling Divine Mother.

Chāmundeshwari: The Goddess Kali (who emanated from Durga Devi) in the fierce form She assumed for the destruction of the demons Chanda and Munda. She is the force of concentration and heart awakening which destroys the superficial mind and elevates it to the highest. Also called Chamunda or Chamundeshwari. As the latter, She is worshipped in a prominent hilltop temple in Mysore, Karnataka.

chandan: Cooling sandal wood paste used in worship.

***Chandi Saptashati*:** (Also known as *Devi Mahatmya* or *Chandi Patha*) A sacred poem of 700 verses, forming an episode of the *Markandeya Purana*. It celebrates Durga Devi's victories over the asuras, demons (our thoughts), and is recited daily in Her temples. Each verse is considered a powerful mantra. See: mantra.

Chandi yāga: (Chandi: fierce form of Devi + yaga: yajna or homa) A ritual fire ceremony dedicated to Chandi Devi.

chandra: The moon.

Chandrasekhara Saraswati, Sri: (1884-1994) His Holiness Chandrasekhara Swamigal headed the Kamakoti Kanchi Math established by Adi Shankaracharya for 87 years.

chapāti(s): A flat whole wheat bread. A staple food for the people.

charana(m): The holy feet of a deity or Guru.

charana dhūli: (charana + dhuli: dust) The sacred dust of a holy person's feet.

charana sannidhi: (charana + sannidhi: being near) Being near the sacred feet of God or a holy person.

chātaka pakshi: (chataka + pakshi: bird) A legendary bird said to live only on raindrops.

Chatur Vedamayi: (chatur: four + Veda + mayi: pervading) Divine Mother, who pervades all the four *Vedas*.

Chenchu Lakshmi: Narasimha Swami's consort in Penusila Kshetram. There, Lakshmi Devi descended in the form of a beautiful tribal girl in order to attract and cool the anger of Lord Narasimha Swami, after He had destroyed the wicked and arrogant King Hiranyakashipu. See: Lakshmi Devi, Narasimha Swami.

Chennāi: Present name for Madras, the capital and important port of the southern state of Tamil Nadu.

choultry: A place where religious functions are held and shelter for pilgrims is provided.

circumambulate: See: pradakshina.

crore: Ten million; when used in the plural, it indicates a countless or infinite number.

Dakshināmūrti: (dakshina: south + murti: form, the auspicious form of Siva that faces south). Lord Siva, who in ancient times manifested as a beautiful, divine youth. In this form, He taught in silence under a tree,

SRI KARUNAMAYI - A Biography

initiating and guiding even the elder sages who were His disciples, by the direct transmission of spiritual energy.

Dakshineshwar: A beautiful Kali temple with nine domes, located in the district of Dakshineshwar in Calcutta on the banks of the Hugly (delta tributary of the Ganga). Sri Ramakrishna Paramahamsa lived and worshipped as the priest of this temple.

darbha: (Also durva or Bermuda grass) Sacred plant, especially to Vishnu, which is used for making offerings during worship.

darbhāsana: A mat woven from darbha grass, especially beneficial to sit on for meditation as it prevents the spiritual energy generated during meditation from flowing into the ground.

Dāridrya Dukha Dahana Stotra: (daridrya: poverty + dukkha: sorrow + dahana: that which burns + stotra) A hymn in praise of Surya, the Sun God, asking for the removal of all kinds of poverty and sorrows.

darshan: (view, sight) To see the auspicious form of a holy person or deity, or be in their blessed presence. Considered a great blessing.

dashāvatāra(s): (dasha + avataras: incarnations) The ten incarnations of Lord Vishnu.

Dasharatha: Father of Sri Rama, a prince of the Solar Dynasty and King of Ayodhya.

Dashehrā: The tenth night after the nine sacred nights of the Navaratri Festival, celebrated in India during October-November. It is also called Vijaya Dashami, the tenth day of victory, commemorating the slaying of the demon Ravana, King of Lanka, by Lord Rama— the victory of good over evil. See: Appendix.

dayā: Mercy, compassion.

Dayā Sāgari: (daya + sagari: One who is in the form of an ocean) Divine Mother, the Ocean of Compassion.

Dayā Lahari: (daya + lahari: wave) Devi, wave of kindness.

Dayāmayi: (Daya mayi: one who pervades) Divine Mother, the personification of compassion.

Deva(s), devatā(s): (< div: to shine) Luminous Lord, God.

Devi: (< div: one who shines) 1. Divine Mother. 2. Formless supreme Consciousness. 3. Shakti, the divine energy that creates, sustains and transforms all life everywhere.

dhāma: Place.

dharma: (< dhri: to hold or retain) Righteousness or virtue; upholding the moral order. The laws of righteousness, or moral living and virtue. Hinduism considers morality to be the natural foundation of the world. See: Sanatana Dharma.

Dharma Devatā: (dharma + Devata) The embodiment of righteousness, which is divine.

SRI KARUNAMAYI - A Biography

Dharma Rāju(a): (dharma + raju: king) Yama, God of Death, is also known as Dharma Raja, King of Righteousness.
dhārmic: Adj. for dharma. See: dharma.
dhoti: A long piece of cloth worn round the waist—the traditional dress of Hindu men.
Dhruva: A young prince who, by his constancy in devotion and meditation won the eternal blessings of Lord Vishnu. After his death, Dhruva was transformed into the Pole Star, known as the Dhruva nakshatra in Hindu astronomy.
dhūli: Dust
dhvaja stambha(m): (dhwaja: flag + stambha(m): pillar, pole). A flagpole.
dhyāna: (meditation) Stilling of the mind by absorption in a single thought, leading to the cessation of all thought. Regular practice of dhyana is the path to samadhi and liberation. See: samadhi.
dhyāna shloka(s): Opening verses of a stotra which paint a beautiful and vivid picture of the divinity praised in the stotra. Reciting these enables the mind to visualize the deity and helps induce a devotional and meditative mood.
Divākara: (diva(s): day + kara: one who makes or brings) A name for the sun, who is the cause of day.
Divine Swan: A name for the supreme Soul, Brahman. The white swan is a symbol of purity and viveka, discrimination. It can separate milk from water—that is, it knows the difference between the eternal and the transitory.
Divya sahaja ātma sthithi: (Divya: divine + sahaja: natural and original + atma + sthithi: state) The divine, pristine, pure, natural and original state of the soul.
Divyātmamayi: (divya: divine + atma + mayi: the essence) Devi as the inner divine soul of all.
Durgā Bhavāni: (< durga: fortress, i.e. one who protects; the inaccessible one + Bhavani) One of the aspects of Parvati Devi, who manifested as Durga in answer to the prayers of the Gods to slay the demon Mahishasura (ego). See: Bhavani.

Ekambareshwara: (eka: one + ambara: the sky + Ishwara: the supreme sovereign) The supreme Lord of infinite space, Lord Siva.

gamyam: (< gam: to go) The goal, destination.
gandharva(s): Celestial musician(s).
Ganesha, Lord: (Ganah: multitude + Isha: lord, i.e., the Lord of all beings) The son of Parvati Devi. He is the

SRI KARUNAMAYI - A Biography

God of wisdom and the remover of obstacles. It is believed that if Lord Ganesha is worshipped at the beginning of any ritual, worship, or new undertaking, it is bound to be successful.

Gaṅgā (Ganges): The holy River Ganga originates in the Himalayan Mountains and enters the sea in the Bay of Bengal. Its water is sacred and purifying. It is used in all pujas, and is also given to the dying.

Gangotri: The almost inaccessible source of the sacred river Ganga, high in the Himalayas in the state of Uttar Pradesh.

Garuda sevā: (Garuda: the eagle, vehicle of Lord Vishnu + seva: selfless service) The annual opportunity for devotees of Vishnu to offer gifts to the Lord for His annual processional march.

Garuda vāhana: (Garuda: eagle + vahana: vehicle, conveyance) The eagle which is the vehicle of Lord Vishnu.

Gautama: A great sage, author of *Gautama Dharma Shastra* and founder of the Nyaya School of Hindu philosophy, which seeks to ascertain the Truth by means of correct logical procedures.

Gāyatri Devi: (ga: one who sings + tra: that which protects + Devi) The effulgent five-faced Goddess of the Sun, who presides over the Gayatri Mantra. She is the wife of Brahma and the mother of the *Vedas*. See: Gayatri Mantra.

Gāyatri kunda: (Gayatri + kunda: pool or pond) The pond located in the Garudachala Hills where Sri Karunamayi did Her tapas, consecrated to Sri Gayatri Devi. See: Gayatri Devi.

Gāyatri Mantra: (gai: to sing or chant + tra: that which protects and liberates + mantra, i.e., the chanting of this mantra protects and leads to liberation) One of the most powerful and sacred mantras of the *Rig Veda*. It addresses its presiding deity, Savitri Devi, Goddess of the Sun, giver of life. Each of its twenty-four seed syllables has a special Gayatri Mantra of its own, with a presiding deity to whom the mantra is dedicated. See: Gayatri Devi.

ghee: Clarified butter. Used in lamps and homas, for worship and cooking.

gingelly oil: Sesame seed oil.

girijan(s): (giri: mountain + jana: people) People who live in mountainous areas.

Godā Devi, Sri: Another name for Andal. See: Andal.

Godāvari River: Name of a holy river in peninsular India.

Gomātā Guha janma bhūh: (Go: cow + mata: mother + Guha: Swami Karttikeya + janma: birth + bhuh: Earth) Parvati Devi Herself, as the sacred cow, the earthly mother of Swami Karttikeya. The cow is looked upon as a mother, for she provides us with milk.

goshālā: (go: cow + shala: covered place; room) A cowshed.

Govinda: (<go: cow; senses) A name of Lord Krishna as the divine

cowherd, who is also master of the senses.

Govinda Rājaswāmi: (Govinda: Lord of cows, master of the five senses + raja: king + swami: master) A respectful term of address for Lord Krishna. See: Govinda.

Guha: A name of Lord Karttikeya. See: Karttikeya.

guna: (fundamental qualities) All objects in prakriti or nature are composed of the three gunas. When they are in balance, there is no manifestation but, when disturbed, creation takes place. The three gunas are: 1. sattva: The first guna, associated with purity, goodness, and peace. 2. rajas: The second guna, associated with activity, passion, anger, etc., and 3. tamas: The third guna, associated with inertia, darkness and ignorance.

Guru(ji), Gurudeva: (gu: darkness + ru: light + ji or deva: terms of respect) The spiritual preceptor; one who leads the disciple from the darkness of ignorance to the light of true knowledge. The true Guru gives mantra initiation and guides the disciple till he achieves liberation. The only way the disciple can "repay" Sri Guru's grace is by total surrender.

Guru Pūrnimā: (Guru + purnima: night of the full moon) The full moon day of the Guru, which usually falls in the month of July. The most auspicious day for a disciple or devotee to be in the presence of the Guru, when the Guru's grace is especially abundant. Sri Guru is venerated by pada puja. See: pada puja.

Hanumāna: (The long-jawed one) The wise and strong monkey chieftain, leader of all the monkeys in Sri Rama's army. He is the ideal devotee, the personification of dasya bhava, unquestioning obedience and total surrender to his master, Lord Rama.

Haridvāra: (Hari: Vishnu + dvara: the door leading to Hari) A sacred town in North India on the banks of the Ganga.

harijan(s): (Hari: God + jana: persons, people) Children of God; a caste of people formerly considered by some to be untouchables.

Himāchala: The Himalayas.

Himālayas: (hima: snow + alaya: abode. The abode of snow) A mountain chain between Tibet and India, running for 1,500 miles east to west. It contains Mt. Everest (Gauri-Shankara), the highest peak in the world, as well as Mt. Kailasa, the Om Parvata, and Lake Manasarovara, locales especially sacred to Lord Siva. Countless yogis have done tapas in this region. See: tapas.

homa: Fire sacrifice. A sacred fire ceremony in which offerings—symbolic of the devotees' thoughts, words and deeds—are made into the fire pit to the chanting of mantras. Also known as yajna.

homa kunda(m): The fire pit in which oblations are offered during a homa.

Hrim: The fourth bijakshara, seed syllable, of the Saraswati Mantra, bestowing energy at the physical, mental, emotional and spiritual levels.

hundi: The collection box into which monetary offerings for God may be placed.

Ishta devatā: (ishta: beloved, respected, honored + devata) The aspect or form of God that is loved and worshipped by the devotee.

Ishwara: (< Ish: the Lord who rules) 1. Lord of the universe. The personal form of supreme Consciousness or Brahman. 2. A name for Siva. See: Siva.

Ishwari: (feminine aspect of Ishwara) Consort of Ishwara, Siva, Lord of the Universe. See: Ishwara, Siva.

jagat: The world.

Jagan Mātā: (< jagat + mata) Devi, the Mother of the whole universe. See: Devi

Jagannātha: (< jagat: + natha: Lord) The Lord of the universe.

Jagat Janani: (jagat + janani) Devi, The Mother of all creation.

jaggery: (<chakara: sugar) Unrefined cane sugar.

jāgrat, jāgrat avasthā: (jagrat: waking + avastha: condition or state) The waking state. The first state of consciousness. See: states of consciousness.

jai, jaya: Salutations to, glory and victory to.

Jammu: One of the northern-most states of India.

jāmun: Black plum.

Janani: (< jan: to produce, give birth) Devi, the Mother of all creation.

Janawāda Kāmākshi: (Janawada: a place in Andhra Pradesh + Kamakshi) An aspect of Parvati Devi, whose temple is located in Janawada. See: Kamakshi.

japa: (japa: to whisper, murmur) Continuous repetition of a mantra, either orally or mentally, which calms and purifies the mind.

japa mālā: (japa + mala: a rosary or chain of beads) A rosary, usually of 108 beads used to count the number of mantra repetitions.

jiva: (< jivan: life) The embodied soul which identifies itself with the body and mind; a living being.

jivan mukta(s): (jivan + mukta: free) Those blessed souls who attain liberation from the endless cycle of birth and death while still in the body. See: moksha.

Jiveshwara: (jiva + Ishwara: Lord) The Lord of all living beings.

jivita charitra: (jivita: living + charitra: story, biography) Life story, biography.

SRI KARUNAMAYI - A Biography

jnāna: (< jna: to know) Spiritual knowledge of the ultimate Reality; the realization that atma and Paramatma are one, and that the manifested universe, apparently so real, is transitory.

Jnāna dāyini: (jnana + dayini: one who gives) Saraswati Devi, or Sharadambika, the bestower of true knowledge.

Jnānākshi: Saraswati Devi, whose eyes are filled with knowledge, and whose glance bestows knowledge.

jowār: A cheap food grain used by the poor.

Jvālāmukhi: (Jvala: light + mukhi: face of) Devi, worshipped as the energy of fire, whose temple is located in the northeast of India in Himachala Pradesh. Here, nine sacred flames continuously burn without fuel or human assistance, erupting from a rockside. It is one of the 18 important Shakti pithas, shrines dedicated to the worship of Divine Mother.

jyoti(s): Light. The flames of lit wicks or camphor.

jyotish: Vedic astrology.

Kabandha: A monstrous demon slain by Sri Rama.

kadamba: A tree dear to the heart of Divine Mother. It is said to flower when rain clouds thunder.

Kailāsa, Mt.: A sacred mountain in the highest ranges of the Himalayas revered as the abode of Lord Siva.

Kaivalya sukha prasādini: (kaivalya: state of oneness + sukha + prasadini: the one who bestows) Devi, who bestows the divine bliss of Self-Realization.

kājal: kohl, collyrium. Black paste applied to beautify the eyes.

Kālāntaka: (kala: time + antaka: one who ends) The Lord of Time and Death, Lord Siva.

kalasha(m): Metal water pot or pitcher. In temple rituals, a kalasha, topped with mango leaves and a husked coconut, represents the deity during special pujas.

Kali yuga: (Kali: black, dark + yuga: age) The present age. See: yuga.

Kālidāsa: (circa 300 or 400 AD) The greatest Sanskrit poet and dramatist, popularly called the "Indian Shakespeare." Originally dull-witted, he was blessed by Saraswati Devi in the form of Kalika Devi and subsequently became one of the "nine gems" or great artists in the court of Vikramaditya, King of Ujjayini.

Kālindi River: A name for the Yamuna River.

kalpa vriksha: A wish-fulfilling celestial tree.

kalyānotsavam: (kalyana: wedding + utsavam: festival) A temple enactment of the marriage of two deities, often celebrated annually.

Kāmadhenu: (kama: desire + dhenu: cow) The wish-fulfilling cow, Surabhi, which emerged from the ocean when it was churned.

SRI KARUNAMAYI - A Biography

Kāmakoti: See: Kamakshi Devi.
Kāmākshi Devi: Devi, who fulfills the desires of Her devotee with a glance. Worshipped at Sri Kamakoti Temple, Kanchipuram, Tamil Nadu, as Raja Rajeshwari, Lalita Tripura sundari, Kamakoti, and the Sri Chakra.
Kānchi, Kānchipuram: One of the seven holy cities. An ancient center of learning and a famous Shakti pitha or shrine. See: Ekambareshwara, Kamakshi Devi.
Kanva Forest: A sacred forest near Amma's ashram named after a great sage who performed severe austerities there for a long time.
Kanva Maharshi: One of the nine brahmarshis (great knowers of Brahman) and author of several hymns in the *Rig Veda*. India was named Bharata varsha after his grandson, Bharata.
Kanva Muni: See: Kanva Maharshi.
karma: (deed) 1. Action, mental or physical. 2. Consequence of such action. 3. (plural) The sum of all mental and physical actions of an individual in this and past lives.
kārmic: (adj.) See: karma.
Karnātaka: State in South India in which the city of Bangalore, where Amma has an ashram, is located.
Kārttikeya: Born as the younger son of Lord Siva and Parvati Devi for the specific purpose of destroying the demon Tarakasura. Commander of the army of the Gods. His vehicle is a peacock. His other names are Guha, Murugan, Shanmukha, and Subramanyam.
karunā: Compassion, mercy.
Karunāmayi, Sri: 1. One who is full of compassion. 2. The name aptly given to beloved Amma, Sri Sri Sri Vijayeswari Devi one winter morning by a poor and shivering worshipper in Varanasi when She spontaneously gave him Her beautiful shawl.
Kāshi: A holy city situated on the banks of the River Ganga in Uttar Pradesh, North India. Also known as Varanasi or Benares. It is believed that people who die there will go to heaven. See: Ganga
Kāshi lingam: A lingam from Kashi. See: Kashi, lingam.
Kashmir: Northernmost state of India. It is prominent in the history of Shaivism, the worship of Lord Siva.
kastūri: Musk.
kilometer: (< kilo: one thousand + meter: to measure) Metric measurement. Multiply by 0.62 to convert to miles.
kimpurusha: A celestial being with a human head and the body of a horse.
kinnara(s): Celestial dancers.
Kolhāpur: A city of temples and palaces in the Northwest corner of Maharashtra State famed as the residence of Maha Lakshmi or Amba Bai.

Krishna, Lord: (the dark one; one who attracts) The eighth incarnation and perhaps the best-loved form of Vishnu, who manifested during the Dvapara Yuga. He is pure Consciousness as the supreme yogi, statesman, warrior and teacher. See: *Bhagavad Gita*, yuga.

Krishnaveni: The sacred Krishna River in Andhra Pradesh, South India.

kshetra(m): Field, place, area, land of.

Kumāra Swami: A name for Karttikeya. See: Kartikkeya.

kumbhaka: Retention of breath during pranayama.

Kumbhakonam: One of the oldest small towns of the South in Tamil Nadu on the banks of the Cauveri.

kumkum: An auspicious red powder used in pujas. It is made by mixing turmeric and lime powder. See: puja.

kumkum archana pūjā: (kumkum + archana + puja) Worship of Divine Mother, where She is offered a pinch of kumkum with each repetition of Her sacred thousand names.

kunda: Pond or pool.

kundalini: (coiled line, snake, serpent power) This powerful spiritual energy lies asleep at the base of the spine in the muladhara chakra in three and a half coils. When she is awakened by the grace of the Guru, she arises gradually through the six chakras, piercing them and causing them to bloom, till she reaches the sahasrara, the thousand-petalled lotus just above the crown of the head. At this stage the devotee achieves enlightenment and the spiritual goal is reached. Regular spiritual practice and right thought and action are imperative for the kundalini to continue her ascent upwards.

kushā: A sacred grass used in pujas and religious ceremonies. Also made into mats for meditation.

L

laddū: A sweet Indian delicacy shaped like a small ball.

lakh: 100,000

laksharchanā: (lakh + archana) Worship or puja performed by repeating the divine name or mantra one lakh times.

Lakshmana: The devoted and faithful younger brother of Sri Rama, who went into voluntary exile with Him for fourteen years. See: Rama.

Lakshmi Devi: Divine Mother in Her auspicious and sustaining form. Luminous Goddess of wealth and all types of abundance, joy and fortune, both spiritual and material. Her consort is Vishnu. She is represented by the seed syllable "Srim" in the Saraswati Mantra.

Lakshmi Narasimha Swāmi: (Lakshmi + Narasimha Swami) Sri Lakshmi as the consort of Lord Narasimha. See: Chenchu Lakshmi.

Lakshmi tulasi: (Lakshmi + tulasi) The sacred tulasi plant, revered as the embodiment of Lakshmi Devi.

SRI KARUNAMAYI - A Biography

Lalitā: (the playful one; the beautiful, elegant, graceful one) The exquisite embodiment of Divine Mother in all Her infinite variety or play, formed of pure sattva. Lalita Devi, also known as Tripura sundari and Raja Rajeshwari, manifested from the sacrificial fire to accomplish the task of the Gods—the destruction of Bhandasura, who symbolizes the embodied soul, ignorant and egoistic, identifying with the physical self. See: Appendix.

Lalitā Parameshwari: (Lalita + Parameshwari: the highest sovereign) Lalita Devi, the supreme ruler of all.

Lalitā Sahasranāma: (Lalita: + sahasra: thousand + nama: names) Hymn of the Thousand Divine Names of Lalita Devi. A unique and faultless Sanskrit composition in 182 rhyming couplets. It was composed by the Goddesses of Speech, Vasini, Vagdevi and others at Devi's command. No commentary can interpret these names adequately. Each name is composed of powerful seed letters saturated with deep meaning.

Lalitāmbā: (Lalita + amba) A loving and intimate form of address for Divine Mother. See: Lalita.

laya: To merge into.

lilā: Play or sport (usually in reference to divine incarnations).

linga(m): (< liyate: to be absorbed + gam: to go, to move) The mark of Lord Siva, in which the universe moves and into which it is absorbed. A highly venerated symbol of the inexpressible nature of the divine Lord Siva. Its elliptical shape is reminiscent of the orbits of the planets, all movement in the cosmos, and also of a flame of light, the light of Consciousness. Linga(m)s may be naturally formed, or sculpted—usually of black stone, marble or pancha dhatu (five metals). There are twelve linga pithas (shrines) in India.

loka(s): Worlds or spheres. Traditionally divided into three: heaven, earth and hell. By another classification, there are seven higher worlds: bhur, bhuvar, svar, mahar, jana, tapas, satya and brahma. Attaining the last, one is not reborn. There are also seven nether worlds or patala lokas, making a total of fourteen lokas.

Loka Mātā: (loka + mata) Universal Mother, mother of all the lokas.

Lokeshwara: (loka + Ishwara) The Lord of all the worlds.

lotus feet: The lotus flower is a symbol of beauty and purity. Since ancient times Eastern poets and writers have used this epithet to describe the loveliness of the face, eyes, hands and feet of the beloved deity. The lotus blooms in the mud pond, but is untouched by it, symbolizing beauty rising above the environment. The drops of water do not adhere to its petals, symbolizing detachment from the world. The lotus asks nothing for itself, but blesses the world by its fragrance and beauty, as does the Divine Mother or Guru. Great spiritual energy flows from the lotus feet of the holy ones, so that touching them destroys all sins and bestows untold blessings. Worshipping the feet mentally, i.e., placing them in the heart, confers even greater benefits.

Mā: Mother.
Madurai: City in Tamil Nadu, where the famed Meenakshi (Parvati Devi) Temple is located.
Māgha: Eleventh lunar month, which corresponds to the winter months of January/February.
mahā: Great.
Mahā Deva: (maha + Deva) The great Lord, a name of Siva.
Mahā Devi: (maha: + Devi: Goddess) The great Goddess.
Mahā Lakshmi: (maha + Lakshmi) The great Goddess Lakshmi. See: Lakshmi Devi.
Mahā Māyā: (maha + Maya) Devi, Creator of Illusion. See: maya.
Mahā Padmeshwari: (maha + padma: lotus + Ishwari) The great Goddess who dwells in the universal lotus, the sahasrara.
Mahā prasāda: (maha + prasada) Great blessing or great gift.
Mahā Saraswati Mantra: (maha + Saraswati + mantra) The great Saraswati Mantra. See: Saraswati Mantra
Mahā Shakti, Mahā Shakti Svarūpini: (maha + shakti + svarupini: of the form of) Devi as the embodiment of supreme energy. See: Shakti.
Mahā Shāntā: (maha + shanta: peaceful one) Devi, the eternally peaceful one.
Mahā Vidyā: (maha + Vidya: highest knowledge) The supreme knowledge of the Self.
Mahā Vishnu: (maha +Vishnu) See: Vishnu.
Mahābhārata: (maha + Bharata: the descendents of King Bharata) The great Sanskrit epic poem which recounts the exploits of the Kauravas and Pandavas and the great war between them. The most important section of the *Mahabharata* is the *Bhagavad Gita*. See: *Bhagavad Gita*, dharma.
mahārishi: (maha + rishi) A great sage or seer. See: rishi.
Maheshwara: (maha + Ishwara) The Great Lord, Siva. See: Siva.
Mahishāsura: (mahisha: buffalo + asura: demon) A buffalo demon, symbolizing the ego, who attempted to fight against Divine Mother, thinking Her to be an ordinary woman. He was destroyed by Her, yet given liberation. See: *Mahishasura Mardini Stotram*.
Mahishāsura Mardini: (mahisha: buffalo + mardini: one who destroys) Durga Devi, the one who destroys the buffalo demon of the ego in us.
Mahishāsura Mardini Stotram: (mahisha: buffalo + asura: demon + mardini: destroyer + stotram: hymn of praise) A hymn of praise by

SRI KARUNAMAYI - A Biography

Adi Shankaracharya, extolling Durga Devi's victory over the buffalo demon, Mahishasura. It symbolizes the difficulty for a seeker to conquer the ego by his own efforts. The twenty verses of the stotra contain the essence of seven hundred shlokas of the *Chandi Saptashati*. See: *Chandi Saptashati*.

mānava putra: (manava: man + putra: son) Mortal beings.

Mandākini: A name for the celestial Ganga.

mandapa(m): (<mandana: to decorate) A pavilion, or a canopy specially erected for the performance of a wedding or religious ceremony.

mandāra kusuma: The exquisitely delicate and beautiful coral-tree flower, found in the gardens of Indra, King of the Gods.

mandir(am): A temple.

mangala: Auspicious, prosperous, fortunate.

mangala dravyam: (mangala + dravyam: materials) Offering of the auspicious materials such as red and yellow powders, kumkum and turmeric.

mangala sūtra: (mangala + sutra: thread, string) Sacred marriage string with black and gold beads put around the bride's neck by the bridegroom at the wedding ceremony, and worn by her as long as her husband lives.

māngalya: Auspicious materials. See: mangala dravya.

Manidwipa: (mani: gems + dwipa: island) Isle of Gems, the abode of Lalita Devi. Situated in the Ocean of Nectar fringed by rows of celestial kalpataru (wish-fulfilling trees). The Ocean of Nectar is represented in the Sri Chakra as the central dot, or bindu, and denotes Brahmananda, the bliss of merging with the Absolute.

Manipura: (mani: gems + pura: city) City of Gems.

mantra(m): (man: to think + tra: to protect or liberate) A mystical formula, the repetition of which protects and liberates, when chanted with the correct pronunciation. A mantra can consist of a single syllable or bijakshara, a series of bijaksharas that have no apparent meaning, or a whole meaningful sentence. Its power is greatly increased when given at initiation by a true Guru. The vibrations set in motion, when the mantra is repeated either orally or mentally, purify the seeker at all levels. Mantra repetition leads to the thought-free state and to union with the Absolute. See: bijakshara.

mantra pushpam: (mantra + puspa: flower) At the end of a puja, the devotee offers flowers to God while chanting special mantras. He symbolically offers himself as a flower at the divine feet of the Lord in complete surrender.

mārga: Path or way.

Mārkandeya Purāna: (Markandeya: a sage + *Purana*: ancient mythological book) One of the eighteen major *Puranas*, Hindu scriptures which describe and celebrate the powers and deeds of the Gods. The *Puranas* are in the form of dialogues between an inquirer and an exponent and are written in verse.

Mātā(ji): Respected Mother.

Māthru: (Telugu) Mother. Amma is known as Sri Mathru Devi.

Māthru chhāyā: (Matru: of the Mother + chhaya: shade) Under the protection of Mother.

mauna sudhā mādhuri: (mauna: silence + sudha: nectar + madhuri: sweetness) The sweet nectar of silence.

māyā: (illusion, deception, appearance) The energy of Brahman, She creates the universe and then draws a veil over the vision of jivatmas (embodied souls) so that they see only diversity, not the one, true underlying reality. This avidya (ignorance) is the cause for worldly attachment and bondage.

Meenākshi: (meena: fish + aksha: eye, i.e., having eyes shaped like a fish) Goddess worshipped chiefly in a famed temple at Madurai, Tamil Nadu, where Her annual marriage to Lord Siva during Chaitra purnima (full moon in March/April) is celebrated with great festivity and devotion.

Mithilā: Ancient city in northeast India, also known as Videha; birthplace of Sita Devi, and the kingdom of Janaka.

moksha: Liberation from samsara, the cycle of births and deaths. This state is attained by the union with supreme Reality, the realization that the jivatma, the embodied soul, and Paramatma are one. Moksha is the culmination of the purusharthas—the four desirable attainments for human beings: dharma (righteousness), artha (wealth), kama (fulfillment of legitimate desires) and moksha.

mudrā: (seal, sign) A symbolic hand gesture. The two most common are the abhaya (protective) and the varada (boon-bestowing) mudras. See: abhaya hasta mudra, varada mudra.

muhūrta: (muhurta: a period of time, according to Indian calculations, equal to 48 minutes) An auspicious time for performing an action.

mūlādhāra: Subtle energy center at the base of spine. See: chakra.

mūla nakshatra: (mula: root, essential + nakshatra: star) Primary star. Also, the name of the nineteenth of the twenty-seven constellations.

Munda: A demon who, along with his brother Chanda, was killed by Goddess Kali. See: Chamundeshwari.

muni: A silent ascetic or sage.

mūrti: Image or idol of a deity or holy person.

Murugan: 1. One of the names of the son of Parvati Devi and Lord Siva. 2. Swami Vijayeswarananda's name given at birth. See: Karttikeya.

SRI KARUNAMAYI - A Biography

Mysore: Town in the state of Karnataka, home of the Chamundeshwari Temple. See: Chamundeshwari.

Mysorepak: A South Indian sweet delicacy.

Nachiketas: A young boy with a rare thirst for true knowledge who went to the home of Yama Raja, God of Death, to seek the answers to his questions about life after death. His inspiring story is told in the *Katha Upanishad*.

Nādamayi: (nada: primal sound + mayi: one who pervades) Devi, the source of sound, who pervades all sound.

nādasvara(m): (nada: sound + svara(m): note of music) A bugle-like musical instrument that is played in temples at the time of arati or on other auspicious occasions.

nādi(s): (tube, vessel, vein) According to Raja yoga, the nadis are nerve channels through which prana, vital life breath, flows to all parts of the body. Nadis are associated with the subtle body, and though they may have some correspondence with their physical counterparts, cannot actually be seen. There are 72,000 nadis, the most important being the sushumna. It runs through the spine from the muladhara (root) to the sahasrara (crown) chakra and is the path taken by kundalini energy, which arises through it. The ida or chandra (moon) nadi lies to the left of the sushumna and the pingala or surya (sun) nadi lies to the right of it. See: kundalini.

nāga: A snake.

naivedya(m): An offering of food presented to a deity.

namah, namo: To bow to; to venerate.

nāmāvali: A garland of names. The sahasranamas, thousand divine names of a deity, and the ashtottaras, 108 names of Gods or holy persons, are called namavalis when each name is chanted separately with an Om at the beginning and namah at the end.

nānnā: (Telugu) Darling child, little one. Term of endearment often spontaneously used by Sri Karunamayi to address one or more of Her devotees.

Narasimha: (nara: man + simha: lion) The fourth incarnation of Vishnu in the form of half-man and half-animal, the head and upper body being that of a lion. Lord Vishnu manifested in this form to kill the arrogant King Hiranyakashipu, who had won a boon that he could be killed by neither man nor beast.

Narasimha Swāmi: (Narasimha + Swami: Lord) In a famed temple located in Penusila, Andhra Pradesh, near Amma's ashram, Narasimha Swami is worshipped as a svayambhu, naturally-formed rock, overlaid with silver. See: Narasimha, Chenchu Lakshmi.

SRI KARUNAMAYI - A Biography

Narmadā Bāneshwara lingam(s): (Narmada: a river in central India + Baneshwara + linga(m)) Auspicious, naturally-formed, small, white stone lingams, elliptical in shape, found only in the bed of the sacred Narmada River. They have a natural polish resulting from the action of river water.

Navadwipa(m): The sacred place in Bengal where the great Krishna devotee, Sri Chaitanya Maha Prabhu was born and lived. His life inspired a resurgence of the devotional form of worship.

Navarātri: (nava: nine + ratri: night) The nine sacred nights before Dashehra or Vijaya Dashami dedicated to Divine Mother. Also known as Sharan Navaratri (9 nights of Saraswati or Sharada). See: Appendix.

neem: One of the trees considered sacred by Hindus. Its leaves have medicinal properties.

nija bhakti: (nija: belonging to + bhakti: devotion) True devotion to the Self.

Nirākārini: (nir: without + akara : form) Divine Mother as formless.

Nirguna: (nir: without + guna: attribute or essential quality) Divine Mother who is beyond attributes. See: guna(s).

nishkāma karma: (nishkama: without desire + karma) The performance of all actions without any expectation.

nyagrodha: The Indian fig tree.

Om: Primal mantra or initial sound vibration that arose prior to creation. All other mantras and sounds have emanated from it. It is the most important bijakshara, and adds to the efficacy of any mantra it precedes.

Omkāra: (Om + kara: the sound of) The sound of Om.

Omkāra pitha: (Omkara + pitha: holy seat or altar) The seat on which Amma sits. It has Om carved on the backrest, indicating Her unity with that sacred sound.

Omkāramaya sharirini: (Omkara + maya: pervading + sharirni: the embodiment of) Devi, the very embodiment of the sacred syllable Om.

Omkāramayi: (Omkara + mayi: of the form of) Divine Mother, who pervades the sacred sound of Om.

Omkārini: (Om + kara + ini: of the form of) Divine Mother, the personification of the sacred mantra, the primal nada, Om.

Ongale bull: Large humpbacked Brahma bull from Andhra Pradesh. Lord Siva's vehicle, Nandi, was of this species.

pāda: Feet.

pāda pūjā: (pada + puja) Ritual worship of the feet of the Guru or holy person. The Guru's spiritual energy is said to be most highly concentrated in the feet. To perform or witness this puja is considered to be a great blessing. The holy feet are washed with water and panchamrita (five auspicious liquids), which become tirtham (holy water). Sprinkling it on the head or drinking it purifies both mind and body. The feet are then anointed with sandalwood paste, kumkum, and turmeric powder and worshipped with incense and flowers while mantras are chanted. Arati is performed to Sri Guru and gifts are offered.

padma: lotus

Padmanābha, Sri: (< padma) A name of Lord Vishnu, from whose navel grew the lotus from which Brahma, the Creator, was born.

padmāsana: (padma + asana: seat) The yogic lotus posture, considered the best for meditation.

Padmāvati Devi: (padma + vati: one who possesses) Lakshmi Devi, who is always seated in the lotus (of the sahasrara), the consort of Lord Venkateshwara. See: Tirupati

Padmeshwari: (padma + Ishwari: consort of the Lord) Sri Lakshmi, consort of Lord Vishnu, who sits on the lotus.

Padmini: A name for Lakshmi Devi.

pallū: Extremity of the sari, sometimes used to cover the head. See:sari.

Pancha bhūtātmika shakti: (Pancha: five + bhuta: the elements + atmika: embodied as + shakti) Devi, the embodiment of the five elements of nature.

pancha brahmāsana: (Pancha: five + Brahma: very great Gods + asana: seat or couch) The couch of Devi is formed by the five great Gods: Brahma, Vishnu, Siva, Ishana and Sadasiva. These gods are the five aspects of divine energy who manifest at the time of creation.

pandāl: Seating area covered with an awning.

pundit: 1. A scholar with a deep knowledge of the *Vedas*, metaphysical knowledge, or any other branch of knowledge. 2. A priest who performs ritual pujas and homas in a temple on behalf of families.

pāpad: A thin and crisp savory wafer made of ground lentils.

para, parama: Supreme.

Para Brahma(n): (para + Brahman) The supreme Absolute—eternal, formless, attributeless, with no change or movement at all. See: Brahma(n).

Para Brahmamayi: The Absolute visualized as feminine energy, pervading all creation. See: Para Brahma(n).

Paramahamsa: (parama + hamsa: swan) Title given to Self-Realized souls, for the white swan is a symbol of purity and viveka, discrimination. It can separate water from milk, that is, it can discriminate between Reality and samsara (the illusory and transitory world).

Paramātmā: (parama + atma) The supreme Soul or Brahman.

SRI KARUNAMAYI - A Biography

Parameshwara: (parama + Ishwara: God) The supreme Lord.
Parameshwari: (parama + Ishwari: Goddess) The supreme Goddess.
Parā Shakti: (para + Shakti) The highest and most powerful primal Energy, beyond which there is no other; i.e., Devi. See: Shakti.
pārāyana(m): Reading aloud the holy scriptures.
pārijāta flower: The delicate and fragrant blossom of a celestial tree produced at the churning of the ocean, with fragrant white petals on a coral stem.
Paripūrna Brahman: (paripurna: complete and full + Brahman) Brahman, with an emphasis on its all-pervasive aspect.
Pārvati Devi: (Daughter of the Mountain; She who dwells in the mountains) The supremely compassionate Divine Mother as dynamic energy. Consort of Siva, She is worshipped through countless names.
Patita Pāvani: (patita: fallen souls, sinners + pavani: one who purifies) Divine Mother, who washes away all sins.
pāyasam: A deliciously flavored semi-liquid sweet pudding made with milk and rice.
Penusila: A sacred rural and tribal forest area in the southern state of Andhra Pradesh where many rishis have done spiritual practices, and where a famed Narasimha Swami Temple is located. Amma, Sri Karunamayi, meditated here for twelve years, and founded an ashram (hermitage) in 1980.
Penusila Kshetram: See: Penusila, kshetram.
pingalā: A nerve channel in the subtle body of human beings. See: nadi.
pipal: (Bodhi tree, Ficus religiosa) A sacred tree with heart-shaped leaves. Lord Buddha attained nirvana, the supreme bliss of liberation, after meditating for a long time under a pipal tree.
pitha(m): (seat or holy center of a deity) There are 108 divine holy centers of worship of Devi, chief of which are eighteen.
pongal: A thick, sweet, milk and rice pudding made specially during Pongal. See: Pongal.
Pongal: The New Year and (rice) harvest season of the people of South India, celebrated in mid-January. See: Sankranti.
Pothana, Bammera (1450-1510): Beloved Telugu poet, born in Bammera village, Andhra Pradesh. A devotee of Siva, he converted to Vaishnavism when, during an eclipse, Lord Rama appeared to him and asked him to translate Sage Vyasa's Sanskrit *Bhagavatam* into Telugu. His translation is majestic and rhythmic, and imparts knowledge of the Divine, along with lessons in ethics and politics.
pradakshinā: Walking around the image of a deity, or homa fire, always keeping it to the right. A method of offering reverential salutations to a deity and washing away one's sins.

pradosham: Thirteenth day of the lunar fortnight.
prāna: Life-giving energy; vital life breath.
Prāna chetanā: (prana + chetana: consciousness) Supreme Consciousness.
Prānadā: (prana + da: One who gives) Devi, the giver of life.
pranām(s): Reverential salutation; bowing with respect.
pranamāmyaham: (pranamami: to offer salutations + aham: I) I offer my salutations.
Prāna rūpini: (prana + rupini: of the form of) Devi, who is the very life breath of all beings.
Pranava(m): The prana or enlivening mantra, Om. It precedes all mantras and enlivens them. It is a symbol of Brahman. See: Om, Omkara.
prānāyāma: (prana + yama: control) Control of life-giving energy or vital force. Yogic technique for regulating the breath. Breathing is closely connected with the mind, and control of breath leads to control of, and finally cessation of, thoughts.
prasāda(m): Blessings, subtle or as blessed food; gift.
prema: Deep love and intense longing for God.
pūjā: Ritual worship of a deity.
pundit: a scholar with a deep and profound knowledge of the *Vedas*, metaphysical knowledge, or any other branch of knowledge.
pūrna Brahma jnāna: (purna: complete + Brahma + jnana) Full and complete knowledge of the ultimate Reality. See: Brahma, jnana.
pūrna jnāna: (purna: full + jnana) Complete knowledge of the Self; Self-Realization.
pūrna kumbha(m): (purna: full + kumbha: water pot) A full water pot, symbolic of auspiciousness, used to welcome or receive an honored guest.
pūrnāhuti: (purna: complete + ahuti: offering) Held aloft for all to see, the purnahuti is the most important offering to the deity made at the end of a homa. It consists of many precious items offered into the homa fire. By witnessing it for even a moment, one gets the entire benefit of the homa.
pūrnimā: Night of the full moon.
Purusha Sūktam: A beautiful vedic hymn that describes how original, infinite and formless divine Consciousness manifested the entire universe out of Itself, and how the one supreme Soul became the millions of individual souls populating all the universes in all ages.

rāga: A mode in classical Indian music.
rāgi: A kind of cheap grain.
Rāja Rājeshwari: (raja: kingdom + Rajeshwari: the ruler of kings, i.e., the supreme empress) Devi, as the supreme ruler, the Empress of all rulers.

SRI KARUNAMAYI - A Biography

rajas: See: guna(s)
rājasic: Adj of rajas. See: guna(s).
Rāma, Sri (Lord): The seventh avatara (incarnation) of Lord Vishnu, born at the end of the Treta Yuga. The eldest son of King Dasharatha and Queen Kaushalya, and husband of Sita Devi, Rama is seen as the ideal son, king, husband and warrior. Throughout His life—from His banishment to the forest on the eve of His coronation, to the separation from His beloved Sita due to public censure—Sri Rama willingly sacrificed His personal interests on the altar of dharma. See: yuga.
Rāma Mantra: (Rama + mantra) The mantra sacred to Lord Rama.
Rāma nāma: (Rama + nama: name) Constant repetition of the holy name "Rama."
Rāma Navami: The birthday of Lord Rama on the ninth day of the month of Chaitra (April), according to the Hindu lunar calendar.
Rama tattva, Sri: (Rama + tattva: essence + Sri) The divine essence of Sri Rama.
Rāmadās, Bhakta (Kancherla Gopanna): Famed Telugu musician saint, who wrote ardent kirtanas, devotional hymns. His intense love for Lord Rama compelled him to divert money from the royal treasury to build a Sri Rama Temple in Bhadrachalam, on the banks of the Godavari River. Imprisoned for 12 years for his misdeeds, he was freed by the same local Nawab when Lord Rama appeared to him in a dream. See: Bhadrachalam.
Rāmakoti: (Rama + koti: crore) The name of Lord Rama written ten million times.
Rāmakrishna Paramahamsa: (1836-1886) One of the greatest spiritual geniuses of modern India. Born in West Bengal, he had his first spiritual experience at the age of six. He was an ardent devotee of Divine Mother as Kalika Devi. Later, his Guru, Totapuri, initiated him in Advaita Vedanta philosophy (the belief that the individual soul and the supreme Soul are one) and nirvikalpa samadhi, which Ramakrishna attained in a single day. He practiced several spiritual disciplines, including Christianity and Islam, and arrived at the conclusion that all paths lead to the same goal, namely the one Reality. His famous disciple, Swami Vivekananda, brought Advaita Vedanta philosophy to the West. See: Advaita, Vedanta, Vivekananda.
Ramana Maharshi: (1879-1950) One of the greatest adepts of jnana yoga in the 20th century. At the age of 16, he experienced an intense fear of death, which prompted him to visualize his own dead body and its cremation. This led to his discovery of the Self

beyond the physical body. He recommended that seekers deeply ponder the question, "Who am I ?" This self-inquiry leads to the recognition of the real Self beyond the ego personality. See: yoga.

Rāmānuja, Sri: (1017-1137) Celebrated philosopher and Vaishnava (devotee of Lord Vishnu) saint of South India. He taught that bhakti, devotion, is the highest ideal, and that all creatures and inanimate things are forms of God.

Rāmāyana: A monumental epic poem originally written in Sanskrit verse by Valmiki. It tells the story of Lord Rama's life from his birth till the establishment of Rama Rajya, the perfect reign of an ideal king. Selfless love of God is praised and high moral values portrayed in its main characters. The *Ramayana* is a lesson in family relationships, and the battle between Rama and the demon king Ravana is an allegory of the battle between good and evil within human beings. See: Rama, Sri (Lord).

Ranganātha Sāi, Sri: (Ranganatha: Lord Krishna + Sai: Lord) An avatara of Lord Vishnu, consort of Andal. See: Andal.

rangavalli: (Telugu) (ranga: color + valli: creeper) A decorative design to beautify the floor. Same as rangoli.

rangoli: Colorful designs of flour, kumkum and turmeric powder, created just outside the front door of a house or building on festive occasions.

rasam: Highly spiced, thin, lentil based South Indian soup.

Ratha Saptami: (Ratha: chariot + saptami: the seventh day of the bright phase of the moon) The saptami in the month of Magha (January-February), dedicated to the worship of the Sun God as the giver of life. The Sun is visualized as riding a chariot across the sky from east to west, hence the name Ratha Saptami.

Rāvana: The King of Lanka, who stole Sita Devi, consort of Lord Rama, from the forest. He was a demon but a very learned one, and a devotee of Lord Siva. He was full of ahamkara (ego) and made his subjects worship him as God. He is one of the leading characters in the great epic, the *Ramayana*. See: *Ramayana*.

Revā: Name of River Narmada.

Rig Veda: (rig: verse + Veda, <vid: to know) See: *Veda(s)*.

rishi(s): (seer) One who sees the shloka, sukta or mantra before composing it. Highly evolved spiritual seers and teachers of the vedic era, who lived lives of wisdom, sacrifice and love. See: maharshi, sapta rishis.

Ritambharatvam: (Rita: Divinity, Truth + bhara: full of + atvam the essence) The essence of eternal divine Truth and bliss.

root chakra: The muladhara chakra. See: chakra, kundalini.

roti: Flat unleavened Indian bread cooked on a griddle.

SRI KARUNAMAYI - A Biography

Rudra: (the howling one) A name of Lord Siva in His destructive, fierce and protective aspect. The *Siva Purana* defines Rudra as one who destroys misery. According to the ancient scriptures, there are eleven aspects of Rudra. See: Siva.

Rudra abhishekam: (Rudra + abhishekam) Anointing of the Sivalingam, accompanied by the chanting of mantras from the *Vedas*, especially the *Sri Rudram*. See: *Sri Rudram*.

Rudra homa: (Rudra + homa) A fire ceremony performed to honor Lord Siva. The sacred text *Sri Rudam* is recited during the homa. See: homa, Rudra, *Sri Rudram*.

Rudra mantra: (Rudra + mantra) The mantra sacred to Rudra. See: Rudra.

rūpa(s): (form; physical beauty) A visible form.

rupee: Basic monetary currency of India.

sādhanā: The regular practice of spiritual disciplines as laid down by the scriptures and one's Guru, which are to be followed by the sadhaka (spiritual seeker) until the attainment of Self-Realization.

sādhu: A holy person or monk who has renounced the world to seek God. A pious person who follows the principles of dharma.

Sage Shuka: The son of Sri Vyasa. He was born an ascetic and philosopher, a being of great purity. He narrated the *Bhagavata Purana* to King Parikshit in seven days so that the king attained liberation at the time when Takshaka, a deadly poisonous serpent, bit him due to a curse.

Sāi, Sāināth: Sri Sai Baba of Shirdi (1835-1918). One of the most universally revered sages of the 20th century. He was beyond all religions. People from every path and walk of life came to get the blessings of this revered saint at Shirdi in Gujarat. Today Shirdi is still a popular pilgrimage site.

sālagrāma: A smooth, black stone of fossilized ammonite, worshiped as a sacred symbol of Lord Vishnu. Authentic salagramas can be found only in the bed of the Gandhaki River in Nepal. The water used for the abhisekham of the salagramas has very powerful vibrations and can heal many diseases. See: abhishekham.

sama drishti: (sama: equal + drishti: vision) Seeing everyone and everything as equal, and the same divine Consciousness everywhere.

samādhi: (to establish, make firm) A state of consciousness beyond the waking, dream and deep sleep states. It involves total absorption in the object of meditation and results in the blissful union with the Supreme or Brahman.

sāmbār: Spicy South Indian lentil soup.

sāmbrāni: Fragrant herbs of copal (a frankincense type resin) used in traditional Indian temples to purify the atmosphere.

Sanātana Dharma: (sanatana: ancient or eternal + dharma) The ancient laws of righteousness which are the foundation for leading a truly moral, virtuous life. Hinduism considers morality to be the foundation of the world. Its tradition is called Sanatana Dharma, meaning that its precepts are true for all time.

Sanātani: (Sanatani: She who is eternal) Devi, who was, is and always will be.

sanctum sanctorum: (< Latin: sanctum: sacred + sanctorum: holy place) The innermost and holiest shrine in the temple where the image of the deity is installed.

sandhyā: (< sandhi: to join) The meeting point of day and night at early dawn and dusk, or twilight. Noon is also called sandhya. Daily prayers are enjoined for these three auspicious times of the day.

sandhyā kālam: (sandhya + kalam: time) At the time of sandhya.

sankalpa: Firm intention or mental resolve.

Sankrānti: A solstice festival in mid-January, celebrated to mark the Northward turning of the sun and its entrance into the zodiacal sign of Capricorn (Makara). See: Pongal.

sannidhi: Nearness.

santripti: Complete satisfaction.

sapotā: Sapodilla fruit of an evergreen tree.

saptami: The seventh day of each half of the lunar month.

sapta rishis: (sapta: seven + rishis: seers) The seven great rishis. They were inspired sages to whom the hymns of the *Vedas* were revealed. The seven rishis were the manas putras (mind-born sons) of Brahma. They are represented in the sky by the constellation of the Great Bear. The names of the sapta rishis vary in different scriptures. See: rishi.

Saraswati Devi: (elegant, the one who flows) Goddess of speech and knowledge, both spiritual and temporal, as well as the creative arts. She is the Mother of Creation in the female Hindu Triad. She holds the *Vedas*, revealing the path of jnana (knowledge) to liberation. The vina (a stringed musical instrument) in Her hands indicates that She is the origin of nada (primal sound). As Her nature is entirely sattvic, She is dressed in pure white and sits on a white lotus. Her vehicle is a pure white swan. One of Her hands is raised in blessing, while the other holds a rosary (mantra power). Her consort is Brahma, the Creator.

Saraswati Mantra: (Saraswati + mantra) The mantra of the Goddess of knowledge containing four very powerful bijaksharas: Om,

Ayim, Srim and Hrim. This mantra purifies the seeker at the physical, emotional, intellectual and spiritual levels, and finally leads to liberation. See: Saraswati.

Saraswati River: Name of a river which was said to have joined the confluence of the Ganga and Yamuna rivers at Prayaga in ancient times. It has now disappeared underground.

sāri: Traditional dress worn by Indian women, made of six yards of soft cotton or silk. It is draped gracefully around the body. In some areas of South and West India, women wear nine-yard saris.

Sarva Sākshini: (sarva: all + sakshini: witness) Devi, who is the witness of all.

sarvajna pitham: (sarvajna: omniscient + pitha: seat or altar of worship) A place of philosophic discussion in Kashmir where Adi Shankaracharaya visited in the early 9th century. With the blessings of Sharada Devi, he defeated all others in debate and ascended this "Seat of Knowledge." At that time he wrote his exquisite *Saundarya Lahari*. See: Adi Shankaracharaya, *Saundarya Lahari*.

Sarvāntarayāmi: (Sarva: all + antara: inner + yami: knower) The Knower of the innermost thoughts of all beings. See: Antarayami.

Satchidānanda: (Sat: That which always was, is and always will be + chit: consciousness + ananda: bliss) A name describing the essential nature of Brahman, which makes it possible for the finite human mind to understand that which is infinite, attributeless, and indescribable.

sattva: See: guna.

sāttvic: Adj. for sattva. See: guna.

Satya: (Truth) That which always was, is, and always will be. The Eternal Brahman; Truth.

Satya ātmā: (satya: + atma) The eternal soul.

Satya loka: One of the worlds or spheres. See: loka(s).

Satyamayi: (Satya + mayi: pervading) Devi, as the very embodiment of Truth.

Satya Nārāyana pūjā: A fast (vrata) observed on the full-moon day for Satya Narayana or Satya Deva, the Lord of Truth and a name for Vishnu, which confers all kinds of auspiciousness and prosperity. Various stories are recited, followed by meditation, and the distribution of prasada.

***Saundarya Lahari*:** (saundarya: splendor, beauty + lahari: wave) The Supreme Wave of Beauty and Splendor. A beautiful poetic hymn of one hundred verses in which the Supreme Being is adored as Tripura sundari or Lalita Devi, Mother of the Universe. Written by Adi Shankaracharya.

sevā: Service.

sevanthi: (Telugu) The chrysanthemum flower.

Shabari: A simple, tribal woman, the very personification of pure-hearted devotion to Sri Rama. When the Lord, drawn by her true and abiding love for Him, came to her humble hut in the forest, she had nothing to offer Him except a few fresh berries. Overcome with love, she tasted each one to make sure that only the sweetest were offered to her beloved Lord. Valuing her deep and simple-hearted emotion, Sri Rama ate each berry with relish. As He left her hut, her life breath also left her body, and Sri Rama lovingly performed her last rites with His own hands. See: Rama.

Shakti: (< shak: to be able) Force, energy, power. The dynamic creative principal envisioned as feminine, and the personification of primal energy. The divine consort of Lord Siva is as inseparable from Him as moonlight from the moon. Siva is the static transcendental principal. Apart from Shakti, He is likened to a corpse. As the dynamic aspect of Brahman, Shakti creates, maintains, and dissolves the universe. In the *Tantras* (scriptures of Devi worship and kundalini yoga), Shakti is of primary importance. In Her three main aspects, She is Iccha Shakti (the power of intention), Jnana Shakti (the power of knowledge) and Kriya Shakti (the power of action). See: Maha Shakti.

shalya: A name of the bilva tree; twig of the bilva tree.

Shāmbhavi: (Sham: peace + bhavi: one who gives rise to) Devi, who blesses all creation with peace.

Shambhu: (Sham: peace +bhu: one who gives) A name for Lord Siva as the peaceful one who bestows peace on all.

shami: Name of a tree said to contain fire.

shāmiānā: Large tent used for outdoor gatherings.

Shankarāchāraya, Adi: (788-820 AD) Born in Kerala, he disappeared at age 32 in the Himalayas. Considered to be an incarnation of Lord Siva, this saint has over 300 literary works to his credit, including the inspirational poem to Devi, *Saundarya Lahari*, and famed commentaries on the *Upanishads*, the *Brahma Sutras*, and the *Bhagavad Gita*. He established monasteries at the four corners of India, which are still functioning today.

Shankari: (< Shankara: one who bestows peace) Devi, the consort of Shankara, Lord Siva.

Shanmukha: (shan: six + mukha: faces) The six-faced one, Swami Karttikeya. See: Karttikeya.

shānti: Peace.

shānti mantras: (shanti: peace + mantras) Opening shlokas of each of the 108 *Upanishads*, chanted for the blessing of peace for all creation.

Shāradā Devi: Holy consort of Sri Ramakrishna Paramahamsa. See next entry.

Shāradā Devi, Sri Shāradāmbā, Shāradāmani: (Sharada: name for Saraswati Devi + Amba: Mother, + mani: jewel) Names of Sri Saraswati as Mother Sharada, Goddess of Knowledge. See: Saraswati Devi.

Shāradāmbikā: (Sharada + ambika: little mother) An intimate and endearing form of address for Mother Saraswati. See Saraswati Devi, Sharada Devi.

shāstra(s): A treatise on any department of knowledge, temporal or spiritual. Sacred scriptures are often referred to as *dharma shastras*.

Shitalā Devi: (She who cools) One of the names of the all-soothing Divine Mother.

Shirdi: A popular pilgrimage site in Gujarat, North India and home of Shirdi Sai Baba. See: Sai, Sainath.

Shivabālayogi: (1935-1994) Sri Shivabalayogi was born as Satayraju at Adivapupeta, Andhra Pradesh, to very poor Saivite weaver parents. At fourteen, Satyaraju had a spontaneous spiritual transformation, when he was initiated into twelve years of tapas.

shloka: (shloka: sorrow, since the first couplet was composed by Valmiki in sorrow at the sight of a bird being killed.) A couplet, often used for hymns of praise, commonly in anushtup chhanda (a meter containing two lines with sixteen syllables in each).

shodashi: (of sixteen) A maiden of sixteen.

Shrāvana: The fifth month of the year (July-August) according to the Hindu calendar.

shruti: (shruti: the revealed word; that which is heard) A name for the *Vedas* and *Upanishads* which, in ancient days, were taught through the word of the Guru as there were no written books.

shuddha: pure.

Shuddha Brahma mayam: (shuddha + Brahma + mayam: pervaded by) Everything pervaded by the Absolute alone.

Shuddha chetanā: (shuddha + chetana: consciousness) Pure Consciousness.

Shuddha vidyā: Pure knowledge.

Shuka, Sage: See: Sage Shuka.

siddha: One who has attained perfection.

siddhi: (attainment, success, achievement of perfection) 1. Being steadily established in samadhi. 2. Mantra siddhi: attaining the full power of a mantra by repeating it a prescribed number of times with faith and devotion.

SRI KARUNAMAYI - A Biography

sindūra: Red powder used for making a mark on the forehead. Also known as kumkum. See: kumkum.
Sitā: (Sita: furrow) Sita Devi is a form of the Divine Mother in the sustaining aspect. During a period of drought, Sita emerged from a furrow in the earth, hence Her name. As the faithful wife of Lord Rama, She experienced, and steadfastly faced, many difficulties and sufferings. These are portrayed in the great epic, the *Ramayana*.
Sitammā: (Sita: wife of Rama + amma: mother) A respectful term of address for Sita Devi.
Siva, Lord: (the kind, friendly, or auspicious one) Siva is the third divinity in the Hindu triad, and has countless names. He is the Lord of Dissolution, not only of the universe at the end of a kalpa (time-cycle), but also of avidya (ignorance). As one who is in constant meditation, Siva is the supreme yogi. He is depicted as having three eyes (omniscience), matted locks (freedom from body consciousness), wearing a tiger skin (victory over the animal nature) and covered in ashes (total renunciation). He also has snakes coiled around His body (control of anger), and holds a trident, symbolic of His mastery over the three gunas and three states of consciousness. Lord Siva is worshipped as the Absolute in the form of the linga(m). See: gunas and states of consciousness.
Siva Ashtottara: (Siva + ashtottara) 108 names of Siva.
Siva nāma: (Siva + nama: name) Constant repetition of the name "Siva."
Siva Shaktyai namah: (Siva + to Shakti + namah: to bow) Salutations to Lord Siva and His consort, Shakti, supreme energy.
Sivalinga: See: linga(m) and Siva.
Sivarātri: (Siva + ratri: night) Also called Maha Sivaratri, which occurs on the 14th day of the dark half of the lunar month in Feb/March. It is celebrated with an elaborate abhishekam of the lingam (using eleven different items) while chanting the *Sri Rudram*. It is observed by an all-night vigil and a fast. See: Siva, *Sri Rudram,* lingam, abhishekam.
Smt: Abbr. for Srimati. A title of respect added to the names of married women; Mrs.
Soham mantra: The supreme divine mantra that every living being repeats unknowingly with every breath throughout life—"So" with the incoming breath and "Ham" with the outgoing breath. The meaning of "Soham" is, "I am That," "I am the supreme Reality." When this sacred mantra is chanted mentally and consciously, it leads the seeker to liberation.
sphatika lingam: (sphatika: crystal, quartz + lingam). See lingam.
Sri: 1. Lakshmi, Goddess of wealth and prosperity, and the consort of

Vishnu. 2. A title of respect added to the names of men as well as deities and eminent persons.

Sri Adi Shankarāchārya: See: Shankaracharya, Adi.

Sri Chakra: (Sri: divine + chakra) A diagrammatic representation utilized in both the mental and ritual worship of Devi as supreme Goddess and Mother of Creation. It represents the macrocosm (universe), and the microcosm, (the individual self), as manifestations of the same shakti or energy. The Sri Chakra has nine enclosures, and is formed by nine intersecting triangles. The bindu in the center signifies Siva-Shakti in union before the manifestation of creation, that is, the complete absence of duality.

Sri Chakra meru: (Sri + chakra + meru: mountain) A three dimensional representation of the Sri Chakra.

Sri Mātā: (Sri: holy + Mata: mother) The Divine Mother who embodies primal Energy, and is Para Shakti, Creator of the Universe. See: Para Shakti.

Sri Pāda Pūjā: Same as pada puja.

Sri Panchami, Vasanta or Basanta (Spring) Panchami: A festival dedicated to Saraswati Devi, Goddess of Knowledge, and held on the fifth day of the bright half of the lunar month of Magha (January/February). Mother Earth and the Ganga are also worshipped on this day.

Srirangam: Tamil Nadu island town near Trichy, location of one of the most revered Krishna Temples, Sri Ranganatha Swami, and a center of bhakti yoga. Ramanuja is buried here. See: Ramanuja.

Sri Rudram: (rudra: fiery, fierce) Rudra is Lord Siva, who though usually referred to as the destroyer, is actually the source of all—Ishwara, the creator, sustainer and destroyer of the manifested universe. *Sri Rudram* occurs in the *Krishna Yajur Veda*, and expounds beautifully His cosmic form and immanence in all sentient and insentient things. Just as watering the roots of a tree nourishes all its branches, leaves, flowers and fruit, chanting the *Rudram* pleases all the Gods and Goddesses, fulfills all wishes and grants liberation. See: *Vedas, Atharva Veda*.

Sri Sailam: A temple pilgrimage spot near Kurnool in Andhra Pradesh. The presiding deities are Mallikarjuna (Lord Siva) and Bhramaramba (Durga Devi in the form of a gigantic bee). It is one of the famed Jyotir Linga shrines and the place where Adi Shankaracharya composed his immortal hymn, *Sivananda Lahari*.

Sri Saraswati bijākshara: See: Saraswati Mantra.

Sri Saraswati Sahasranāma: (Sri + Saraswati + sahasranama: a thousand divine names) The Thousand Divine Names of Saraswati Devi.

Sri Sūktam: An eloquent vedic hymn of praise to Lakshmi Devi. Its high poetic quality distinguishes it from a stotra.

Srim: (< Sri: Lakshmi Devi) Bijakshara for the Goddess of Auspiciousness, Lakshmi Devi. The third seed syllable of the Saraswati Mantra. Devotional repetition of Srim endows the sadhaka or seeker with divine light, physically, mentally and spiritually.

Srimad Bhāgavatam: Tenth book of the *Bhagavata Purana*, which describes in great detail and with supreme devotion, the life of Lord Krishna, one of best-loved incarnations of Vishnu. It was written by Vyasa. After classifying the *Vedas* and writing many philosophical works, he could not find peace of mind. The sage Narada then appeared to him and suggested that if he wrote a book on love of God, his heart would find bliss and peace.

Sri Mathru Devi: A reverent name for Amma. See: Mathru

Shringeri: Location of one of the four famous maths established by Adi Shankaracharya on the Tunga River in Karnataka. See: Shankaracharya.

Sripura(m): (Sri: Devi + puram: city) Name for Manidwipa, blissful, ambrosial land of Divine Mother. Also refers to the innermost triangle in the Sri Chakra, in the center of which Divine Mother dwells as the bindu (dot).

srishti: Creation.

Shruti: (Shruti: that which is heard; the revealed word) Name given to the *Vedas* which were not written down, but were revealed to the ancient sages in meditation, as sound. Their knowledge was handed down from Guru to disciple through hearing and memorizing.

states of consciousness: The states of awareness are generally classified as: 1. jagrat: waking. 2. svapna: dreaming. 3. susupti: deep sleep. 4. turiya: beyond these three—the thoughtless state of samadhi. 5. turiyatita: beyond turiya, in which a yogi stays continuously in bliss, totally unaware of the body or the manifested universe. Also called sahaja sthiti. See: samadhi.

sthiti: Maintenance of creation, state.

stotra: A hymn of praise consisting of several verses or shlokas.

Subramanya: See: Shanmukha.

Sugriva: A monkey leader, and younger brother of Bali, who befriended Sri Rama.

sukha(m): Happiness (worldly); bliss (spiritual).

supreme Consciousness: See: Para Brahma.

sūrya: The sun.

Sūrya Bhagavān: (surya + bhagavan: God) The Sun God.

sushumnā: See: nadi(s).

sushupti: Deep sleep. See: states of consciousness.
Suvah loka: The celestial realms. See: loka.
svapna: (dream) The dream state. See: states of consciousness.
svasvarūpa: (sva: one's own + svarupa: form) One's true inner Reality.
swāmi(ji): (swami: lord) 1. A mode of address used for a monk. 2. A title of respect that follows the name of a spiritual master or revered holy man.
Swāmiji: An affectionate and respectful form of address for Swami Vijayeswarananda. See: Vijayeswarananda.

T

Tāi: (Tamil) Divine Mother.
Takshaka: (snake) A very poisonous snake which bit King Janamejaya due to a curse, causing his death.
tāla: Indian musical term meaning, rhythm or beat.
Talli: (Telugu) Mother or Divine Mother.
tālukā: A subdivision of a district.
tamarind: A tropical Asian tree with pods containing an edible sour pulp.
tamas: See: guna.
tāmasic: Adj. for tamas. See guna.
Tānjore: Former capital of the Chola Empire on the banks of the Cauveri River in Tamil Nadu. Location of a great temple and the Saraswati Mahal Library, with over 30,000 rare Sanskrit volumes.
tapas: (tapas: glow, heat) Severe ascetic practices and austerities undertaken to purify the body and mind, along with an intense desire for union with God. Meditation is the highest form of tapas.
tapasvini: A woman who performs tapas.
tapovana: A forest in which people have performed or are performing tapas.
Tāta: (Telugu) Grandfather.
tattva: Essence; the five basic elements of nature.
tattva drishti: (tattva: essence + drishti: vision) The ability or understanding to see the essence of things—oneness.
Tattvādhikā: (Tattva: the five basic elements + adhika: more than) Devi, who is beyond the five elements of nature.
Tattvamayi: (Tattva: the five basic elements + mayi: pervading) Devi, who pervades the five elements of nature.
tavā: An iron griddle for cooking flat bread.
tejas: Radiance. The luster or glow that appears on the face of a sadhaka (seeker) who practices spiritual discipline.
Telugu: Language spoken by the people of Andhra Pradesh in South India. It is a soft, sweet language derived primarily from Sanskrit and the native Dravidian.

third eye: The ajna chakra, subtle energy enter between the eyebrows. See: chakra (ajna)

Thiruppavai: Sacred poetic composition of 30 verses, written before the age of 15 by Andal, a saint of Tamil Nadu, in which she pictures herself to be a cowherd girl or gopi, yearning to merge with Sri Villiputtur (Lord Krishna) for all eternity. The poem is recited with great devotion in all Vaishnavite Tamil Nadu temples, especially during December-January. See: Andal.

thousand petalled lotus: Subtle energy center which is just above the crown of the head. See: chakra (sahasrara), kundalini, nadi.

throat chakra: Subtle energy center at the base of the throat. See: chakra (vishuddhi), kundalini, nadi.

Thyāgarāja: (1767-1847) A famous poet saint of Andhra Pradesh in southern India. He composed hundreds of songs in praise of Sri Rama, his adored deity. Steeped in the purest, deep devotion, these kirtanas (devotional songs) are remembered and sung even today.

tilaka(m): Auspicious mark placed between the eyebrows to honor or bless. It indicates an awareness of the divinity within that person.

tirtha(m): Holy water.

Tirumala (Hills): Seven hills spread over 100 square miles, representing the seven hoods of the serpent Shesha at Tirumala where the famed shrine of Lord Venkateshwara is located in Andhra Pradesh.

Tirupati: The famed and richest pilgrimage center in the world, located in Andhra Pradesh where Lord Vishnu is worshipped as Balaji or Sri Venkateswara. See: Venkateswara.

Tiruvannamalāi: A pilrimage center in South India where the ashram of Sri Ramana Maharshi is situated. Also the site of the holy mountain Arunachala. See: Ramana Maharshi

Treta yuga: See yuga.

tri: three

tribhuvana: (tri + bhuvana: worlds, lokas) The three lokas. See: lokas.

Trichy (Tiruchi): An ancient historical city in Tamil Nadu on the banks of the Cauveri River, site of a famed 100 pillared Rock Temple. This whole temple has been carved out from solid rock.

trigunas: (tri + gunas: fundamental qualities) All objects in prakriti or nature are composed of the three gunas. See: gunas.

Trimūrti: (tri + murti: image) An image of the Lord, showing Him in His three aspects of the Hindu triad, Brahma, Vishnu, and Maheshwara (Siva).

Tripurāntakam: (Tripura: the three cities + antakam: one who ends) Lord Siva, detroyer of all the triads such as the three gunas, the three states of consciousness etc.

SRI KARUNAMAYI - A Biography

Tripura sundari: (tripura + sundari: the beautiful one) Divine Mother as the lovely Lalita Devi, who dwells in the bindu (point in the center) of the Sri Chakra and is the ruler of the three cities or lokas as well as the three states of consciousness (waking, dreaming and deep sleep). See: states of consciousness.
tulasi: Sacred basil plant.
turiya: See: states of consciousness.
turmeric: (< M.Latin terra: land + merita: deserved) Indian plant. Its yellow root has germicidal properties. It is ground and widely used in Indian cooking. Considered auspicious and used in all pujas.
tyāga: Sacrifice, renunciation.

udumbara: An Indian berry-bearing tree popularly known as gulara.
Umā Devi: A name for Goddess Parvati, consort of Lord Siva.
Umā Maheshwari: (Uma + maha + Ishwari: consort of the Lord) Parvati Devi, the Consort of Lord Siva.
Upanishads: (upa: near +nishad: sitting: to sit near) Ancient revealed texts attached to the end of the *Vedas*. They were taught to the aspirants while seated near the feet of the Guru, hence their name. They contain the essence of Hindu philosophy—Advaita, the oneness of all creation. They declare with one voice that the individual soul and the supreme Soul are one. They also deal with metaphysical inquiry regarding the origin of the universe, the nature of God and the soul, and the connection between mind and matter. There are 108 major *Upanishads*.

Vaikuntha: The abode of Lord Vishnu. This paradise is sometimes described as situated on Mount Meru, the Hindu Olympus, and at others in the Northern Ocean.
Vaishnavi Devi: Devi as the consort of Vishnu.
Vaishnavi Devi Temple: The famed pilgrimage site is located in the North Indian state of Jammu inside a sacred cave. In the form of a five foot rock, Sri Vaishnava Devi is believed to be a composite of the collective energies of Sri Kali, Sri Lakshmi and Sri Saraswati Devi, born of the tejas of the divine triad, Lords Siva, Vishnu and Brahma.
Vālmiki: (< valmiki: anthill) Renowned Sanskrit poet and sage; he is the author and some-time participant in the famous epic, the *Ramayana*. He sheltered the banished Sita Devi at his ashram and educated Her twin sons, Lava and Kusha. In his youth, however,

SRI KARUNAMAYI - A Biography

Valmiki was a dacoit (robber) called Ratnakara. His meeting with and initiation by the sapta rishis into the reversed Rama Mantra transformed his life. He meditated for so long that termites built an anthill around his body; hence, his name.

vana sampada: (vana: forest + sampada: wealth) Forest wealth.

varada mudrā: (varada: bestowing boons + mudra: hand gesture) A hand gesture associated with deities, the palm turned outward, pointing down, symbolic of the bestowal of boons. See: mudra.

Vasishtha, Maharshi: A celebrated vedic sage, one of the sapta rishis, the seven great sages, who meditated in the hills near Amma's Penusila ashram. He was the son of Brahma, the creator. In the *Ramayana* he is the kula Guru (family priest) of King Dasharatha, father of Sri Rama. A famous religious treatise, *Yoga Vasishtha*, was written by him as a series of answers to the questions posed by the disillusioned young Rama, who perceived the world as maya.

vāstu shastra: (vastu: dwelling, site + shastra: science) A revealed science concerned with the five elements and the four directions and their proper order and balance. Its purpose is to ensure auspiciousness and health to people in their dwellings and work places. East and North are important, for the sun rises in the East, and North is the center of the magnetic pole.

Vasundharā: The Earth.

vāyu: Air.

***Veda(s)*:** (vid: to know) The four ancient holy books which are the foundation of Sanatana Dharma (later known as Hinduism). They are in the form of hymns, which were revealed as sound to the rishis, whose names they bear. Hence, the *Vedas* are known as the *Shrutis*, or "what was heard." The four *Vedas* are: *Rig, Yajur, Sama,* and *Atharva*. 1. *Rig Veda*: It is the oldest, longest and most important *Veda*. The *Yajur* and *Sama Vedas* are derived from it. Its hymns praise the personifications of the powers of nature, e.g., Surya (the sun), Agni (fire), Varuna (water) and Indra (king of the gods). 2. *Yajur Veda*: (yajur: rhythmic prose + *Veda*) Its hymns and prayers are mostly derived from the *Rig Veda*. It is the manual used by priests performing yajnas and other ritual ceremonies and has two parts—the Taittariya and Vajasneyi. The former is known as the Krishna (black) *Yajur Veda*, and the latter as the Shukla (white) *Yajur Veda*. 3. *Sama Veda*: (saman: chant or melody + *Veda*) This *Veda* is written entirely in metric verses which are chanted or sung during homas, along with each offering. Many of the invocations are addressed to Soma (the moon), and others to Agni (fire), Indra (king of the gods), etc. 4. *Atharva Veda*: (the Atharvans: a class of intellectual priests + *Veda*) The fourth *Veda*, of later origin, contains a mixture of prose and verse, and deals with material life, i.e., the attainment of prosperity, good health, victory over enemies, etc.

Veda jnāni: (*Veda* + jnani: knower) One learned in the *Vedas*.

Veda Mātā: (*Veda* + Mata: mother) Saraswati Devi, Mother of the *Vedas*. Divine Mother, the giver of true knowledge.

Vedamayi: Devi, the embodiment of the *Vedas*.

Vedānta: (Veda + anta: end or conclusion) The ultimate wisdom of the Vedas contained in the *Upanishads*. See *Upanishads*.

Veda vana vasini: (Veda + vana: forest + vasini: dweller) The Divine Mother who dwells in the vast forests of vedic knowledge.

vedic: Adj, for *Veda*.

***Vedic shāstras*:** (vedic + shastras) See: *Vedas*, shastra.

Venkateshwara, Lord: The eight foot, black granite, self-manifested image of Lord Vishnu at Tirupati in Andhra Pradesh. He wears coverings over both eyes, His gaze being too powerful for mortals to bear. See: Vishnu, Tirupati.

Vibhishana: Younger brother of Ravana, who left him and joined Sri Rama. He was crowned king of Lanka after Ravana's death at the hands of Sri Rama. See: Ravana.

vibhūti: (divine power) Sacred ash from the homa or yajna fire, highly charged with mantra power. Applied between the eyebrows, it activates and energizes the ajna chakra. Taken internally it has the power to cure diseases. See: chakra.

vidyā: (learning) Knowledge, of which there are two types: the lower or material wisdom, and the higher, or spiritual wisdom and true knowledge. See: Atma Vidya.

Vijaya Dashami: (vijaya: victory + dashami: the tenth day, i.e., victory on the tenth day) See: Appendix.

Vijayawādā: One of the foremost towns of Andhra Pradesh, containing the ancient Kanaka Durga temple.

Vijayeswarānanda: (vijay: victory + Ishwara: Lord + ananda: bliss, i.e., the victorious Lord of Bliss) Spiritual son and cousin-brother of Sri Karunamayi. From his twenties, his life has been totally dedicated to the service of Amma. "Swamiji," as he is affectionately known, travels with Amma, translates Her discourses, and is the administrator of Her ashrams and missions.

Villiputtur: A place in Tamil Nadu named for Lord Krishna and a kingdom where Andal (Sri Goda Devi) lived. See: Andal.

vinā: A stringed musical instrument that has a long fretted fingerboard with resounding gourds at each end. Held in the divine hands of Saraswati Devi, the sound of the vina symbolizes nada, the primal sound. See: Saraswati.

Vishālākshi: Devi who has large eyes. A name for Devi.

Vishnu, Lord: (<vis: to pervade) The second God of the Hindu triad, the embodiment of sattva guna, purity, peace and goodness. He is the preserving power of the universe, the Self-existing and all-pervading Lord. His consort is Lakshmi Devi. He is depicted as blue in color and four-armed, holding the conch, discus, mace and a lotus flower. He reclines on the serpent Shesha Naga or Adi Sesha, and His vehicle is Garuda, the eagle. See: Lakshmi Devi, Venkateshwara.

Vishvāmitra: A celebrated sage who was born a kshatriya (of the warrior or ruling class), but by intense tapas, austere practices, raised himself to the status of a true brahmin, a knower of Brahman. He is one of the sapta rishis, the seven great sages, and was the first to hear the Gayatri Mantra from Devi Herself. See: Gayatri Mantra.

Vishva shānti: (vishva: world + shanti: peace) World peace.

Vishvanātha: (Vishva: world + natha: lord) Lord of the world, Lord Siva. See: Siva.

Vivekānanda, Swāmi: (viveka + ananda: bliss. One who enjoys the bliss of discrimination) (1863-1902) Born Narendranath Dutta, this young lawyer became the chief disciple of Sri Ramakrishna Paramahamsa, and brought the knowledge of advaita philosophy to the West. He was universally acclaimed for his exposition of Vedanta (precepts of the *Vedas*) at the Parliament of World Religions (1893) in Chicago. See: Ramakrishna Paramahamsa, advaita, Vedanta.

Vyāsa Maharshi: (vyasa: collector, compiler + maha: great + rishi) The compiler of the *Vedas* and author of several great scriptural texts: the *Brahma Sutras*, the *Srimad Bhagavatam*, the *Mahabharata*, and the eighteen major *Puranas* (ancient legends).

waistees: (Telugu) Dhotis. See: dhoti.

yāga shālā: (yaga: a yajna or homa + shala: covered place) A place where yajnas or homas are performed.

yajna rakshā: (yajna: sacrificial fire ceremony + raksha: protection) The sacred ash or vibhuti from the homa or yajna fire, which protects when applied to the forehead, as it is highly charged with mantra power. See: homa.

yājniks: Brahmins who perform homas. See: homa.

Yamunā River: A river near Vrindavana, the location of many of Lord Krishna's bala lilas (childhood episodes), and also of the mystic rasa lila (cosmic dance) with the gopikas (milkmaids).

Yashodammā: (Yashoda + amma: mother) Foster mother of Lord Krishna and wife of the cowherd Nanda.

yoga: (<yuj: to yoke or join) Path of union with God. There are traditionally four yogas: 1. Bhakti yoga, devotion to God. 2. Jnana yoga, intellectual approach through knowledge and Self-inquiry. 3. Karma yoga, selfless actions offered to God, and 4. Dhyana yoga, meditation on God.

yogi: An adept or one who practices yoga. See: yoga.

yogic: Adj. for yoga.

yogini: A woman who practices yoga.

yuga: Period of time referred to in epic scriptures or *Puranas*. There are four yugas, each preceded and followed by a period of "twilight" called sandhya, wherein one yuga gradually fades away and the other gradually begins. 1. Sat or Krita Yuga is the age of righteousness, which corresponds to the Greek Golden Age. 2. In Treta Yuga, sacrifices commence, but righteousness decreases. 3. In Dvapara Yuga, righteousness decreases still further. Few adhere to the truth and diseases and calamities assail them. They then offer sacrifices or practice austerities to get relief from suffering. 4. In Kali Yuga, (the present age) righteousness declines to only twenty-five percent. As a result, calamities, diseases, hunger and corruption, etc. are prevalent, and there is great suffering. One cosmic cycle of these four yugas is called a maha yuga, and is said to consist of 4,320,000 solar years.

zari border: (zari: gold and silver thread + border: edging) An ornamental edging of gold or silver thread.